Free Lunch on Wall Street

Free Lunch on Wall Street

Perks, Freebies, and Giveaways for Investors

Charles B. Carlson, CFA
Editor, *Dow Theory Forecasts*

McGraw-Hill, Inc.

New York San Francisco Washington, D.C. Auckland Bogotá
Caracas Lisbon London Madrid Mexico City Milan
Montreal New Delhi San Juan Singapore
Sydney Tokyo Toronto

Library of Congress Cataloging-in-Publication Data

Carlson, Charles B.
    Free lunch on Wall Street : perks, freebies, and giveaways for
investors / Charles B. Carlson.
        p.   cm.
    Includes index.
    ISBN 0-07-009978-2 (acid-free paper) :   —ISBN
0-07-009979-0 (pbk. : acid-free paper) :
    1. Stocks.   2. Discount.   3. Free Material.   4. Gifts.
5. Stockholders.   I. Title.   II. Title: Perks.
HG4661.C327   1993
658.8'2—dc20   93-22809
                                                              CIP

1 2 3 4 5 6 7 8 9 0   DOC/DOC   9 9 8 7 6 5 4 3

ISBN 0-07-009978-2 [HC]
ISBN 0-07-009979-0 [PBK]

*The sponsoring editor for this book was David Conti, the editing supervisor
was Kimberly Goff, and the production supervisor was Pamela A. Pelton. This
book was set in Palatino. It was composed by McGraw-Hill's Professional Book
Group composition unit.*

Printed and bound by R. R. Donnelley & Sons Company.

This book is printed on recycled, acid-free paper containing a
minimum of 50% recycled de-inked fiber.

This publication is designed to provide accurate and authoritative information in regard to the subject matter covered. It is sold with the understanding that the publisher is not engaged in rendering legal, accounting or other professional service. If legal advice or other expert assistance is required, the services of a competent professional person
should be sought.
            *—From a declaration of principles jointly adopted by a committee of the
                      American Bar Association and a committee of publishers*

To Denise

Contents

Dow Theory Forecasts
Dow Jones News/Retrieval
Wall Street Journal
Barron's
Forbes
Quicken software
The Low Priced Stock Survey
Retire ASAP software
Business Week
QuoTrek
Morningstars' *5-Star Investor*
Bottom Line Personal
Worth
Metastock software
Microsoft Excel
America Online
Andrew Tobias' Managing Your Money software
Daily Graphs
CompuServe
Financial World

Preface

Most of us would agree that one of our favorite snacks when we were growing up was *Cracker Jack*, those caramel-covered popcorn and peanut treats that wreaked havoc with our dental fillings. And I think most of us would also agree that it wasn't so much the taste that we liked.

It was the prize inside. The little something extra. The Freebie. Perk. Lagniappe.

And even though many of us no longer eat *Cracker Jack*, we still haven't lost our love for freebies.

That's what this book is all about.

My impulse for writing this book, aside from my own love for freebies, perks, and giveaways, was the interest shown in this subject over the years by readers of *Dow Theory Forecasts*, the investment newsletter I edit. In answering readers' questions about which companies offer perks and freebies, I was surprised that there wasn't a primary source for this information. Until now.

I'm sure an academician would say that a discount or freebie is hardly a reason for an individual to buy stock in a particular company. I suppose that's true. However, I think the way a company treats its shareholders says a lot about the character of the company and management. Does the company perceive the shareholders—the owners of the corporation—to be important? Or are they just nuisances? True, shareholder discounts on company products or a shareholder dividend reinvestment plan may not be as important in determining the investment value of a firm as its finances or earnings-growth prospects. But they are additional pieces of information that can be added to the investment decision process.

And if you come across two potential investments that are identical by every financial yardstick, but you discover, because of information in these pages, that one of the companies takes better care of its shareholders than the other, then this book will have done its job.

Charles B. Carlson

Acknowledgments

I would like to thank the readers of *Dow Theory Forecasts* for their questions and comments concerning this subject. Also, a special thanks to the companies that provided the discount coupons in the back of the book.

Thanks go to my editor at McGraw-Hill, David Conti, for his suggestions and comments, as well as to Rian Fried of *The Clean Yield* newsletter for his help on socially responsible investing.

I greatly appreciate the help from the entire staff of Dow Theory Forecasts, Inc., especially Avis Beitz, Bob Evans, Tom Pressler, Al Rayski, Randy Roeing, Veronica Ambuul, David Hill, and Rich Moroney.

I would be remiss if I didn't give special thanks to Monica Taylor for her efforts on this book. Monica has had to put up with me on two books now, and I couldn't have done either without her.

Finally, a special thanks to colleague Elberta Miklusak for her assistance and FREE LUNCH sign, which acted as my muse when the words stopped flowing.

Introduction

I wonder if this describes your typical day:

You get out of bed. You shower, dress, and hop into your company car. On the way to work you make some phone calls on your car phone—paid for by the company—and arrive at work to park in your reserved parking space. You meet with your staff for an hour. You get back in your company car and head to the local airport. You board the company jet—the jet you used last month for that Canadian fishing trip with your buddies—and fly to another meeting in a city one hour away. After the meeting, you return home on the company jet just in time to make your tennis date at the health club, whose membership is paid by the company.

After tennis, you return to work in your company car. At 6 p.m. you call it a day. As you head home in your company car you make reservations, via your company-paid car phone for that evening at the country club, the membership of which is paid by the company. At dinner, you meet with your financial planner—whose services are paid by your company—to discuss the tax implications of exercising the $600,000 in stock options given to you by the company. You ask for advice on where to invest some of the $1.3 million in salary you'll earn this year.

Following dessert and an after-dinner drink, you bid your financial planner farewell and return home in your company car. You make a call on your company-paid car phone to tell your wife you're on the way. You arrive home, greet your family, and retire to your den to review various life insurance policies paid for by the company. Satisfied that your affairs are in order, you retire to bed for a good night's rest.

Sound familiar? I didn't think so. And yet, that lifestyle may not be all that uncommon for corporate CEOs and presidents. Indeed, *The*

Wall Street Journal reports that, according to Towers Perrin compensation consulting company, median CEO total pay for 350 of the largest companies in the country was $1.3 million in 1991. That figure includes salary, bonuses, and long-term incentives. Of the 121 chief executive officers in the sample that exercised stock options, the median gain was $690,720.

And that $1.3 million in total compensation seemed rather paltry compared to the really big bucks for those at the top of the heap. Anthony J. F. O'Reilly, the head of H. J. Heinz, reportedly had total compensation of $74.8 million in 1991, of which over $71 million stemmed from gains on stock options. Leon C. Hirsch, the chief at U.S. Surgical, pulled down $22.6 million, with $20.8 million in stock options. Richard Eamer, the boss at National Medical Enterprises, reaped nearly $17 million in total compensation, including $8.4 million from stock option gains and $7.1 million in various long-term payouts.

CEO pay wasn't too bad in 1992, with Hirsch of U.S. Surgical pulling down nearly $61 million (Hirsch's wife, U.S. Surgical vice president Turi Josefsen, earned nearly $27 million) and Toys 'R Us chief Charles Lazarus receiving more than $64 million in salary, bonus, and options compensation.

And the perks don't stop with salaries and compensation. According to Hay/Huggins Co., a tracker of corporate perks and fringe benefits:

- 70 percent of companies surveyed in 1991 provided company cars or car allowances for executives.
- 44 percent provided executive parking.
- 35 percent provided country club memberships.
- 33 percent provided financial planning services.
- 30 percent paid for mobile telephones.
- 19 percent offered paid spouse travel expenses.
- 17 percent had available company aircraft.
- 13 percent provided chauffeurs.
- 6 percent paid for personal legal services.

Chances are, if you own stock, you're probably a shareholder in one or several of these companies. In other words, you're one of the owners. That's right. An *owner*.

Amazingly, most individual investors forget this fact. Your ownership of stock should give you certain rights, so it would seem. However, just try to get some of the same perks and freebies bestowed upon the top brass in your companies. You and I both know you won't get past the receptionist.

My little scenario isn't intended to bash corporate honchos and their generous perks. It is intended to make a point: Shareholders should get more out of investing in a company than a dividend check and the hope that the stock rises in price. You should be able to enjoy some of the perks, indeed, the power that comes with ownership.

Sure, it's a bit unrealistic to expect to have access to the corporate jet, or to earn what the CEO makes, or to dine at the country club on your company's buck. But it's not too much to ask to be able to derive certain other benefits of ownership. As an owner, you should be able to purchase your company's products or services at a discount. You should be able to tour the facilities. You should be able to buy stock in your company at a discount—just like the CEO. You should have some say in how the company is run.

Pie-in-the-sky thinking, you say. There are no companies that offer such perks and freebies, right? Think again.

In fact, there are many companies that know shareholders are the real owners: Companies where it is, indeed, possible for shareholders to buy products or services at a discount. Companies that permit shareholders to tour the facilities. Companies that allow shareholders to buy stock directly from the company without paying a brokerage commission. Companies that offer shareholders an opportunity to buy stock at a discount to the market price. Companies that make it easier for shareholders to have direct input into how the company is managed.

Where are these companies? In the pages before you.

You are now holding in your hands the most complete guide available to investor perks, freebies, and giveaways. As you'll see, my definition of perks is rather encompassing. It includes the obvious freebies, such as gifts for new shareholders or discounts on products or services. My definition of perks also includes other types of benefits that are less "concrete" but no less important, such as:

- The good feeling some investors get in knowing that their corporations are doing their best to protect the environment.

- The ability to have your voice, no matter how small, heard when it comes to running your company.

- The satisfaction you may derive by knowing that your firm gives back to the community.

Along the way, the book also discusses other types of perks for investors, such as the ability to buy stock at rock-bottom commissions; cheap or free financial research; strategies for buying closed-end funds at a discount; the best ways for cutting fees for credit cards and bank accounts; even how to muscle a free meal from your broker, financial adviser, or insurance agent. The book even includes a complete directory of over 400 companies that offer various perks, freebies, and discounts for investors.

And the perks don't stop there. At the end of this book, you'll find discount coupons for *The Wall Street Journal, Barron's, Forbes, Business Week, Dow Jones News/Retrieval*, Microsoft *Excel, Money, Quicken*, and 20 more leading financial publications, software, and database products. (See the back of the book for a complete listing of companies as well as their coupons.) These coupons are valued at nearly $1000, which makes this book perhaps the best investment you'll make this year.

Most people, myself included, are a bit skeptical when it comes to freebies. After all, you don't get something for nothing. So why do some companies offer their shareholders perks, freebies, and giveaways? Actually, companies benefit greatly by doing so, as you'll soon read in Chapter 1.

Free Lunch
on Wall Street

1

What's in It for the Company?

To say that **Walt Disney** has been a good holding for investors over the last decade would be an understatement. Shares of the entertainment company have soared from a split-adjusted price of under $3 per share in 1984.

But Disney shareholders not only made money with their shares, they also saved money. That's because Disney shareholders who join the Magic Kingdom Club Gold Card Program receive discounts of up to 30 percent on Disney accommodations, theme parks, and merchandise.

Ralston Purina's performance hasn't been as impressive as Disney's, but the stock of this pet food maker hasn't been a dog. The stock has moved up sharply since trading for about $5 per share in 1981. But the gains don't stop there. Shareholders of Ralston Purina receive discounts on lodging, ski rentals, ski lessons, and lift tickets at the company-owned Keystone Resort ski area in Keystone, Colorado.

J.P. Morgan & Co. has become synonymous with quality in the banking field. Shareholders have benefited from the company's strong market position, with the stock posting big gains since bottoming below $12 in 1982. But participants in Morgan's dividend reinvestment plan (DRIP) did even better by purchasing shares at a 3 percent discount to the market price.

Wrigley, William, Jr. Co. dominates the chewing gum market with such popular brand names as *Doublemint, Spearmint, Juicy Fruit, Big Red, Extra,* and *Hubba Bubba.* And while Wrigley may not be a favorite with dentists, the stock's performance has put a smile on the faces of shareholders. The shares have skyrocketed since trading at a split-adjusted price of $2 in 1982. As if that weren't enough, Wrigley makes sure its shareholders have plenty of the product on hand. The company sends each shareholder 20 packs of gum every year.

Disney, Ralston Purina, Morgan, and Wrigley are just a few of the companies that offer shareholders something extra for being an owner. These perks range from something as modest as Wrigley's gum freebie to savings of potentially hundreds of dollars for Disney shareholders. And freebies include the ability to buy stock at a discount—as in Morgan's DRIP—or the "feel-good" perk of investing in companies that have strong charitable programs or are sensitive to social concerns.

Interestingly, many individuals are not aware that such perks, freebies, and giveaways are available in selected companies. Such unawareness probably stems from the fact that most companies offer shareholders—the true owners—nothing more than perhaps a dividend check and the hope of stock-price appreciation. Of course, some economists and academicians would argue that the stock's return to a shareholder is all that should be expected from stock investments. I disagree. Shareholders, large or small, deserve to be treated like owners, not like the unwanted stepchildren of corporate management. Some companies understand who the real owners are and treat them accordingly; others do not. My aim is not to lambaste those firms that have chosen not to offer shareholder perks. Rather, I hope that, by showing how shareholder perks and freebies help the corporation as well as the shareholder, more companies will adopt perk programs.

Something for Nothing?

There's skepticism in all of us when it comes to perks and freebies. After all, you don't get something for nothing. That's true with corporate perks and freebies. Shareholders aren't getting something from the company for nothing. Indeed, firms that offer shareholder perks benefit in several ways.

Diverse Shareholder Base

One reason companies offer perks is to achieve a diverse shareholder base of institutional and individual investors. Obviously, shareholder discounts on corporate products and services attract individual investors to a company.

Why would companies want individual investors? First, a large contingent of individual investors decentralizes ownership. A wide shareholder base makes it more difficult to acquire large blocks of stock for a hostile takeover. Also, with institutional investors becoming more proactive in influencing corporate management, some corporations want individual investors, who are more likely to side with management or be quiet on controversial issues.

Another reason companies like individual shareholders is that small investors tend to be more loyal and long-term oriented than institutional investors. Presumably, a large contingent of individual investors means that the stock is less apt to undergo huge price swings that may occur in institutionally dominated companies.

Building a diverse shareholder base means having the stock appeal to a variety of investor types. Take the growth of socially responsible investing (SRI), for example. SRI, which is discussed in Chapter 8, covers firms that behave in a "socially responsible" manner. Such companies may have generous policies when it comes to charitable contributions or community involvement. Socially responsible companies take extra precautions to be environmentally friendly. Such social agendas are a perk in the sense that shareholders in these companies may derive a certain benefit from knowing that they and the company share similar philosophies when it comes to community involvement and the environment.

I can remember, not that long ago, when socially responsible investing was often looked upon with a snicker or sneer from Wall Street's establishment. But that's no longer the case. Social investing has mushroomed to become a billion-dollar investment business. Since money talks on Wall Street, corporations have begun to take notice of the clout being wielded by socially responsible investors and investment groups. Indeed, many companies are finding it advantageous to develop their social consciences in order to attract some of this money and diversify their shareholder base.

Shareholder as a Customer

Another reason companies offer perks is to solidify relationships with investors. It is important to remember that shareholders are also potential customers. Companies bank on the belief that a shareholder is more likely to purchase the company's products and services. For a company whose products sell in competitive consumer markets, it is truly in the firm's best interest to have as many individual investors as possible.

Offering shareholders a discount on a product or service is the most obvious way of converting a shareholder into a customer, but there are other ways as well. **McDonald's,** the fast-food giant, offers a dividend reinvestment program (DRIP) for shareholders. The program permits current shareholders to purchase stock directly from the company for as little as $50 at a time up to $75,000 annually and pay no commissions. McDonald's actively promotes its program, with 60 percent of the company's 127,400 shareholders enrolled.

In an industry as competitive as fast food, having a close relationship with some 76,000 DRIP participants can provide a nice competitive advantage. Indeed, if each of these DRIP investors bypasses Wendy's or Burger King each week to have a $5 meal at McDonald's, that means an additional $19.8 million in annual revenues for the Golden Arches. Remember that many of these shareholders are the head of a household, which means that $5 could easily grow to $20 or more a week, which translates to $79 million or more annually in additional revenues for McDonald's.

Exxon is another example of a company that has exploited the benefits of offering perks to investors. Exxon initiated a program in 1992 that permits individuals to buy stock directly through Exxon, even for first-time purchases. Exxon's program has other interesting wrinkles, including an Individual Retirement Account option in the dividend reinvestment plan. The company will allow you to invest directly through the company, without paying commissions, and have these investments credited to an IRA.

The early response to the direct-purchase plan was sensational. With only limited publicity, the company reported that over 50,000 calls were received in the first month of the program, and more than 25,000 enrollments were processed. In the program's first year, 187,000 new accounts signed up. Presumably, these 187,000 new enrollees are now buyers of at least some of Exxon's products and services. Also, these new enrollees are excellent prospects for Exxon charge cards, which increases the potential revenues coming from this source. Clearly, Exxon's program is a win-win situation for shareholders and the company.

Akin to cementing relationships with shareholders/consumers are the perks companies offer suppliers and employees. For example, many companies offer employee stock ownership programs that enable employees to accumulate shares in their company without paying commissions and usually at prices below the market. Obviously, such programs act as incentives for employees and, hopefully, spur productivity and improve employee retention. Some companies have similar programs for suppliers. **Mobil** has been seeking approval from the Securities and Exchange Commission to implement a program that gives Mobil's some 5500 U.S. dealers and distributors the opportunity to invest monthly in Mobil shares through a "dealers and distributors plan." The plan works basically like a dividend reinvestment plan. Contributions to the voluntary investment program will be collected at the same time Mobil collects the dealers' and distributors' payments for deliveries of gasoline. Such programs help cement relationships with suppliers and foster supplier goodwill and involvement.

Shareholder as a Guinea Pig

Test-marketing a product can be expensive. Fortunately, companies have a built-in test group called shareholders. Shareholders represent an interesting test market for new products. Shareholders are more likely to provide candid feedback on a new product, especially since the success of the new product may impact their investment. Shareholders are also accessible via company communications and dividend payments. Therefore, it is easy to get discount coupons for new products and services into their hands and track responses. Common corporate freebies such as discount coupons on new products that accompany a dividend check, or perhaps pull-out product coupons in the quarterly or annual report, not only provide a nice perk for shareholders but are also an effective way to test and build demand for new products.

Good Public Relations

Companies realize that offering shareholder perks and freebies is good public relations. **Ben and Jerry's Homemade** ice cream is one of the best-known companies when it comes to socially responsible investing. The company gives a generous 7½ percent of pretax profits to various charities. The firm has its "Traveling Show" touring bus, complete with vaudevillian performers, which travels across the country raising money for nonprofit organizations. The company's social agenda is a feel-good perk for shareholders. However, "Traveling Show" and the firm's social programs also generate ample public relations for the firm. Such PR is probably the cheapest, and most effective, advertising that money can buy in terms of building brand awareness. Yes, Ben and Jerry's social programs and charitable activities are to be admired. But don't underestimate the amount of ice cream—Ben and Jerry's sold more than $130 million worth in 1992—that is sold due to favorable PR.

Another twist on this notion of "perks for PR" is seen in the aforementioned Exxon direct-purchase plan. It's no secret that Exxon's Valdez tanker incident wasn't exactly a positive PR development for the company. Although Exxon probably wouldn't admit it, I can't help but wonder if the firm's decision to offer a direct-stock purchase program—a program that is highly desirable to investors—wasn't partly a PR move to help repair the company's image with individual investors. Judging from the results—remember that the firm added 187,000 new accounts in the program's first year—it appears that at least a few investors have forgiven the company.

Cheap Equity Capital

Dividend reinvestment plans are an attractive perk for shareholders. These programs, explained in Chapter 3, permit current shareholders to buy stock directly from the company, usually without paying commissions. Stock is purchased in two ways: with dividends that are reinvested in additional common shares and through optional cash investments that investors send directly to the company. These optional cash payments can be as little as $10 to over $100,000 per year in some plans. An especially attractive kicker in about 10 percent of the 900 programs is the ability to buy stock at a discount to the market price—the ultimate "free lunch" (such discounts are discussed in Chapter 5).

Obviously, shareholders benefit nicely from DRIPs. But what do companies get out of offering this perk? Plenty.

First, since shareholders are reinvesting dividends, companies retain the money for investment purposes. This helps cash flow, which can come in handy during rough times.

Second, dividend reinvestment plans, due to their very nature, provide regular buying support for the stock. Such support is generally desired from a corporate standpoint, as it means that there are ready-made buyers who will step in to buy shares at least quarterly. This may help support the stock.

Third, as we saw with Exxon and McDonald's, corporate perks that promote stock ownership, such as DRIPs and direct-purchase programs, have the ability to turn shareholders into customers, which translates into increased sales.

But perhaps the biggest benefit a company receives from offering a dividend reinvestment program is that a DRIP provides a cheap source of equity capital. Companies have a number of ways of raising capital to run their operations. Two common ways are to issue bonds and common stock. These issuances, or *offerings* as they are called, are usually underwritten by an investment bank. The names of Wall Street's leading investment banks are probably familiar to most of you—**Merrill Lynch**, **Goldman Sachs**, and **Salomon Brothers**, for example. For their efforts in organizing the offering and acting as the lead manager for the syndicate assembled to sell the bonds or stocks, the investment bank takes a cut of the action. This cut generally totals at least 3 percent of the money raised and can easily run to 7 percent or more. When talking about stock or bond offerings in the hundreds of millions of dollars, the fees to investment banks are not inconsequential.

However, a company can dodge the investment banker's bite by issuing shares through a dividend reinvestment plan. Companies that have DRIPs usually have two options in acquiring the shares to be used in the program. First, companies may go into the open market to buy shares for DRIP participants. In this way, the company is merely acting as a broker of sorts, and no new shares are created. Second, a firm may issue new shares to DRIP participants. In this instance, the money that shareholders invest through the DRIP goes directly into the company coffers. These funds can be used to retire debt, fund research and development, improve plant and equipment, etc. When a company issues new shares through a DRIP, it acts as its own underwriter and pockets the fees it would otherwise pay to the investment bankers.

Potomac Electric Power, a utility in and around the nation's capital, provides a good example of just how much money can be saved by using a DRIP to raise equity capital. In 1990, Potomac Electric Power raised $29.1 million in equity capital via its DRIP. According to a company spokesperson, the estimated costs of running the DRIP for the year were around $268,000, or less than 1 percent of the equity raised through the plan. Compare those numbers to the expenses incurred for the firm's common stock offering of 4.91 million shares in February 1991. The shares were priced at $21⅜, with the underwriter receiving roughly 69 cents per share, or more than $3.38 million. Fees for such things as printing, lawyers, and accounting services totaled another $145,000. In all, the firm incurred costs of over $3.5 million to raise $101.5 million—or about 3½ percent of the equity raised in the offering.

Thus, the costs to raise equity in this manner were nearly four times as great, in percentage terms, as raising equity via a DRIP. And keep in mind that Potomac Electric Power, because of its strong finances, has a fairly low cost of capital. An indication that DRIPs are effective money-raising tools is that heavy users of capital, particularly utilities and banks, dominate the list of companies offering DRIPs. In fact, electric utilities alone account for nearly 10 percent of all DRIP programs. Clearly, companies can save quite a bit of money by raising equity capital through DRIPs.

The amount of money that a firm can raise through a DRIP can be quite large, especially if a company entices shareholders to invest by offering a discount. For example **South Jersey Industries,** a natural gas utility, amended its DRIP in April 1990 to provide for the purchase of newly issued shares at a 5 percent discount from the market price. South Jersey stipulated that, in addition to reinvested dividends, optional cash payments of up to $30,000 annually qualified for the discount. A generous program, especially when you take into account that South Jersey Industries is an attractive investment aside from the discount.

Investors turned out in droves. In fact in June 1990, plan participants purchased approximately 479,000 new shares of common stock for almost $8 million. To slow down the stream of money, the firm amended the DRIP in August 1990, this time lowering the discount to 3 percent on reinvested dividends and optional cash payments and setting a maximum on optional cash payments of $1000 per quarter.

Chase Manhattan is yet another example of a company that has effectively exploited a discount in its DRIP to draw in capital. According to *The New York Times,* Chase Manhattan raised $92 million in the first half of 1992 by offering a 3 percent discount on optional cash payments. Taking a cue from Chase Manhattan, **Citicorp**—a company that always seems to be in need of capital—in 1992 began offering a 2½ percent discount on shares purchased through optional cash payments in its DRIP. With many companies scrambling for inexpensive ways to raise capital, look for additional firms to employ a discount in a DRIP to raise equity capital.

Conflict of Interest?

The relationship between shareholder and customer can take on an interesting twist when the company is a utility and the shareholder is also a ratepayer. Currently, there are a number of utilities— **Dominion Resources, Philadelphia Suburban, Carolina Power & Light, Connecticut Energy, New Jersey Resources, Oklahoma Gas & Electric, Centerior Energy, Central Maine Power, Northern States Power, Duke Power, Florida Progress, Hawaiian Electric Industries, Minnesota Power & Light, National Fuel Gas, New York State Electric & Gas, Nevada Power, Puget Sound Power & Light, SCANA, San Diego Gas & Electric, Montana Power, Southwest Gas, Union Electric, United Water Resources, WICOR,** and **Wisconsin Energy**—that permit their customers to buy stock directly, even for first-time purchases.

Philadelphia Suburban, a water utility, has been one of the more successful utilities to implement this strategy. In 1992 alone, the firm raised about $25 million by selling stock directly to customers. Some of the funds were used to retire high-interest debt. Had Philadelphia Suburban gone through an investment bank, the costs could easily have been 3 to 5 percent of the amount raised, much higher than the costs of doing it without Wall Street's help.

But a cheap source of equity capital may not be the only reason utilities want customers to be shareholders. If customers own stock in a utility, it presents a most interesting conflict of interest. On the one hand, as a rate-paying customer, you want the lowest rates possible. On the other hand, as a shareholder, high rates aren't so bad for business or dividend payments. Could it be that utilities, such as Philadelphia Suburban, want as many ratepayers as possible to become shareholders since shareholders will be less likely to object when it comes time to ask for a rate hike?

You might think I'm reaching here, but I don't think so. One reason is that I've talked with people in the utility industry, and they have hinted that, yes, having ratepayers as shareholders does make for an interesting relationship. Furthermore, I received a letter from an individual who owns stock in his utility company. The gentleman stated that he doesn't mind higher utility rates since that usually means higher dividends.

Revenge Factor

Another benefit a company may derive from offering a DRIP/direct-purchase program is that the plan provides a way to gain a little revenge on Wall Street. To say that investors, corporate America, and Wall Street have a tenuous relationship would be an understatement. On the one hand individual investors and corporations need brokers and investment bankers to gain access to financial markets. Yet both investors and corporations often feel like money trees for Wall Street firms. Also, plenty of resentment remains due to the merger and acquisition mania, balance sheet leveraging, and insider trading scandals of the '80s—activities for which many investors and companies blame Wall Street.

Therefore it's not a stretch to believe that any time investors and corporations can "stick it" to brokers and investment bankers, they will do so. Direct-purchase plans and self-underwritings via DRIPs are effective ways for investors to gain a little revenge on Wall Street and save brokerage commissions and underwriting fees in the process. A further examination of how dividend reinvestment plans can be a "win-win" situation for investors and corporations is provided in Chapter 3.

2
Leaders
of the Perks

My first contact with corporate perks was through a shareholder welcome package from **Bristol-Myers Squibb** (unfortunately, Bristol-Myers Squibb no longer offers this perk). The package came to my house unannounced and, I might add, unexpectedly since I had purchased five shares of stock only in order to enroll in the company's dividend reinvestment plan.

The gift box was filled with company products, including skin-care lotions, deodorants, and pain relievers. I'm just guessing, but I bet the goodies were worth well over $20—not a bad "dividend" on an investment of just a few hundred dollars.

I learned that Bristol-Myers Squibb wasn't alone in providing a welcome package for new shareholders. In fact I soon discovered that, in addition to free gifts, some companies give shareholders such perks as discounts on products and services, deals on holiday gift packages, special rates on hotel and resort stays, memberships in exclusive shareholder clubs, and free food at the annual shareholder meeting.

In pure dollar terms, some of the deals are quite generous. Since investors usually need only one share to be eligible for perks, the savings from the perks and discounts often exceed the price of the single share of stock. For example, around the Christmas holiday, **Tandy** shareholders receive a 10 percent discount on purchases up to $10,000 at its *Radio Shack* stores. If you were planning to buy yourself expensive computer and electronic gear and junior some video equipment for Christmas totaling $5000, your savings from owning just one share would be $500.

Granted, not all perks are created equal. Some companies spoil shareholders with especially attractive perks and freebies; others tease them with modest discounts. This chapter focuses on the "leaders of the perks"—companies that offer the best investor perks, freebies, and giveaways.

I've divided this chapter based on types of perk and freebies. Since I've already discussed Bristol-Myers Squibb's package for new shareholders, let's look at other firms that welcome new shareholders with more than just open arms.

Rolling Out the Welcome Mat

A number of companies take special care in making a strong first impression on new shareholders. For example:

- **Minnesota Mining & Manufacturing** gives new shareholders a welcome package consisting of such products as *Post-it* notes, tape, sandpaper, and other household products.

- **Colgate-Palmolive,** the marketer of *Colgate* toothpaste, *Mennen Speed Stick, Baby Magic* lotion, *Hill's* pet food, *Ajax,* and *Fab,* sends new shareholders about $15 in discount coupons.

- **Gerber Products,** the baby food maker, sends new shareholders discount coupons and a catalog offering discounts on baby products.

- **Kellogg,** the cereal maker with such leading brands as *Frosted Flakes, Rice Krispies, Frosted Mini-Wheats, Special K, Froot Loops, Apple Jacks, All-Bran, Pop-tarts,* and *Eggo,* provides new shareholders coupons on its products and has been known to provide other gifts, such as a recipe book.

- **Quaker Oats,** in addition to including discount coupons with some quarterly reports, gives new shareholders a packet of discount coupons on the firm's products, which include *Cap'n Crunch* and *Gatorade.*

Companies usually make welcome perks available only to shareholders of record. If you're interested in receiving most company perks, have the stock registered in your name, not the street name or brokerage name.

Where's the Beef?

Privately held companies are often quite generous toward new shareholders who have the opportunity to buy into the firm. One of the more unique welcome packages comes from **Tonga Capital,** a closely held corporation located in Covina, CA. All new shareholders of Tonga receive a sampler package of the company's lean, low-cholesterol beef products (retail value $25). And as a shareholder you're entitled to receive a 10 percent discount on low-fat, low-cholesterol beef. Orders are delivered frozen in insulated containers directly to shareholders' doors.

Shareholder Holiday Gifts and Discounts

A number of corporations get into the holiday spirit by giving shareholders special gifts or making available special holiday packages of products at greatly reduced prices. For example **General Mills,** which markets *Betty Crocker* desserts, *Gold Medal* flour, and *Yoplait* yogurt, and operates *Red Lobster* and *Olive Garden* restaurants, makes available to shareholders a special holiday package of products and coupons— retail value $50—for just $18.95 (price includes UPS delivery to any location within the continental United States). Forms are usually mailed at the beginning of November with the dividend checks. Products featured in the 1992 holiday box included:

- *Multi Grain Cheerios*
- A *Breakfast Pack* cereal assortment
- Strawberry *Gushers* fruit snacks
- *Gold Medal* blueberry muffin mix pouch
- Mushroom and wild rice *Hamburger Helper*
- Cheddar-flavor *Potatoes Express*
- *Betty Crocker Sunkist* lemon bars
- Butter-flavor *Pop Secret*
- Peanut butter-flavor *IncrediBites*

The box also contained coupons for $5 off meals at both *Red Lobster* and the *Olive Garden,* and 100 free points in the Betty Crocker catalog. The package even included *Betty Crocker's Easy Entertaining Cookbook.*

Kimberly-Clark is another company that gives its shareholders the opportunity to purchase a holiday goody bag at a reduced price. The company at one time canceled this program. However, clamor from disappointed shareholders caused the company to reinstate the holiday perk. In the past the package has contained an assortment of Kimberly-Clark products, such as *Kleenex* tissues, *Huggies Baby Wipes*, stationery and envelopes, dinner napkins, *Kleenex* pocket pack, handkerchiefs, and a five-year calendar, as well as samples of new products. The firm charges $12 per box.

Scott Paper, a maker of tissues, paper towels, and toilet paper, makes available discount shareholder gift boxes at Christmas and throughout the year. Last year's box cost $10.

Wrigley, Wm., Jr., the chewing gum producer with such popular brands as *Doublemint, Spearmint, Juicy Fruit, Big Red, Extra, Orbit, Freedent, Big League Chew,* and *Hubba Bubba,* offers the perfect holiday gift for a child or grandchild. Each year in December, the company sends all shareholders a free box containing 20 packs (100 sticks) of gum chosen by the CEO. The flavor changes each year.

If your tastes run toward the upscale, **Brown-Forman** offers an attractive holiday special. In recent years the company has provided a 50 percent discount on certain *Lenox* holiday china and ornaments for shareholders. In addition, the company has provided a 50 percent discount on its *Hartmann* luggage. A pamphlet showing the products for sale is usually sent to shareholders in the fall.

Finally, as if we don't eat enough around the holidays, **Hershey Foods** helps its shareholders and their friends and family to consume even more calories. For shareholders who call 800-544-1347 and request a copy, the company sends a holiday catalog featuring its products. Shareholders can order gifts for friends and relatives, and Hershey will ship the package directly to the recipient.

Shareholder Discounts on Products and Services

Corporations realize that shareholders can be their best customers. Thus, it's not uncommon for companies to provide shareholders with discounts on products and services. An interesting shareholder discount is offered by **Moto Photo,** the operator of photo-processing stores. Shareholders receive a complimentary Moto Photo club membership. Club members receive discounts on film, film processing, picture frames, and special gifts, as well as special deals on cruises and car rentals.

Federal National Mortgage Association ("Fannie Mae") provides a special perk for investors, even those who don't own its stock. The firm, which is a government-sponsored company that is the largest mortgage lender in the U.S., has in the past given away copies of a software program called *Remic Master* (202-752-6604). The software provides assistance in understanding the complicated mortgage-backed securities market. The name "Remic" comes from the term given to real estate mortgage investment conduits. The Remic is the most popular type of collateralized mortgage obligation (CMO). The software program lets you work out yield and total returns on these investments based on various economic assumptions. The company warns that the software is for "investment professionals and institutional investors." Still, because of the popularity of CMOs with individual investors—many of whom have no clue what they are buying when they purchase a CMO—the software may be useful even for small investors.

A Cable-Ready Investment

TV Communications Network (303-751-2900), a small developer of wireless cable television systems, gave shareholders in its hometown market of Denver a special treat. The company installed equipment, waived deposit fees, and offered two free months of its wireless cable TV service for every 4000 shares of stock (the issue is a penny stock trading on the OTC "pink sheets") that an investor held for a year. In addition, two more months of free service were given for each additional 4000 shares held. Thus, if you held 24,000 shares of stock, you received 12 months free service for every year the stock was held.

Entertainment Perks for Shareholders

Several companies in the entertainment and recreational markets provide special perks for shareholders. **Disney, Walt** shareholders may join Disney's Magic Kingdom Club Gold Card Program at a reduced rate. The two-year Gold Card membership costs shareholders $39, a 20 percent savings from the price for nonshareholders. The Gold Card entitles holders to a variety of freebies, perks, and discounts, including:

- Plastic membership card, embossed with the individual's name
- A custom tote bag
- Luggage tags
- Vacation video
- Free subscription to a Disney magazine
- Special "members-only" toll-free number to call to book reservations
- Reduced prices on tickets to all theme parks
- 10 to 30 percent discounts on select hotel accommodations
- Discounts on *National Car Rental* as well as cruises on *Premier, Royal Caribbean*, and *Norwegian Cruise* lines
- Discounts on select *Delta* flights
- Discounts on merchandise purchased at Disney stores throughout the country

For further information on Disney's Magic Kingdom Club Gold Card program, call 714-490-3939.

Additional companies that offer perks on entertainment and recreation include the following.

- **American Recreation Centers,** an operator of bowling alleys, primarily in California, Oklahoma, Kentucky, and Texas, provides shareholders with a number of special perks. First, shareholders of 500 or more shares receive a "distinguished shareholder pass." This pass entitles the holder to five free games of bowling *per day* at any of the company's bowling centers. In addition, "distinguished shareholders" receive a 20 percent discount from published prices in the *Right Start* children's catalog. (American Recreation is the majority shareholder in Right Start, Inc., a direct-mail marketer of products for infants and children.)

- **Anheuser-Busch Cos.,** a brewer and theme-park concern, permits shareholders of at least one share to join the company's Theme Parks Club. Membership entitles you to receive 10 to 15 percent discounts on admission at the company's theme and amusement parks, including *Busch Gardens* in Tampa and Williamsburg, VA; *Sea World* in San Diego, Orlando, and San Antonio; *Water Country USA* in Williamsburg; *Shirley Plantation* in Charles City, VA; *Cypress Gardens* in Winter Haven, FL; and *Adventure Island* in Tampa. Membership also entitles you to discounts on select hotels in the Williamsburg area, meals at *Old San Francisco Steak House* in four Texas locations, and auto rentals at *National Car Rental*.

"Liquid" Dividends for the Thirsty Investor

Anheuser-Busch may be the "King of Beers," but **Portland Brewing** is certainly tops with its shareholders. The Portland, OR, micro-brewer gives new meaning to the phrase "investment liquidity." The company's shareholders receive a card worth a free pint of ale *per day* at the firm's pub adjacent to its brewery. But before you dial your broker, be aware that only Oregon residents are eligible to become stockholders. For further information call 503-222-7150.

- **Santa Anita Companies,** the operator of Santa Anita race track in California, doesn't guarantee winners for shareholders, but it provides the next best thing: free admission. Shareholders with 100 shares or more receive 30 complimentary Club House admission tickets each year; shareholders with less than 100 shares receive six tickets. Tickets are sent automatically to California residents, but shareholders who reside out of state may request tickets in writing. (The company's address is in the perk directory at the back of the book.)

Shareholders Rest Easy With These Perks

Publicly traded hotel and resort companies offer some of the more attractive shareholder perks:

- **Marriott** has a generous shareholder perk program. Shareholders receive $10 off weekend stays at certain *Marriott* hotels. In addition, shareholders receive a 10 percent discount on stays at the firm's *Fairfield Inn* chain (discount good every day of the week) and a 10 percent discount on weekend stays at the company's *Courtyard* hotels.

- You might not associate skiing with a dog food company. Nevertheless, **Ralston Purina** shareholders who like deep powder and turtleneck sweaters receive a nice perk from the company. Ralston Purina owns Keystone Resort in Keystone, CO. Shareholders are eligible for discounts up to 30 percent off accommodations at the ski resort. In addition shareholders receive up to $10 off lift tickets, as well as discounts on ski lessons and rentals.

- **CSX** is best known on Wall Street for its railroad operations. However, the company also operates one of the most prestigious resorts in the country—The Greenbrier, located on 6500 acres in White Sulphur Springs, WV. Throughout the year, The Greenbrier offers CSX shareholders "House Parties" featuring discounted rates and special activities. In 1992 the company held four "House Parties" around Easter, Fourth of July, Labor Day, and Thanksgiving. In addition, shareholders receive a special offer entitling them to a one-time 10 percent discount on the resort's "Modified American Plan" rates. Reservations are accepted on a space-available basis. The offer doesn't apply during "House Parties" or if a shareholder is attending a conference being held at The Greenbrier. For information call 800-624-6070.

▪ **Bay Area Holdings** has gone through a variety of transformations over the last decade. Today the firm's main asset is the Union Hotel in Benicia, CA, located near the Napa Valley. Stephen Lipworth, who heads the company, told me that he's trying to build greater awareness of the company among investors. Mr. Lipworth also told me that, while he's never been approached about it before, he would be willing to give discounts on hotel stays to shareholders. If you have an interest in the stock, or already own it and want a deal on your next visit to the Union Hotel, give Mr. Lipworth a call at 707-746-0368.

Dividend Perks

Receiving a dividend check is one of the more pleasurable perks of stock ownership. Companies nearly always pay dividends quarterly. However, wouldn't it be nice to receive a dividend check every month instead of every three months? After all, our bills come monthly, not quarterly. One company that sends shareholders a dividend check every month is **Winn-Dixie Stores,** an operator of supermarkets in the Sunbelt. The firm has paid dividends since 1934, with the dividend increasing annually for nearly 50 years—a New York Stock Exchange record.

Citizens Utilities has perhaps the most attractive dividend policy in the market. The company supplies electric, gas, telecommunications, water, and wastewater services to residents in Arizona, California, Colorado, Hawaii, Idaho, Illinois, Indiana, Louisiana, Ohio, Oregon, Pennsylvania, Vermont, and Washington. This blend of operations has served the company well, with Citizens Utilities posting higher annual earnings and dividends for over four decades—an outstanding record for any company, let alone a utility.

Citizens Utilities' dividend policy gives shareholders the opportunity of taking stock or cash. The company has two classes of stock:

Series A and Series B shares. The shares differ in two ways. First, Series A shares are convertible into Series B shares, but B shares are not convertible into A. Second, while Series A shares pay stock dividends, Series B shareholders have the annual option of receiving stock dividends or enrolling in the stock-dividend sale plan. This plan offers B holders the opportunity to have their quarterly stock dividends sold in the market at a minimal commission, with the net proceeds of the sale distributed to them each quarter.

This arrangement is attractive from a tax standpoint because if a stockholder does not want cash he or she can receive stock dividends, which will accumulate tax-free until the shares are sold.

This Perk Is Child's Play

Shareholder perks are not reserved exclusively for U.S. companies. A number of Canadian and overseas-based companies offer shareholders freebies and discounts. One of the more interesting international perks is offered by **Irwin Toy,** a Toronto-based maker of toys traded on the Toronto and Montreal stock exchanges. Many of the company's shareholders are children. The firm takes a special interest in its young shareholders and each year holds a formal shareholder meeting for the youngsters. Following the meeting, the children play with the firm's products. Each child is given a questionnaire and asked to rate the toys. In effect, the meeting serves as a giant focus group for the company, giving corporate executives important feedback. In the past, the company has given the youngsters a free gift as well as literature on stock market investing. Scott Irwin told me that about 1200 kids come to the annual meeting. For further information call 416-533-3521.

More Perks to Come

Hopefully, this chapter has whetted your appetite, and you're ready to discover additional investor perks, freebies, and giveaways. The rest of this book covers such perks as commission-free investing (Chapter 3) and buying stocks at a discount (Chapter 5), to freebies available at the annual shareholders' meeting (Chapter 6) and financial perks off Wall Street (Chapter 9). I'll even tell you when a free lunch is really no free lunch at all (Chapter 10).

I've also hidden a few investor freebies of my own throughout the book to reward careful readers. Each of these "buried treasures" comes with its own "code words." If you're lucky enough to find one or all of these freebies, send a note with the code words, along with a business-size, self-addressed stamped envelope, to me at 7412 Calumet Avenue, Hammond, IN 46324-2692. I'll send you the freebie promptly.

3

Who Says You Have to Pay Brokerage Fees?

The Perk of Commission-Free Investing

The average pay of a stockbroker in 1992 was $114,000, according to *The Wall Street Journal*. That pay comes largely from the commissions you pay every time you buy or sell stocks, bonds, and other investments. Those are commissions you pay regardless of whether your investment skyrockets or plummets. In other words, the only person guaranteed to make a profit when you trade is your broker.

But it doesn't have to be that way. Several ways exist to eliminate the broker when buying and selling investments.

Broker Bashing?

Before I discuss various commission-free investing strategies, I want to say something right up front. My book, *Buying Stocks Without a Broker* (McGraw-Hill), didn't exactly endear me to the brokerage community.

I've taken a fair amount of heat from brokers over the last few years due to my position on commission-free investing.

However, as I said in *Buying Stocks Without a Broker* and as I'll say again: I have no bone to pick with brokers. The brokerage industry has brought millions of individuals into the market and has helped educate investors on the merits of stock investing. Certainly, a brokerage commission is a small price to pay if the broker steers you into a stock that increases nicely over time. For novice investors, full-service brokers can provide a needed source of advice on stock selection and portfolio allocation. Clearly, brokers serve many important functions, and the good ones are well worth the commissions they receive.

But my point—and what brokers often fail to recognize whenever I bring up the topic of buying stocks without a broker—is that the investment world is changing. The wealth of relatively inexpensive financial information and services readily available to individuals via magazines, newsletters, television, newspapers, and electronic databases has created a more confident and aware individual investor. These investors want to call their own shots. You only have to look at the growth of discount brokers and deep-discount brokers over the last decade to see that more and more investors are comfortable making their own investment decisions. These self-reliant investors should be rewarded for making their own decisions in the way of low- or no-commission investing.

Death of the Middleman

Brokers also must realize that, to a large extent, what is happening in the financial markets is occurring throughout the business world—the death of the middleman. Stockbrokers are middlemen, putting buyers and sellers together and taking a fee for their efforts.

There was a time when middlemen served an essential role in the marketplace. Communications and information were expensive, and middlemen had the contacts needed to get products and services into the hands of those who wanted them. However, as telecommunications and computing power have become much more advanced and inexpensive, the role of the middleman has diminished.

You see it in retailing. For example **Wal-Mart**, in November 1991, sent a letter to its suppliers stating that it would no longer deal with their independent sales representatives—the middlemen between consumer goods producers and retailers—but only with the suppliers' own top executives. Eliminating the 3 to 5 percent middlemen fees helps keep Wal-Mart's prices down.

You see it in real estate. You're starting to see it in insurance with "low-load" products. You see it in mutual funds, where no-load mutual funds have become the investment of choice for millions.

And you see it in the stock market. The movement toward commission-free stock investing has been a logical progression over the last two decades. First there were full-service brokers. Then came "May Day"—May 1, 1975—the day the Securities and Exchange Commission eliminated fixed commissions. "May Day" opened the door to negotiated rates and a new kid in town—discount brokers. Through the years, full-service and discount brokers found a new enemy: deep discounters, who are discussed in Chapter 4. During this time, "no-load" mutual funds were growing in popularity. Finally, the progression has been completed with the emergence of what I call "no-load" stocks™ as well as the reawakening of investors to dividend reinvestment plans (DRIPs).

No-Load Stocks™

The term "no load" has become commonplace in investor vernacular due to the growth of no-load mutual funds over the last 15 years. No-load funds, which are discussed later in this chapter, are mutual funds that do not have any sales fees attached to them. While no-load funds have many attractions, their primary draw, in my opinion, is convenience. "No-load," especially to small investors, means no brokers and no brokerage fees. In short, "no-load" really means "no-hassle" investing.

If only investing in individual common stocks were as simple! Well, the fact is "no-load" stocks™ do exist, but don't expect to hear about them from your broker.

No-load stocks™ come in two types: those that are open to all investors and those that are open only to corporate customers or residents in the state in which the company is headquartered.

Investing in no-load stocks™ is as easy as investing in no-load mutual funds. All it requires is calling or writing the company and requesting information and an application. Once the information has been received, investors merely have to fill out the application form and return it to the company along with their check for the initial investment. Some no-load stocks™ have initial investment minimums of as little as $20. Following the initial investment, investors may make additional purchases with optional cash payments and reinvested dividends. In most cases the companies charge no fees for these services, and those that do have only nominal fees.

The number of no-load stocks™, especially those open to all investors, pales in comparison to the thousands of stocks on the three major exchanges. However, the list is not without quality issues.

My favorite no-load stock™ is **Exxon.** The company's program permits initial investment with just $250. After the initial investment, investors may make stock purchases with as little as $50 per week up to $8000 per month.

Another interesting no-load stock™ is **Atmos Energy,** a natural gas utility serving parts of western Texas, Louisiana, and Kentucky. The company initiated its direct-purchase program in 1992. Initial purchases may be made with a minimum investment of $200. Thereafter, investments may be as low as $25 up to $60,000 per year.

While investors benefit greatly from direct-purchase programs, benefits also flow back to the companies. Direct-purchase programs help solidify relations with shareholders, which can translate into supporting company management and buying more of the company's products. Direct-purchase programs are effective ways to raise equity capital cheaply. Many no-load stocks™ are utilities—traditionally heavy users of capital. When utilities sell stock directly to customers they are, in effect, underwriting their own stock offering. Issuing shares in this manner is considerably less costly than using an investment bank to float a secondary stock offering. Also, selling stock directly to utility customers turns a ratepayer into a shareholder, which can be helpful when it comes time to seek higher utility rates.

The fact that high-profile companies, such as Exxon and **Texaco**, have direct-purchase programs has fueled interest in these programs from both investors and corporations. Given the benefits companies derive from direct-purchase programs, it's a good bet that more companies will start direct-purchase plans. In fact, I've been told by a number of securities transfer agents that the number of no-load stocks™ will accelerate over the next few years.

Curiously, I haven't heard much from the brokerage community concerning no-load stocks™, other than the occasional hate letter I receive from brokers in response to *Buying Stocks Without a Broker.* With only a very small percentage of companies offering no-load stock programs, brokers probably see them more as an "oddball" investment than as a real threat to their turf.

But no-load mutual funds were an "oddity," too. It will be interesting to see if history repeats itself.

Here is a list of "no-load" stocks™, with telephone numbers. Interested investors should contact the companies for information and prospectuses explaining the programs.

Firms that permit initial stock purchases directly:

Arrow Financial Corp.
(518-793-4121)

American Recreation Centers, Inc.
(916-852-8005)

Atlantic Energy, Inc.
(609-645-4506)

Atmos Energy Corp.
(800-382-8667)

Central Vermont Public Service Corp.
(permitted in less than half the states)
(802-773-2711)

Citizens First Bancorp, Inc.
(201-670-2456)

Dial Corp.
(800-453-2235)

Exxon Corp.
(800-252-1800)

First Alabama Bancshares, Inc.
(800-638-6431)

Grace, W.R. & Co.
(407-362-2000)

Interchange Financial Services
(201-703-2265)

Johnson Controls, Inc.
(414-287-3956)

SCANA Corp.
(permitted in 44 states)
(800-763-5891)

Texaco, Inc.
(800-283-9785)

The following firms permit initial purchases for customers of the corporation or residents of the state in which the company operates:

Bancorp Hawaii, Inc.
(808-537-8239)

Carolina Power & Light Co.
(800-662-7232)

Centerior Energy Corp. (OH)
(800-433-7794)

Central Maine Power Co.
(800-695-4267)

Connecticut Energy Corp.
(203-382-8156)

Dominion Resources, Inc. (VA)
(800-552-4034)

Duke Power Co. (NC)
(800-488-3853)

Florida Progress Corp.
(813-824-6416)

Hawaiian Electric Industries, Inc.
(808-537-9988)

Meridian Bancorp, Inc. (PA)
(215-655-2437)

Minnesota Power & Light Co.
(218-723-3974)

Montana Power Co.
(800-345-6767)

National Fuel Gas Co. (NY & PA)
(716-857-7706)

Nevada Power Co.
(800-344-9239)

New Jersey Resources Corp.
(908-938-1230)

New York State Electric & Gas Corp.
(800-225-5643)

Northern States Power Co. (MN, MI, ND, SD, WI)
(800-527-4677)

Oklahoma Gas & Electric Co.
(800-395-2662)

Philadelphia Suburban Corp.
(215-527-8000)

Puget Sound Power & Light Co. (WA)
(206-462-3719)

San Diego Gas & Electric Co.
(619-696-2020)

Southwest Gas Corp. (NV)
(702-876-7280)

Union Electric Co. (MO)
(800-255-2237)

United Water Resources, Inc. (NY & NJ)
(201-767-2811)

WICOR, Inc. (WI)
(414-291-7026)

Wisconsin Energy Corp.
(800-558-9663)

General Motors has an interesting direct-purchase program. Former GM shareholders of record, but not investors who held the stock in street name, can become GM shareholders again by investing directly through GM. General Motors "E" and "H" shareholders may also purchase GM stock directly by enrolling in the GM DRIP. Dividends from the E and H shares may be reinvested in additional GM common, and E and H shareholders may also make optional cash payments to purchase GM stock. For further information about these GM purchase programs, call 212-791-3909.

The list of no-load stocks™ changes frequently, and I'm sure new companies have been added since this book was published. To receive an updated list of no-load stocks™, send a note with the code words "No-Load Stocks™," along with a business-size, self-addressed stamped envelope, to me at the address given at the end of Chapter 2.

Dividend Reinvestment Plans

The next best thing to no-load stocks™ are "nearly" no-loads, better known as dividend reinvestment plans (DRIPs). In fact, no-load stocks™ are really extensions of companies' DRIPs.

In a nutshell DRIPs, offered by around 900 companies and closed-end funds, allow current shareholders to purchase stock directly from the company, bypassing the broker and brokerage commissions. Investors purchase shares with dividends that the company reinvests for them in additional shares. Most DRIPs also permit investors to make voluntary cash payments directly into the plans to purchase shares.

DRIPs have many attractions for individual investors:

- Most companies charge no commissions for purchasing stocks through their DRIPs, and those that do charge only a nominal fee.

- Nearly 100 companies have DRIPs that permit participants to purchase stock at discounts to prevailing market prices. These discounts are usually 3 to 5 percent and may be as high as 10 percent. This discount feature, which is explored more fully in Chapter 5, is the closest thing to executive stock options for individual investors that exists in the market.

- Most DRIPs permit investors to send optional cash payments (OCPs), in many cases for as little as $10, directly to the company to purchase additional shares. If your investment isn't enough to purchase a whole share, the company will purchase a fractional share, and the fractional share is entitled to that fractional part of the dividend. OCP gives small investors the ability to buy attractive blue-chip stocks when they otherwise might not be able to afford them.

Joining a DRIP is easy. Once you have selected a particular stock, check to see if it has a DRIP. My book, *Buying Stocks Without a Broker* (available in bookstores or by calling 219-931-6480, has a complete directory of programs with addresses, phone numbers, and plan specifics. Also, contact the shareholder relations department of the company of interest to verify that it has a DRIP.

Once you have identified a company with a DRIP, in most cases you have to become a shareholder of record to enroll. This is an important point. You must have the stock registered in your name, not brokerage or "street" name. Once you are a shareholder of record, contact the company for a DRIP application and prospectus. The prospectus provides all the details about the program, including fees, if any; optional cash payment minimums and maximums; investment dates; and eligibility requirements. Chances are, the company will contact you once it has your name as a registered shareholder.

Nuts and Bolts

Although DRIPs are fairly straightforward investments, investors should be aware of the following nuts and bolts:

- Most DRIPs do not charge any fees to participate. However, there is a trend developing in the industry toward the implementation of fees for purchasing shares through the plans. For example, **Bristol-Myers Squibb** toward the end of 1992 implemented a series of fees in its DRIP. The company now charges a fee of 4 percent of the dollar amount of dividends being reinvested (maximum $5 per transaction). The firm also charges 4 percent of the amount invested via optional cash payments (maximum of $25). It is important that you know what the fees are before joining the DRIP.
- Know the number of shares needed to enroll in the DRIP. Most plans require only one share. But Bristol-Myers Squibb, for example,

raised its minimum to 50 shares. Since it costs money to service DRIP investors, it's not surprising that companies are raising their minimums in order to weed out what they feel are "marginal" investors. Check with the company beforehand concerning share requirements for enrollment so there are no surprises when it comes time to join the program.

- DRIPs differ between companies. Some DRIPs purchase stock with optional cash payments once a month, while others do so once a quarter or even once a week. The timing of purchases may differ. Some firms buy on the first business day of each month, while others purchase stock on the 15th of each month. Some DRIPs permit investors to take possession of some of their dividends while reinvesting the remainder, while others require that all dividends be reinvested. Some programs allow individuals to make optional cash payments without reinvesting dividends, while others do not. How do you find out the particulars? Call the company, talk to the shareholder relations department, and get a copy of the plan prospectus.

- Dividends that are reinvested for additional shares are still considered income for tax purposes. The 1099 form that you receive from the company each year gives you this information. Also, DRIP investing requires maintaining good records, especially to determine the cost basis of stock for tax purposes when it comes time to sell. Good record keeping is very important. Companies and their transfer agents provide regular statements that help investors keep track of the DRIP holdings.

- Investing in DRIPs limits your flexibility to some extent. For example, shares are purchased usually once a month. Let's say you like a stock at today's price. By the time the stock is purchased with your optional cash payment, the stock may have risen in price. The ability to transact a buy with the speed that is possible through a broker is lost in a DRIP. The same is true on the sell side, when it may take 5 to 10 trading days for a sell transaction to be conducted. That's why the programs are suited for long-term investing and not trading. Over time, fluctuations in price should even out and not have much of an impact on your portfolio's performance.

Getting the First Share

A potential stumbling block to joining a DRIP is that in most programs you already have to be a shareholder of the company in order to enroll. Brokers offer one avenue for getting that first share, although the fees to purchase one share of stock will be quite high in percentage terms of the total investment. However, investors should realize that once the initial investment has been made through the broker, they will never again need a broker to purchase stock in that company.

Investors may also obtain the first share via the "buddy system." For example, let's say that someone you know has stock in **McDonald's**. You can go through McDonald's transfer agent to have your friend transfer one of his or her shares into your name. After the transfer, you are now a shareholder of record and able to participate in the DRIP.

A variation of the buddy system is getting perhaps five investors together to purchase a total of five shares in a company. Splitting up the brokerage commission on a five-share investment makes each investor's commission relatively small. Following the purchase, go through the transfer agent and have the five shares transferred into the individual names of the five members of the group. Once this has been done, each investor may enroll in the DRIP and begin making investments with reinvested dividends and optional cash payments.

A cottage industry has developed over the last few years to help customers bypass the brokerage community to buy stock for DRIP enrollment. The best known is run by the **National Association of Investors Corporation (NAIC),** located in Royal Oak, MI. For NAIC members ($32 annual membership fee), the organization will buy one share of stock in over 100 companies for a one time charge of $5 per company. I have generally heard good things about the organization, especially when it comes to helping individuals establish and operate investment clubs. For further information, contact the organization at P.O. Box 220, Royal Oak, MI 48068 (313-543-0612).

Two other organizations that offer assistance in obtaining the initial share in order to enroll in DRIPs are **Moneypaper** and **First Share.** Moneypaper (914-381-5400) has a program similar to NAIC but covers a greater number of stocks. However, Moneypaper charges $15 to $20 per purchase, and it can take two months or more to enroll in DRIPs using the program. First Share acts as a clearinghouse for investors who want to purchase one share in a particular company in order to join the DRIP. First Share maintains a database of members' holdings. Let's say you want to purchase one share in Merck & Co. First Share can put you in touch with a Merck shareholder, and the two of you will negotiate the sale of one share. First Share takes a finder's fee for its efforts. For further information, call 800-683-0743.

Letting the Little Guy Play

The most obvious benefit of DRIP investing is the ability to buy shares without paying brokerage fees. However, I believe that the biggest benefit is that the programs allow anyone, including small investors, to participate in the stock market. Many individuals wrongly believe that the market is a rich person's game, especially if you want to buy expensive blue-chip stocks. In fact, any investor can begin a stock accumulation program in hundreds of quality stocks via DRIPs. Indeed, it's not a stretch to call DRIPs the most powerful investment tool available to small investors.

Below is a sampling of quality issues with DRIPs that permit optional cash investments of as little as $10:

Abbott Laboratories	New York Times Co.
American Cyanamid Co.	Norfolk Southern Corp.
Atlantic Richfield Co.	Northern States Power Co.
Clorox Co.	PepsiCo, Inc.
Coca-Cola Co.	Pfizer, Inc.
Dow Chemical Co.	Philip Morris Companies, Inc.
Equifax, Inc.	Quaker Oats Co.
Gannett Co., Inc.	Roadway Services, Inc.
General Electric Co.	Sara Lee Corp.
General Mills, Inc.	SCEcorp
Genuine Parts Co.	Sherwin-Williams Co.
Gillette Co.	Thomas & Betts Corp.
McGraw-Hill, Inc.	VF Corp.
Minnesota Mining & Manufacturing Co.	Walgreen Co.
	Warner-Lambert Co.
Mobil Corp.	Weis Markets, Inc.
Monsanto Co.	

For big market players, below is a sampling of stocks that permit optional cash payments of at least $60,000 per year:

American Express Co.	Coca-Cola Co.
American Home Products Corp.	Colgate-Palmolive Co.
Amoco Corp.	Dow Chemical Co.
Anheuser-Busch Companies, Inc.	Exxon Corp.
Atlantic Richfield Co.	Gannett Co., Inc.
Bausch & Lomb, Inc.	General Electric Co.
Bob Evans Farms, Inc.	Johnson Controls, Inc.
Brooklyn Union Gas Co.	McDonald's Corp.
Browning-Ferris Industries, Inc.	Mobil Corp.

Morgan, J.P., & Co., Inc.

Nalco Chemical Co.

Pall Corp.

PepsiCo, Inc.

Philip Morris Companies, Inc.

Potomac Electric Power Co.

Rochester Telephone Corp.

SCEcorp

Texaco, Inc.

Woolworth Corp.

Wrigley, William, Jr. Co.

Partial Dividend Reinvestment and OCP-Only Plans

Companies provide a variety of options within their dividend reinvestment plans that increase the flexibility and usefulness of the programs. For example, let's say you'd like to reinvest some of your dividends but would like to take possession of some as well. Many companies offer partial reinvestment, which allows you to receive some cash and reinvest the remainder.

For investors who need the dividend income but would still like to make optional cash payments, many companies provide an "OCP-only" option in their DRIPs.

Safekeeping Services

Certificate safekeeping services are another DRIP-related perk. Many companies with DRIPs allow investors to send certificates to the company for safekeeping. Most companies don't charge for this service, and those that do usually have fees of only $5. Safekeeping services alleviate the need to pay for a safety deposit box in order to hold stock certificates. Such services eliminate the possibility of lost or stolen stock certificates. Below is a partial list of companies that offer safekeeping services in their DRIP:

Abbott Laboratories

AFLAC, Inc.

Air Products and Chemicals, Inc.

Allegheny Power System, Inc.

AlliedSignal, Inc.

Aluminum Company of America

American Electric Power Co., Inc.

American Express Co.

American General Corp.

American Greetings Corp.

American Home Products Corp.

American Recreation Centers, Inc.

American Telephone and Telegraph Co.

Ameritech Corp.

Amoco Corp.

AMP, Inc.

ARCO Chemical Co.

ASARCO, Inc.

Atlanta Gas Light Co.

Atmos Energy Corp.

Avon Products, Inc.

Baker Hughes, Inc.

Baltimore Bancorp

Banc One Corp.

Bank of Boston Corp.

Barnett Banks, Inc.

Bausch & Lomb, Inc.

Bay State Gas Co.

BB&T Financial Corp.

Bell Atlantic Corp.

BellSouth Corp.

Bemis Company, Inc.

Beneficial Corp.

Block, H & R, Inc.

Bob Evans Farms, Inc.

Boise Cascade Corp.

Bristol-Myers Squibb Co.

Brooklyn Union Gas Co.

Browning-Ferris Industries, Inc.

Campbell Soup Co.

Capital Holding Corp.

Carolina Power & Light Co.

Centerior Energy Corp.

Central Louisiana Electric Co., Inc.

Central Maine Power Co.

Central Vermont Public Service Corp.

Chase Manhattan Corp.

Chrysler Corp.

CIGNA Corp.

Cincinnati Bell, Inc.

CIPSCO, Inc.

Citicorp

Clorox Co.

Coca-Cola Co.

Colgate-Palmolive Co.

Colonial Gas Co.

ConAgra, Inc.

Connecticut Energy Corp.

Connecticut Natural Gas Corp.

Consolidated Natural Gas Co.

Consolidated Rail Corp.

CoreStates Financial Corp.

CPC International, Inc.

Crane Co.

Crompton & Knowles Corp.

Dayton Hudson Corp.

Delta Air Lines, Inc.

Dominion Resources, Inc.

Donaldson Company, Inc.

Donnelley, R.R., & Sons Co.

Dow Chemical Co.

Du Pont, E.I., de Nemours & Co.

Eastern Utilities Associates

Eastman Kodak Co.

Ecolab, Inc.

EG&G, Inc.

Emerson Electric Co.

Equifax, Inc.

Exxon Corp.

First Chicago Corp.

First Union Corp.

Florida Progress Corp.

FPL Group, Inc.

Freeport-McMoRan, Inc.

Fuller, H.B., Co.

General Mills, Inc.

General Motors Corp.

Georgia-Pacific Corp.

Gillette Co.

Glaxo Holdings Plc

Grace, W.R., & Co.

Graco, Inc.

Green Mountain Power Corp.

Handy & Harman

Hannaford Bros. Co.

Harcourt General, Inc.

Harris Corp.

Harsco Corp.

Hawaiian Electric Industries, Inc.

Hershey Foods Corp.

Home Depot, Inc.

Hubbell, Inc.

Huntington Bancshares, Inc.

Indiana Energy, Inc.

International Business Machines Corp.

International Multifoods Corp.

ITT Corp.

Jefferson-Pilot Corp.

Johnson & Johnson

Johnson Controls, Inc.

Jostens, Inc.

Kellogg Co.

Kemper Corp.

Kerr-McGee Corp.

Kimberly-Clark Corp.

Kmart Corp.

Knight-Ridder, Inc.

Lincoln National Corp.

Liz Claiborne, Inc.

Louisiana Land & Exploration Co.

Louisiana-Pacific Corp.

Lowe's Companies, Inc.

Marsh & McLennan Companies, Inc.

Maytag Corp.

McDonald's Corp.

MCN Corp.

Media General, Inc.

Merck & Co., Inc.

Millipore Corp.

Minnesota Mining & Manufacturing Co.

Mobil Corp.

Morgan, J.P., & Co., Inc.

Motorola, Inc.

National City Corp.

National Medical Enterprises, Inc.

National Service Industries, Inc.

NationsBank Corp.

New England Electric System

New York State Electric & Gas Corp.

New York Times Co.

Newell Co.

NYNEX Corp.

Oklahoma Gas & Electric Co.

Old National Bancorp

Pacific Telesis Group

Pall Corp.

Paramount Communications, Inc.

Penney, J.C., Company, Inc.

Pennsylvania Power & Light Co.

Pentair, Inc.

Peoples Energy Corp.

PepsiCo, Inc.

Pfizer, Inc.

Phelps Dodge Corp.

Philadelphia Electric Co.

Philip Morris Companies, Inc.

Piedmont Natural Gas Co., Inc.

Pitney Bowes, Inc.

Potomac Electric Power Co.

Premier Industrial Corp.

PSI Resources, Inc.

Public Service Co. of Colorado

Quaker Oats Co.

Ralston Purina Co.

Raytheon Co.

Rochester Telephone Corp.

Rubbermaid, Inc.

Ryder System, Inc.

St. Paul Companies, Inc.

San Diego Gas & Electric Co.

Sara Lee Corp.

SCANA Corp.

SCEcorp

Schering-Plough Corp.

Sears, Roebuck and Co.

Shawmut National Corp.

Sherwin-Williams Co.

SmithKline Beecham Plc

Smucker, J.M., Co.

Southeastern Michigan Gas
Enterprises, Inc.

Southwest Gas Corp.

Southwest Water Co.

Southwestern Bell Corp.

Stanhome, Inc.

Stride Rite Corp.

Tambrands, Inc.

TECO Energy, Inc.

Texaco, Inc.

Texas Utilities Co.

Thomas & Betts Corp.

Time Warner, Inc.

Toro Co.

Transamerica Corp.

Tribune Co.

TRW, Inc.

UGI Corp.

Union Electric Co.

Union Pacific Corp.

United Water Resources, Inc.

UNUM Corp.

Upjohn Co.

USF&G Corp.

UST, Inc.

U S West, Inc.

V. F. Corp.

Wachovia Corp.

Walgreen Co.

Warner-Lambert Co.

Wells Fargo & Co.

Wendy's International, Inc.

Weyerhaeuser Co.

Whitman Corp.

Wisconsin Energy Corp.

WMX Technologies, Inc.

Worthington Industries, Inc.

WPL Holdings, Inc.

Wrigley, William, Jr. Co.

Zurn Industries, Inc.

Individual Retirement Accounts

DRIPs are perfect for long-term investing, which make them perfect for an individual retirement account. Unfortunately, it's difficult to hold DRIPs in an IRA. In order to have stocks in a self-directed IRA, you have to have a custodian for the account. Brokerage firms, which are the custodians for many self-directed IRAs, usually won't offer custodial services for an IRA with DRIP since they don't get commissions each time stock is purchased in a DRIP. Other custodial agents, such as banks, may provide such services, but their numbers are extremely low.

Fortunately, a few companies have implemented DRIPs with an IRA option. **Exxon** offers an IRA with its DRIP and charges an annual administrative fee of $20. **Atmos Energy** and **Connecticut Energy** are additional companies that offer a DRIP with an IRA option. Both charge an annual $35 administrative fee. I'm sure many companies are watching these programs to evaluate whether it's worthwhile to offer a DRIP with an IRA option.

Automatic Withdrawal/Direct Deposit of Dividends

An attractive service offered by a growing number of DRIPs is electronic funds transfer to and from shareholders' accounts. For example, **Pacific Telesis Group** has made monthly optional cash investments easy by providing automatic supplemental contributions of a minimum of $50 per month via direct electronic funds transfer from a participant's bank account. **Exxon** is another company with direct electronic funds transfer for optional cash payments.

Many companies offer the ability to have dividends directly deposited into shareholders' bank accounts via electronic fund transfer. Direct deposit helps eliminate delays that may occur due to slow postal delivery. The program also eliminates lost dividend checks. Below is a list of companies that, according to my research as well as research done by the National Automated Clearing House Association and Standard and Poor's, offer electronic direct deposit of dividends:

Allegheny Power System, Inc.	Atlantic Energy, Inc.
Aluminum Company of America	Atlantic Richfield Co.
American Brands, Inc.	Atmos Energy Corp.
American Express Co.	Avnet, Inc.
American General Corp.	Avon Products, Inc.
American Greetings Corp.	Ball Corp.
American Telephone and Telegraph Co.	Baltimore Gas and Electric Co.
Ameritech Corp.	Bancorp Hawaii, Inc.
Amoco Corp.	Bard, C.R., Inc.
AmSouth Bancorp.	Barnett Banks, Inc.
Atlanta Gas Light Co.	Baxter International, Inc.

Bay State Gas Co.

BB&T Financial Corp.

BCE, Inc.

Bell Atlantic Corp.

Black Hills Corp.

Boatmen's Bancshares, Inc.

Bob Evans Farms, Inc.

Boise Cascade Corp.

Borden, Inc.

Bristol-Myers Squibb Co.

Brooklyn Union Gas Co.

Brown-Forman Corp.

Carolina Power & Light Co.

Central Louisiana Electric Co., Inc.

Central Maine Power Co.

Chevron Corp.

CIGNA Corp.

CILCORP, Inc.

Cincinnati Bell, Inc.

CIPSCO, Inc.

Coca-Cola Co.

Colgate-Palmolive Co.

Comerica, Inc.

Connecticut Energy Corp.

Consolidated Edison Co. of New York, Inc.

Consolidated Natural Gas Co.

Consumers Water Co.

CoreStates Financial Corp.

Corning, Inc.

Crestar Financial Corp.

CSX Corp.

Dana Corp.

Dean Foods Co.

Disney, Walt, Co.

Dow Chemical Co.

Dow Jones & Co., Inc.

Duke Power Co.

E-Systems, Inc.

Eastman Kodak Co.

Empire District Electric Co.

Energen Corp.

EnergyNorth, Inc.

Equifax, Inc.

Equitable Resources, Inc.

Exxon Corp.

Fifth Third Bancorp

First Alabama Bancshares, Inc.

First Bancorporation of Ohio

First Commerce Corp.

First Fidelity Bancorp.

First Michigan Bank Corp.

First of America Bank Corp.

First Security Corp.

First Union Corp.

First Virginia Banks, Inc.

Firstar Corp.

Fleet Financial Group, Inc.

Fourth Financial Corp.

Freeport-McMoRan, Inc.

Fuller, H.B., Co.

General Motors Corp.

Gerber Products Co.

Graco, Inc.

Green Mountain Power Corp.

Hannaford Bros. Co.

Hawaiian Electric Industries, Inc.

Hormel, Geo. A., & Co.

Household International, Inc.

Huntington Bancshares, Inc.

Idaho Power Co.

IES Industries, Inc.

Inco, Ltd.

Indiana Energy, Inc.

International Paper Co.

Iowa-Illinois Gas & Electric Co.

ITT Corp.

Johnson & Johnson

Johnson Controls, Inc.

Jostens, Inc.

KeyCorp

Kimberly-Clark Corp.

Kmart Corp.

LG&E Energy Corp.

Lincoln National Corp.

Marshall & Ilsley Corp.

MCN Corp.

MDU Resources Group, Inc.

Mellon Bank Corp.

Merck & Co., Inc.

Meridian Bancorp, Inc.

Middlesex Water Co.

Minnesota Mining & Manufacturing Co.

Minnesota Power & Light Co.

Mobile Gas Service Corp.

Nalco Chemical Co.

National City Corp.

National Fuel Gas Co.

NBD Bancorp, Inc.

Nevada Power Co.

New England Electric System

New York State Electric & Gas Corp.

NICOR, Inc.

Nordson Corp.

Norfolk Southern Corp.

North Carolina Natural Gas Corp.

Northern States Power Co.

NYNEX Corp.

Oklahoma Gas & Electric Co.

Oneida Ltd.

Orange & Rockland Utilities, Inc.

Pacific Telesis Group

PacifiCorp

Pall Corp.

Panhandle Eastern Corp.

Pennsylvania Power & Light Co.

Pentair, Inc.

Peoples Energy Corp.

Pfizer, Inc.

Phelps Dodge Corp.

Philadelphia Electric Co.

Philip Morris Companies, Inc.

Piccadilly Cafeterias, Inc.

Piedmont Natural Gas Company, Inc.

PNC Bank Corp.

Potomac Electric Power Co.

PPG Industries, Inc.

Procter & Gamble Co.

Public Service Co. of Colorado

Public Service Enterprise Group, Inc.

Puget Sound Power & Light Co.

Quaker Oats Co.

Supervalu, Inc.

Synovus Financial Corp.

U.S. Bancorp

Gift-Giving Programs

Some DRIPs make it easy to give stock as gifts. **Exxon**'s program has a gift-giving feature, as does **Texaco**'s. Under Texaco's program, you can open an Investor Services Plan account in a person's name, and the company provides you with a gift certificate to give the recipient.

Even if a company doesn't have a formal "gift-giving" feature to its DRIP, it's easy to give shares as a gift by transferring one of your shares to the individual. For example, if you transfer one of your shares to your child or grandchild, McDonald's will give you a mock "stock certificate" that you can give the child.

Save Commissions on the Sell Side

Dividend reinvestment plans not only save you money when you buy stock, but also when you sell. Most DRIPs permit investors to sell stock directly from the plan, and the fees for selling are usually much lower than you'd pay by going through a broker. That's because the company sells shares in bulk and gets volume discounts unavailable to small investors.

In some cases, it is even possible to sell stock through the company without paying any brokerage commission. A few DRIPs permit this, as do companies that conduct what are called "odd-lot" buybacks of stock. Odd lots are holdings of less than 100 shares in a stock. Odd-lot holders cost the company money since quarterly and annual reports must be mailed to them. A company with many odd-lot holders may want to eliminate them by offering to buy back all of the shares from stockholders who own fewer than 100 shares. Companies will often charge little or no commission to buy back the shares.

An interesting example of an odd-lot buyback was **Fibreboard Corp.,** a manufacturer of lumber and insulation products. In December 1991, the company offered to buy back all of the shares owned by stockholders who had holdings of fewer than 100 shares. The company charged no commissions for the service. Through the program, participating holders had the option of automatically donating their cash proceeds to one of six nationally recognized charities or taking the cash. The firm stated that the plan was in response to inquiries by odd-lot shareholders who had requested assistance in selling their small number of shares in the open market. In some cases the minimum brokerage commission, often about $40, actually exceeded the value of the shares to be sold. The firm also received requests from stockholders, who asked the firm to assist them in donating their shares to charity. Fibreboard felt that by pooling any donations made by stockholders, a more significant and meaningful contribution could be made to the named charities.

Many of Fibreboard's shareholders fell into the odd-lot category following the spin-off of the company from Louisiana-Pacific in 1988. When a company is spun off, shareholders often receive a small holding in the newly created firm. Such companies are prime candidates to offer an odd-lot buyback program.

A company that offers a continuous odd-lot buyback program is **U S West.** The regional telephone issue offers owners of fewer than 100 shares the option of selling their stock through the company. U S West charges a fee of $6 per account plus $0.06 per share. The deal is a good one for investors who may have only, say, 25 shares. In this instance, the fee would be $7.50—well below minimum brokerage commission rates.

If you're holding odd lots in an issue in which you have no intention of rounding up your position—perhaps you got them via a spin-off—and you would like to sell, contact the firm to see if an odd-lot buyback program is offered.

Choosing a DRIP

Of course, just because a company offers a DRIP and related perks doesn't make it a good investment. The bottom line with any investment is the quality of the firm's financial position, prospects for earnings growth over the next several years, dividend-growth potential, and the strength and defensibility of its industry position. These factors need to be assessed before buying any investment. Chances are, with some 900 companies offering dividend reinvestment plans, at least a few of the companies that survive your investment-selection process will offer DRIPs.

For guidance on the best DRIPs, I've selected what I feel are quality DRIP holdings divided by industry groups. The addresses and phone numbers for these companies are available in the perk directory in Chapter 11. Companies change plans frequently. Thus, always check with the company and obtain a DRIP prospectus before investing.

Aerospace and Defense
Raytheon Co.

Agribusiness
ConAgra, Inc.
Ralston Purina Co.

Apparel Manufacturers
Liz Claiborne, Inc.

Russell Corp.
V.F. Corp.

Appliances
Whirlpool Corp.

Auto Parts
Genuine Parts Co.

Banking
Banc One Corp.
Bancorp Hawaii, Inc.
Central Fidelity Banks, Inc.
Dauphin Deposit Corp.
Fifth Third Bancorp
First Alabama Bancshares, Inc.
First Bancorp. of Ohio
First Michigan Bank Corp.
First Virginia Banks, Inc.
Firstar Corp.
Mark Twain Bancshares, Inc.
Marshall & Ilsley Corp.
Morgan, J.P., & Co., Inc.
NBD Bancorp, Inc.
Wachovia Corp.

Brewing
Anheuser-Busch Companies, Inc.

Broadcasting
CBS, Inc.

Building Supplies
PPG Industries, Inc.
RPM, Inc.
Sherwin-Williams Company
Weyerhaeuser Co.

Chemicals
Air Products & Chemicals, Inc.
American Cyanamid Co.
Crompton & Knowles Corp.
Dow Chemical Co.
Du Pont, E.I., de Nemours & Co.
Fuller, H.B., Co.
Loctite Corp.
Monsanto Co.
Nalco Chemical Co.

Communications
American Telephone & Telegraph Co.
Ameritech Corp.
Bell Atlantic Corp.
BellSouth Corp.
Cincinnati Bell, Inc.
Communications Satellite Corp.
GTE Corp.
Northern Telecom Ltd.
NYNEX Corp.
Pacific Telesis Group
Rochester Telephone Corp.
Southern New England Telecommunications Corp.
Southwestern Bell Corp.
Sprint Corp.
U S West, Inc.

Containers and Packaging
Bemis Co.

Cosmetics and Toiletries
Gillette Co.
Tambrands, Inc.

Discount and Variety
Home Depot, Inc.
Lowe's Companies, Inc.

Drug Chains
Rite Aid Corp.
Walgreen Co.

Drugs
Abbott Laboratories
American Home Products Corp.
Bristol-Myers Squibb Co.
Glaxo Holdings Plc
Lilly, Eli, & Co.

Merck & Co., Inc.

Novo-Nordisk A/S

Pfizer, Inc.

Schering-Plough Corp.

Warner-Lambert Co.

Electric Utilities

Consolidated Edison Co. of New York, Inc.

Duke Power Co.

IPALCO Enterprises, Inc.

Minnesota Power & Light Co.

Northern States Power Co.

Orange & Rockland Utilities, Inc.

Potomac Electric Power Co.

San Diego Gas & Electric Co.

SCEcorp

Southern Indiana Gas & Electric Co.

TECO Energy, Inc.

Wisconsin Energy Corp.

WPL Holdings, Inc.

Electrical Equipment

Emerson Electric Co.

General Electric Co.

Hubbell, Inc.

Premier Industrial Corp.

Thomas & Betts Corp.

Electronics Components

AMP, Inc.

Avnet, Inc.

Filter Products

Pall Corp.

Financial Services/Broker

Federal National Mortgage Association

Food

Campbell Soup Co.

CPC International, Inc.

Dean Foods Co.

General Mills, Inc.

Gerber Products Co.

Heinz, H.J., Co.

Hershey Foods Corp.

Hormel, Geo. A., & Co.

Kellogg Co.

Quaker Oats Co.

Sara Lee Corp.

Smucker, J.M., Co.

Wrigley, William, Jr. Co.

Food Chain

Fleming Companies, Inc.

Giant Food, Inc.

Hannaford Brothers Co.

Weis Markets, Inc.

Winn-Dixie Stores, Inc.

Health Care

Bard, C.R., Inc.

Bausch & Lomb, Inc.

Baxter International, Inc.

Johnson & Johnson

Medtronic, Inc.

Household Furnishings

Rubbermaid, Inc.

Industrial Products

Crane Co.

Keystone International, Inc.

Insurance

CIGNA Corp.

General Re Corp.

Jefferson-Pilot Corp.

Lincoln National Corp.

Marsh & McLennan Companies, Inc.

Liquor

Brown-Forman Corp.

Multi-industry

Corning, Inc.

Dexter Corp.

Dial Corp.

Harcourt General, Inc.

Honeywell, Inc.

McKesson Corp.

Minnesota Mining & Manufacturing Co.

Paramount Communications, Inc.

Time Warner, Inc.

Natural Gas

Atmos Energy Corp.

Brooklyn Union Gas Co.

Consolidated Natural Gas Co.

Indiana Energy, Inc.

South Jersey Industries, Inc.

Natural Resources

Phelps Dodge Corp.

Oil

Amoco Corp.

Atlantic Richfield Co.

Chevron Corp.

Exxon Corp.

Mobil Corp.

Texaco, Inc.

Paper

International Paper Co.

Kimberly-Clark Corp.

Scott Paper Co.

Pollution Control

Browning-Ferris Industries, Inc.

Safety-Kleen Corp.

WMX Technologies, Inc.

Zurn Industries, Inc.

Printing

Donnelley, R.R., & Sons Co.

Publishing

Dow Jones & Co., Inc.

Gannett Co., Inc.

Knight-Ridder, Inc.

McGraw-Hill, Inc.

New York Times Co.

Tribune Co.

Rails

Consolidated Rail Corp.

CSX Corp.

Norfolk Southern Corp.

Union Pacific Corp.

Real Estate Investment Trust

Washington Real Estate Investment Trust

Restaurants

Bob Evans Farms, Inc.

McDonald's Corp.

Retail Department Stores

Dayton Hudson Corp.

Kmart Corp.

Limited, The, Inc.

May Department Stores Co.

Penney, J.C., Co., Inc.

School Supplies

Jostens, Inc.

Services

Block, H & R, Inc.

Equifax, Inc.

National Service Industries, Inc.

Rollins, Inc.

Soap Companies

Church & Dwight Co.

Clorox Co.

Colgate-Palmolive Co.

Procter & Gamble Co.

Soft Drink

Coca-Cola Co.

PepsiCo, Inc.

Steel

Nucor Corp.

Worthington Industries, Inc.

Technology

Intel Corp.

Motorola, Inc.

Tobacco

American Brands, Inc.

Philip Morris Companies, Inc.

Universal Corp.

UST, Inc.

Trucking

Roadway Services, Inc.

Water Utilities

American Water Works Co., Inc.

United Water Resources, Inc.

Investors who would like more information on DRIPs should read my book, *Buying Stocks Without a Broker,* which discusses DRIPs in depth and provides model DRIP portfolios and specific DRIP recommendations. The book also provides a complete directory of all programs, with addresses, phone numbers, plan specifics, and performance ratings. For continuous coverage of DRIPs, let me plug my monthly newsletter, *DRIP Investor* (7412 Calumet Ave., Hammond, IN 46324-2692). The newsletter has a special focus on new DRIP plans as well as new "no-load" stocks™. A discount coupon for a subscription to *DRIP Investor* is in the back of the book.

Foreign Companies With DRIPS

A number of foreign companies offer DRIPs, providing U.S. citizens with an easy way to invest in foreign stocks for little or no commission.

Historically, overseas investing has been pretty much the private domain of institutional investors with access to foreign exchanges. However, that situation has changed with the growth of American Depositary Receipts, better known as ADRs.

ADRs are issued by U.S. banks against the actual shares of foreign companies held in trust by a branch or correspondent institution overseas. Oftentimes, ADRs are not issued on a share-for-

---

(Continued)

share basis. Instead, one ADR may be the equivalent of five or ten ordinary shares of the company.

ADRs have become popular in recent years. One reason is convenience. Investors can buy and sell ADRs like ordinary shares, eliminating the need for currency translations. Commissions to purchase ADRs are smaller than would be charged if the securities were purchased on foreign markets. Since ADRs trade in the U.S., transactions are usually settled within five days. On some foreign exchanges, settlement of trades can take two weeks or longer. Dividends on ADRs are paid in U.S. dollars.

There are two types of ADRs: sponsored and unsponsored. Unsponsored ADRs are created in response to investors' demand. The foreign company okays the creation of the ADR but does not play an active role in the program. In a sponsored program, the foreign company appoints a bank to service its ADR holders. The company pays for the cost of the program and agrees to provide ADR holders with financial reports. Only sponsored ADRs may be listed on the New York and American Stock Exchanges.

Although ADRs offer plenty of pluses for investors, there are some things to consider before investing. Currency fluctuations will impact ADRs. When local currencies strengthen versus the dollar, the return on the ADR is boosted. Thus, if you own shares in a country whose stock market is rising and whose currency is strengthening against the dollar, you're getting a double-powered boost to your portfolio. Conversely, if the dollar is strengthening against the nation's currency of your ADR, returns will suffer.

Another consideration is that accounting norms differ between countries. Thus, interpreting financial data may be difficult.

A number of quality foreign companies offer DRIPs for U.S. investors. This is an interesting way to accumulate stock in overseas firms. The table below lists ADRs, representing several countries, that offer DRIPs. Investors who are interested in DRIPs of foreign securities should first obtain prospectuses.

ADRs offering DRIPs:

British Airways Plc (Airlines) (800-428-4237)

British Petroleum Co. Plc (Energy) (800-428-4237)

Broken Hill Proprietary Co. Ltd. (Resources) (212-648-3143)

Glaxo Holdings Plc (Drugs) (800-524-4458)

Marks & Spencer (Retailing) (800-428-4237)

National Australia Bank Ltd. (Banking) (212-648-3143)

News Corp. Ltd. (Media/Entertainment) (212-657-7322)	Volvo AB (Automobiles) 212-754-3300)
Novo-Nordisk A/S (Drugs) (800-428-4237)	Westpac Banking Corp. (Banking) (800-428-4237)
SmithKline Beecham Plc (Drugs) (800-428-4237)	Willis Corroon Group Plc (Insurance) (800-428-4237)

Commission-Free Investing in U.S. Treasury Securities

The U.S. Treasury offers investors a perk by selling treasuries directly without charging a commission.

For those of you who may not be familiar with treasury securities, they come in three flavors: treasury bills, notes, and bonds. Treasury bills are short-term obligations with a term of 1 year or less. Treasury notes have maturities of 1 to 10 years. Treasury bonds have maturities greater than 10 years.

The securities differ in the minimum denominations in which they are issued. Notes maturing in 4 years or longer, as well as all bonds, are usually available in minimum denominations of $1000. Notes maturing in less than 4 years are issued in minimum denominations of $5000. Treasury bills are sold in minimum amounts of $10,000.

One final difference is the payment of interest. Treasury notes and bonds pay interest twice a year. Treasury bills do not pay a stated interest rate. Rather, bills are sold at a discount to par, and the difference between the purchase price of the bill and the amount that the owner is paid at maturity (par) represents the interest.

Treasury securities are popular for several reasons. First, since treasuries are backed by the full taxing power of the federal government, the interest and return of principal are fully guaranteed. Also, interest earned on treasury securities is exempt from state and local taxes, although it is subject to federal income tax.

Treasury securities are sold via an auction process. Notices of upcoming auctions are featured in *The Wall Street Journal*. Treasury bills are usually auctioned weekly, and most notes and bonds are auctioned quarterly.

Most investors buy treasury securities from a broker or bank. Fees differ, but it is not unusual to pay $70 or more to purchase a $10,000 treasury security. In addition, your bank or broker may charge you a safekeeping fee for holding the treasury certificate. But investors who are willing to spring for some stamps and stationery can pocket those commissions by going directly to the Federal Reserve Board.

If you live near a Federal Reserve Bank (see Fig. 3-1 for addresses and phone numbers of Federal Reserve Banks and Treasury servicing offices), you may apply in person to buy treasuries directly.

If you don't live near a Federal Reserve branch, you can still buy treasuries via the mail by sending in a new account form—one can be obtained by writing or calling the Federal Reserve Bank nearest you—and a letter with the following information (this procedure is for purchasing notes or bonds):

- Name and address
- Telephone number
- Type and amount of securities desired
- Whether the bid is competitive or noncompetitive (I'll explain this shortly)
- Preference for form in which securities are to be issued, name(s) for registration, and the social security number(s)
- Direct deposit information—name of purchaser's financial institution, routing number of financial institution, account name, number, and type (checking or savings)
- Purchaser's signature—you should also include the payment, either in cash, certified personal check, bank check, or check issued by credit union, made payable to the Federal Reserve Bank where the information and payment are being sent. On the outside of the envelope write, "Tender for Treasury Notes [or Bonds or Bills]." Make sure that your payment arrives prior to the auction date listed in the paper.

The procedure for purchasing treasury bills is similar, with just a few wrinkles. Applications, or tenders, may be obtained at the Federal Reserve Bank. If you apply without using a tender, you should send a new account form and the same information required for notes and bonds. In addition you should include:

- The maturity desired—13, 26, or 52 weeks
- The face amount of bills being purchased
- Whether you want to reinvest the funds at maturity
- Your telephone number during business hours

Payment for treasury bills may be in the form of cash; checks issued by banks, savings and loans, or credit unions; certified personal checks; and matured U.S. Treasury notes or bonds. On the outside of

APPENDIX A

ADDRESSES AND TELEPHONE NUMBERS OF FEDERAL RESERVE BANKS AND TREASURY SERVICING OFFICES

For In-Person Visits	For Written Correspondence	For In-Person Visits	For Written Correspondence
Atlanta 104 Marietta Street, N.W. Atlanta, GA 404-521-8653 404-521-8657 (recording)	FRB Atlanta 104 Marietta Street, N.W. Atlanta, GA 30303	**Denver** 1020 16th Street Denver, CO 303-572-2477 303-572-2475 (recording)	Denver Branch FRB of Kansas City PO Box 5228 Terminal Annex Denver, CO 80217
Baltimore 502 South Sharp Street Baltimore, MD 301-576-3553 301-576-3500 (recording)	Baltimore Branch FRB of Richmond PO Box 1378 Baltimore, MD 21203	**Detroit** 160 West Fort Street Detroit, MI 313-964-6157 313-963-4936 (recording)	Detroit Branch FRB of Chicago PO Box 1059 Detroit, MI 48231
Birmingham 1801 Fifth Avenue, North Birmingham, AL 205-731-8702	Birmingham Branch FRB Atlanta PO Box 830447 Birmingham, AL 35283-0447	**El Paso** 301 East Main Street El Paso, TX Call Dallas 214-651-6362 214-651-6177 (recording)	El Paso Branch FRB of Dallas PO Box 100 El Paso, TX 79999
Boston 600 Atlantic Avenue Boston, MA 617-973-3810 617-973-3805 (recording)	FRB of Boston PO Box 2076 Boston, MA 02106	*Helena*—The Helena Branch of the Federal Reserve Bank of Minneapolis does not deal in Treasury securities. Persons in the area served by the Helena Branch should instead contact the Minneapolis office listed in this Appendix.	
Buffalo 160 Delaware Avenue Buffalo, NY 716-849-5079 716-849-5030 (recording)	Buffalo Branch FRB of New York PO Box 961 Buffalo NY 14240	**Houston** 1701 San Jacinto Street Houston, TX 713-659-4433 713-652-1688 (recording)	Houston Branch FRB of Dallas PO Box 2578 Houston, TX 77252
Charlotte 530 East Trade Street Charlotte, NC 704-358-2410 or 2411 704-358-2424 (recording)	Charlotte Branch FRB of Richmond PO Box 30248 Charlotte, NC 28230	**Jacksonville** 800 West Water Street Jacksonville, FL 904-632-1179	Jacksonville Branch FRB of Atlanta PO Box 2499 Jacksonville, FL 32231-2499
Chicago 230 South LaSalle Street Chicago, IL 312-322-5369 312-786-1110 (recording)	FRB of Chicago PO Box 834 Chicago, IL 60690	**Kansas City** 925 Grand Avenue Kansas City, MO 816-881-2783 or 2409 816-881-2767 (recording)	FRB of Kansas City Attn. Securities Dept. PO Box 419440 Kansas City, MO 64141-6440
Cincinnati 150 East Fourth Street Cincinnati, OH 513-721-4787 Ext. 333	Cincinnati Branch FRB of Cleveland PO Box 999 Cincinnati, OH 45201	**Little Rock** 325 West Capitol Avenue Little Rock, AR 501-372-5451 Ext. 288	Little Rock Branch FRB of St. Louis PO Box 1261 Little Rock AR 72203
Cleveland 1455 East Sixth Street Cleveland, OH 216-579-2490	FRB of Cleveland PO Box 6387 Cleveland, OH 44101	**Los Angeles** 950 South Grand Avenue Los Angeles, CA 213-624-7398 213-688-0068 (recording)	Los Angeles Branch FRB of San Francisco PO Box 2077 Terminal Annex Los Angeles, CA 90051
Dallas 400 South Akard Street Dallas, TX 214-651-6362 214-651-6177 (recording)	FRB of Dallas Securities Dept. Station K Dallas, TX 75222	**Louisville** 410 South Fifth Street Louisville, KY 502-568-9236 or 9231	Louisville Branch FRB of St. Louis PO Box 32710 Louisville, KY 40232

Figure 3-1

Addresses Continued

For In-Person Visits	For Written Correspondence	For In-Person Visits	For Written Correspondence
Memphis 200 North Main Street Memphis, TN 901-523-7171 Ext. 622 or 629 Ext. 641 (recording)	Memphis Branch FRB of St. Louis PO Box 407 Memphis, TN 38101	**Portland** 915 S.W. Stark Street Portland, OR 503-221-5932 503-221-5921 (recording)	Portland Branch FRB of San Francisco PO Box 3436 Portland, OR 97208-3436
Miami 9100 N.W. 36th Street Miami, FL 305-471-6497	Miami Branch FRB of Atlanta PO Box 520847 Miami, FL 33152-0847	**Richmond** 701 East Byrd Street Richmond, VA 804-697-8372 804-697-8355 (recording)	FRB of Richmond PO Box 27622 Richmond, VA 23261-7622
Minneapolis 250 Marquette Avenue Minneapolis, MN 612-340-2075	FRB of Minneapolis PO Box 491 Minneapolis, MN 55480	**Salt Lake City** 120 South State Street Salt Lake City, UT 801-322-7944 801-322-7911 (recording)	Salt Lake City Branch FRB of San Francisco PO Box 30780 Salt Lake City, UT 84130
Nashville 301 Eighth Avenue, North Nashville, TN 615-251-7100	Nashville Branch FRB of Atlanta 301 Eighth Avenue, North Nashville, TN 37203	**San Antonio** 126 East Nueva Street San Antonio, TX 512-978-1305 or 1309 512-978-1330 (recording)	San Antonio Branch FRB of Dallas PO Box 1471 San Antonio, TX 78295
New Orleans 525 St. Charles Avenue New Orleans, LA 504-586-1505 Ext. 293 or 294	New Orleans Branch FRB of Atlanta PO Box 61630 New Orleans, LA 70161	**San Francisco** 101 Market Street San Francisco, CA 415-974-2330 415-974-3491 (recording)	FRB of San Francisco PO Box 7702 San Francisco, CA 94120-7702
New York 33 Liberty Street New York, NY 212-720-6619 24-hour recording: 212-720-5823 (results) 212-720-7773 (new offerings)	FRB of New York Federal Reserve PO Station New York, NY 10045	**Seattle** 1015 Second Avenue Seattle, WA 206-343-3605 206-343-3615 (recording)	Seattle Branch FRB of San Francisco PO Box 3567 Terminal Annex Seattle, WA 98124
Oklahoma City 226 Dean A. McGee Avenue Oklahoma City, OK 405-270-8652	Oklahoma City Branch FRB of Kansas City PO Box 25129 Oklahoma City, OK 73125	**St. Louis** 411 Locust Street St. Louis, MO 314-444-8665 or 8666 314-444-8602 (recording)	FRB of St. Louis PO Box 442 St. Louis, MO 63166
Omaha 2201 Farnam Street Omaha, NE 402-221-5636	Omaha Branch FRB of Kansas City PO Box 3958 Omaha, NE 68102	**United States Treasury** Washington, DC Bureau of the Public Debt 1300 C Street, S.W. Washington, DC 202-287-4113 Device for hearing impaired: 202-287-4097	 Mail Inquiries to: Bureau of the Public Debt Washington, DC 20239-1000 Mail Tenders to: Bureau of the Public Debt Washington, DC 20239-1500
Philadelphia Ten Independence Mall Philadelphia, PA 215-574-6675 or 6680	FRB of Philadelphia PO Box 90 Philadelphia, PA 19105-0090		
Pittsburgh 717 Grant Street Pittsburgh, PA 412-261-7863 412-261-7988 (recording)	Pittsburgh Branch FRB of Cleveland PO Box 867 Pittsburgh, PA 15230-0867		

Figure 3-1 (Cont.)

the envelope should be written, "Tender for Treasury Bills." Once the auction occurs, the securities that are purchased, along with any future interest payments, are credited to the purchaser's account at the Federal Reserve Board.

One final note. When purchasing treasuries, individuals may specify if bids are competitive or noncompetitive. Competitive bids specify the yield the purchaser is willing to accept. With competitive bids, individuals run the risk of paying more than the noncompetitive price if their bid is accepted. Competitive bids also run the risk of being shut out from the auction if the bid is not accepted. It is suggested that individuals make noncompetitive bids and accept the yield established at the auction.

An informative book on buying treasuries directly, *Buying Treasury Securities,* is available for $4.50 (send a check) at Federal Reserve Bank Richmond, Public Service Department, P.O. Box 27622, Richmond, VA 23261.

Commission-Free Investing Through No-Load Mutual Funds

Another way for individuals to invest without brokerage fees is through a "no-load" mutual fund. Briefly, mutual funds, operated by investment companies, take in funds from many individuals, commingle the money, and buy a portfolio of stocks that they manage. Mutual funds are divided into closed-end funds and open-end funds. Closed-end funds, which are discussed in Chapter 5, sell only a certain number of shares in the fund to the public via an initial public offering. After the shares are sold, the fund is "closed" and no new shares are issued. A closed-end fund trades on one of the exchanges, and the fund's price is determined by the laws of supply and demand in the market.

Open-end funds differ from closed-end funds in a number of areas. First, an open-end fund continuously issues new shares to the public and redeems shares at the fund's net asset value—the market value of the firm's portfolio of stocks minus short-term liabilities. Also, open-end funds don't trade on the various stock exchanges. The value of the fund depends solely on the returns of the shares held in the portfolio.

It used to be that mutual funds were either "load" funds—funds sold by brokers and financial advisers and carrying a sales charge—or "no-load" funds—funds purchased directly from investment companies without sales charges. Simple enough, right? Unfortunately, over time the lines have blurred between what constitutes a "load" and "no-load" fund. As we shall soon see, there are "no-load" funds that actually cost investors more than certain "load" funds. Furthermore, major differences exist across no-load funds.

Fees, Fees, and More Fees

What has created a confusing mess for mutual fund investors is the emergence of a variety of fees and expense arrangements in the industry over the last decade. Not only are there up-front load charges to consider, but many mutual funds also have back-end charges and 12b-1 charges, not to mention management expenses that can vary widely. Let's look at each of these charges.

Management Expenses.   All mutual funds, regardless of whether they are load or no-load, charge management expenses. These are the fees that cover the administration and management of the fund. Management expenses can run from as little as 0.10 or 0.20 percent for an index fund—a fund that replicates one of the major market indexes and doesn't require active management—to 2 percent or more. Surprisingly, if you ask most mutual fund investors how much they pay in management fees, they probably don't know, which is exactly what the mutual fund providers want. Indeed, since these expenses are deducted each year from shareholders' holdings, they represent a fairly "painless" expense. But what investors fail to realize is that these expenses, over time, take a huge bite out of the portfolio.

Load Fees.   As mentioned, load fees are the charges investors pay up front when they purchase a mutual fund. Load fees range from 2 percent up to 8½ percent of the amount invested. These fees usually compensate the brokers who sell the funds. There seems to be a trend in the mutual fund industry toward reducing or even eliminating load fees, as investors have become sensitive to these types of charges. That's not surprising since load fees are the most obvious fee when purchasing a fund. However, what mutual fund companies have been doing is upping less obvious charges, such as...

12b-1 Fees.   12b-1 fees, which range from 0.5 percent to 1 percent or more, are charged by mutual funds supposedly to help pay for marketing expenses. The regulatory justification for permitting these fees, which are charged by no-load as well as load funds, is that the charges pay for advertising, which brings more money into the mutual fund, which helps to achieve greater economies of scale, which lowers management expenses for existing shareholders. Thus, 12b-1 charges are really in the existing shareholders' best interests, according to some in the mutual fund industry.

Unfortunately, 12b-1 fees have not done what they promised. Despite record inflows of money into mutual funds over the last decade, management expenses have actually increased during that time. Who really benefits from 12b-1 fees? The mutual fund companies.

Back-end Fees.   Back-end fees are a type of redemption fee that some mutual funds charge investors who sell funds that have been held for a relatively short period of time. For example, a mutual fund may charge a 5 percent back-end fee on assets that are sold after one year, with a sliding scale of charges occurring until, say, the fifth year, when the back-end charge is dropped altogether.

Rising Expenses

A disturbing trend in the mutual fund industry over the last decade has been the increase in fees. According to Morningstar, the mutual fund rating service, the expense ratio for the average equity fund climbed nearly 32 percent in the decade ending with 1990.

Why has this happened? One reason is that mutual fund investors have let fund operators get away with hiking fees. Rising expenses were easy to slide through when stocks were rising at an annualized rate of 18 percent for the period. What's an extra 0.5 percent here, or 0.4 percent there, in expense fees, when the funds are rising so rapidly? Who'd notice?

The mutual fund industry has done a masterful job in creating a high "fog" level when it comes to fees. Mutual funds have come up with clever ways to disguise fees, hiding them behind such terms as "contingent deferred sales charges" and "asset-based" fees. Mutual funds know that it's a rare investor who will sit down with a mutual fund prospectus, cut through the jargon, and really see just how much money is being lifted from his or her pocket each year in fees.

Another way mutual funds crank up the "fog" level is by implementing a variety of different classes to cover the same mutual fund. For example, a few years ago, **Merrill Lynch** launched its Short-Term Global Income Fund with two options: "A" shares, with a 3 percent load charge, and "B" shares, with no load charge but half a percentage point more in annual fees plus a declining back-end redemption charge. Which fund is better? It depends on how long you hold the fund. If you're a buy-and-hold investor, you'll probably be better off in the "A" shares.

Another tactic in the industry is the development of "hub-and-spoke" funds. Hub-and-spoke funds are basically the same mutual fund sold under different names to different types of investors. For example, Franklin Adjustable U.S. Government Fund is one of the "spokes" of the Institutional Adjustable U.S. Government Fund, which acts as the "hub." What makes hub-and-spoke funds so attractive to companies that manage them is that they can charge different fees for each of the spokes. Thus, one spoke may be a load fund carrying a 3 percent charge, another spoke may carry a larger fee, and one of the spokes may be marketed as a no-load fund. In effect, investors pay different fees for the same investment. Hub-and-spoke funds present one more factor to consider when buying a mutual fund.

Buying No-Load Funds Through a Broker

No, the headline isn't a mistake. It is possible to buy certain no-load mutual funds—without paying a brokerage fee—by going through a broker.

Charles Schwab, the giant discount broker, allows investors to purchase more than 80 no-load funds offered by such fund families as **SteinRoe**, **Invesco**, **Janus Group**, **Founders**, **Berger Associates**, **Dreyfus**, and **Neuberger & Berman**. Schwab doesn't charge a brokerage fee for the service. Investors benefit by having one-stop shopping for potentially all of their mutual fund needs. Free lunch, right?

Perhaps, but there is a catch. Schwab is charging the fund families a very small annual fee on the assets they manage through the program. The big question is, who will really end up paying this fee? Will the participating fund families pass the fee along to the customers with increased 12b-1 or management expenses? Obviously, the participating mutual funds are hoping that Schwab's marketing clout garners them a bounty of new money. If this is the case the companies may eat the Schwab charge since they'll be making it up many times over in increased fees off the larger asset base. However, if new money doesn't roll in at the expected rate, look for the mutual fund companies to pass the Schwab charge on to investors in the form of higher annual management expenses.

What's an Investor to Do?

The overriding factor in choosing any investment, including mutual funds, is the quality and return potential of the investment. A load fee is a small price to pay for a mutual fund that skyrockets in value. Conversely, a no-load fund with low management expenses that goes nowhere is a poor investment. Here are some factors to consider when choosing a mutual fund:

- Studies have shown that, on average, load funds don't outperform no-loads. According to Morningstar, the mutual fund rating service (a coupon for a free copy of Morningstar's *Five-Star Investor* newsletter is in the back of the book), for the five-year period ended May 1992, pure no-load equity funds delivered an average annual return of 8.3 percent. Funds with 12b-1 charges returned 8.49 percent; those with a front-end load, 8.49 percent; and those with back loads, 7.3 percent. And among bond funds, pure no-loads offered the highest five-year returns. All things equal, investors should preference no-load funds, especially if you don't need the higher service level often provided by load funds.

- As the Morningstar study indicates, never buy a bond fund that charges a load fee. It's tough to recoup the load fee versus a no-load bond fund.

- Don't just look at the load fee—look at management and 12b-1 expenses as well. Annual fees can have an even greater impact on a fund's performance than a load fee, as the example below indicates:

$10,000 initial investment, 10 percent annual return

Years	No-load, with 1.5 percent mgmt. fee	3 percent front-end load; 0.5 percent mgmt. fee
1	$10,835	$10,616
2	11,739	11,619
3	12,719	12,718
4	13,782	13,919
5	14,932	15,234

In this example, the fund with the load fee but lower annual expenses is the better investment if the fund is held for longer than three years. Moral of the story: Look at annual management expenses and annual 12b-1 fees as closely as you do load fees. In many cases, a no-load fund with above-average annual expenses may cost you more over the long term than a load fund with modest annual expenses. Management expenses of over 2 percent for a stock fund and over 1 percent for a bond fund can be considered excessive. Where are these fees stated? In the mutual fund's prospectus, which should be must reading prior to any mutual fund investment.

- Beware of funds sold by brokerage firms. Put yourself in a broker's shoes. Where would you focus most of your mutual fund research— on funds that pay sales fees, or those that don't? An example of the broker's plight was provided in an interesting article in *The New York Times.* The article stated that the Prudential Government Securities Trust Intermediate-Term Series had an outstanding record among all short-term bond funds. Prudential at one time paid a 2 percent commission to brokers who put customers in the fund. But in 1986, the load fee was dropped. Curiously, despite the strong performance of the fund, assets in the fund started to drop. What was happening? Basically, Prudential brokers had stopped selling the fund, opting to sell other funds carrying load fees.

   Overall, brokerage firms can generate as much as $7000 per broker from the sale of in-house mutual funds. That is a lot of incentive to push the broker's own funds. Does that mean investors should always avoid brokerage mutual funds? Not necessarily, but it does make sense to shop around to see if a no-load fund with a similar investment style and low expenses exists.

For readers who would like to receive a special report, *The High Cost of Mutual Funds,* send a note with the code words "Mutual Fund Fees," along with a business-size, self-addressed stamped envelope, to me at the address given at the end of Chapter 2.

True No-Load Funds

As a starting point for mutual fund investments, investors may want to investigate mutual funds marketed by members of the 100 percent No-Load Mutual Fund Council. The organization, founded in 1989, identifies funds that have no-load fees, 12b-1 fees, contingent sales charges, long-term redemption charges, exit fees, or dividend reinvestment charges. For further information about the Council, call 212-768-2477.

   One mutual fund family that I particularly like is **Vanguard**. Vanguard's funds traditionally have among the lowest management expenses in the industry. For further information about Vanguard funds, call 800-662-7447.

4

If You Must Use a Broker, Here Are Ways to Ease the Pain

And Get Perks and Freebies in the Process

Unfortunately, despite the many options discussed in Chapter 3, it may not always be possible to avoid the broker. However, for times when a broker is needed, ways exist to limit his or her bite and receive a freebie or two in the process.

There's an old saying that investments aren't bought—they're sold. That statement has many implications for individual investors. If you know how a broker operates—how he or she is compensated, for example, or what products generate the biggest commissions—you are better equipped to deal with brokers and limit their take.

The only way a broker is compensated is if you do something, either buying or selling. It's in the broker's best interest to generate activity. They feed off your action and die by your inaction. If you aren't generating demand, they'll do it for you. You don't buy securities; they are sold to you.

And if I'm a broker selling securities, I might as well sell you the investments that generate the biggest commissions for me.

Now before I get death threats from brokers, I'm not saying that all brokers abide by the "stick-it-to-the-customer" line of thinking. However, such conflicts of interest are inherent in the brokerage system, which is too bad for both brokers and clients. Nevertheless, the broker-client conflict is a fact of life, and it's up to investors to keep their brokers honest. Being an investing neophyte doesn't absolve you from your responsibility of overseeing your broker's activities. Ask yourself the following questions:

- Is the broker taking my best interests to heart?

- Are there other investments that would meet my needs just as well but carry lower commissions?

- Why is my portfolio filled with mutual funds operated by the broker's firm?

- Are these the best funds, or are they the funds that pay him or her the most?

Checking Up on Your Broker

There are several ways to keep your broker honest. For example, you shouldn't feel bashful about checking up on your broker's background and credentials. The National Association of Securities Dealers is one source for such information. The association records disciplinary actions by various securities regulators as well as criminal convictions. However, it doesn't have on file pending actions. Nevertheless, a quick call here may provide some pertinent information. The toll-free number is 800-289-9999.

Another source for background checks is the North American Securities Administrators Association. To find out who handles requests in your state, call 202-737-0900.

If you're active in the commodities market, it's worth a call to the National Futures Association's "Disciplinary Information Access Line" (DIAL) at 800-676-4632.

Remember that a clean slate at these sources doesn't necessarily mean that your broker is clean. Current complaints may not be registered, and information is sometimes incomplete. Nevertheless, the phone calls are toll-free in most instances. Thus it's cheap insurance, and insurance you really can't afford to be without.

Don't be afraid to ask your broker questions, and pay attention to his or her responses.

Fog Level Revisited

The "fog level" in terms of mutual fund fees was discussed in Chapter 3. What this term means is that fee structures are made so complicated, so "foggy," that discerning the true cost of an investment is virtually impossible. That's why it's important to know and understand the cost of every investment you buy. Don't settle for jargon, such as "load" fees, "redemption" fees, or "wrap" fees. It's up to you to get your broker to tell you exactly what all of these fees mean and how they will impact your portfolio.

Take the "wrap" account, for example. This has become one of Wall Street's hottest products. In a "wrap" account, brokers take in money from customers and place it with a private money manager. The clients are charged a flat fee, usually 2 to 3 percent of assets, but do not pay for commissions generated by the money manager. Clients get personal money management without having to worry about "churning" in their account, all for a flat fee. Sounds great, right? Maybe not.

First, fees of 2 to 3 percent can be a rather stiff price to pay—$3000 annually on a $100,000 investment—especially if a no-load mutual fund with low expenses can meet your needs. Second, keep in mind the nature of this transaction. Your broker takes your money and places it with another manager. Why would a broker do this? One line of thought is that giving your money to an outside manager somehow reduces your broker's risk level should the manager do poorly. Your broker can always blame the manager for poor performance and take your money elsewhere. Your broker insulates himself to a certain extent from accountability.

You should also be aware of any financial arrangements between your broker and the firm he recommends to manage your account. Does your broker get a "referral" fee—a kickback—for every account he brings? Is the money manager your broker's tennis buddy? Is your broker keeping good tabs on the performance of the money manager?

Some "wrap" programs have been quite profitable for investors, and as with any investment, it is performance that counts. For investors who trade frequently and who would exceed the 2 to 3 percent wrap fee in commissions alone, "wraps" may make sense. Still, when you consider that you start out each year 3 percent in the hole due to the "wrap" charge—and stocks may rise only 7 percent or so after inflation in an average year—"wrap" programs lose a lot of their luster. Again, don't be afraid to question your broker. It's your money.

While we're on the subject of fees, I think it's appropriate to discuss some of the new fees brokers are charging customers. It's not enough that investors pay commissions. Brokers want them to pay even more of their overhead bill. Some brokers now charge "inactive" fees of $40 or more. These are fees charged to investors who don't meet some arbitrary level of trading each year. There are fees to issue stock certificates. There are fees to send out trade confirmations. There are administrative fees. There are fees when you fire your broker and move your account to another brokerage firm. So when evaluating a prospective broker, don't stop at the commission schedule—find out if other types of fees are charged as well.

Negotiate, Negotiate, Negotiate

The important thing to remember about fees and commissions is that nothing is set in stone. Sure, some brokerage firms may have a fairly strict policy about minimum commission levels and certain mandatory fees. However, that doesn't mean that you can't try to negotiate down some of the fees.

Obviously, negotiating works better from a position of strength. A broker's established customer will have a greater ability to negotiate more preferential commissions and fees than a new client. Likewise, a customer with big bucks is in the position to bargain for better rates than an odd-lot purchaser.

The market environment also impacts a customer's clout. If the market is hot and volume is heavy, chances are brokers will be less willing to negotiate fees than if the market stinks. In the latter environment, all commissions and fees are negotiable, regardless of the size of your wallet.

My experience suggests that full-service brokers have greater flexibility in setting commissions than discount brokers. For very small purchases, say a couple of shares to get started in a dividend reinvestment program, your best bet may be a full-service broker.

Perks and Freebies From Your Broker

Brokers have a number of items at their disposal to entice you to trade with them. However, these perks and freebies may be put on hold by the broker unless you ask for them or the broker feels compelled to offer them in order to gain your business.

Many full-service brokers have *Value Line* and *Standard & Poor's* research information available for clients' use. But you'll probably have to ask for them in order to get them. Full-service brokerage firms have a number of computer services that may be available. Say you want a list of all stocks priced at $15 per share and under with P-E ratios of 20 or less and dividend yields of 2 percent or more. Your broker should be able to run that screen through a computer program at his or her firm to come up with a list for you.

Another perk that's available at most full-service brokers is personalized counseling and asset-allocation programs to meet a variety of needs—retirement, estate planning, college educations, etc. Merrill Lynch, for example, has a CollegeBuilder program that helps determine the best way to save for college based on your children's ages.

We've mostly been discussing full-service brokers. Customers of full-service brokers have greater leverage in obtaining certain perks since they are paying for these services with higher commissions. However, customers of discount brokers are not without the ability to receive certain freebies and perks as well.

A number of discount brokers, including **Charles Schwab** and **Jack White & Co.**, offer no-fee IRA accounts. This is an extremely attractive perk, given the usual $25 and up fees for providing custodial services for an IRA. A number of discounters also offer check-writing privileges. Two discounters, Schwab and **Fidelity**, offer commission discounts on trades done electronically. Both firms have services that let you punch in orders on your phone—Fidelity's is called TouchTone Trader and Schwab's is TeleBroker—and receive a 10 percent discount on commissions. Both firms also offer computerized trading—Fidelity's is called On-Line Express (FOX) and Schwab's is the Equalizer System—that entitles users to discounts off regular commission rates.

Money-Back Guarantee From a Broker?
Well, Sort of...

Discount broker **Quick & Reilly** offers customers an interesting perk—a money-back guarantee. But before you get too excited, there are strings attached. The guarantee doesn't apply to the success or failure of the investment. If you buy a stock that goes from $20 to $4, don't expect to get your money back. The guarantee applies only to the service aspect of the trade. A complaint that would qualify would be a foul-up on the broker's part in transferring stock or delivering stock certificates. The broker won't pay a refund if the trade is poorly executed.

Admittedly, the guarantee is a bit thin in terms of coverage. Nevertheless, it's interesting that other brokerage firms haven't jumped on the bandwagon. I guess that asking for guarantees on anything in the financial markets—even good service—is too much to expect.

Below is a list of perks, freebies, and giveaways that might be available from your broker. Don't be afraid to ask for them, especially if you're currently using a full-service broker.

- Free research reports, including *Value Line* and *Standard & Poor's* sheets. Also, I've known brokers to pay for subscriptions to investment newsletters and business magazines for certain clients.
- No-fee IRAs. Schwab and Jack White, for example, have lifetime, no-fee IRAs for accounts with at least $10,000.
- Certain mutual funds may waive their minimum initial investment requirements, especially when it comes to saving for college educations. **Dreyfus** (800-TAX-FREE) waives the minimum fee on some of its funds, provided that you agree to a $100 automatic monthly investment. Fidelity reduces its minimum on certain funds if the money is being used to open a Uniform Gifts or Transfers to Minors Act (UGMA/UTMA) account.
- Preretirement, estate, college education, and other financial planning programs are available at most full-service brokerage firms.
- Many full-service brokers will provide computer asset allocation and stock and mutual fund screening services for customers upon request.
- Many brokerage firms, including discounters, provide a check-writing feature. Check with your broker as to availability and cost, if any.
- Ask your broker to "sweep" your account on a more frequent basis. "Sweeping" is the term used to collect cash in your accounts, such as dividends, and "sweep" it into your money market account at the firm so you can earn interest. "Sweeps" are often done monthly. However, you might be able to persuade your broker to do it weekly.
- Most brokerage firms permit investors to get quotes on stocks over the phone for free. In some cases, this is done through an automated system.
- A nice perk is tapping into *Dow Jones News/Retrieval, CompuServe,* or any of the other news and information databases used by brokers. Do you want the latest news on one of your holdings? It's perfectly acceptable, if you deal with a full-service firm, to call up your broker and ask him or her to check the various information databases for "hot" news stories.
- A number of brokers, such as Schwab and Jack White, now sell no-

load funds directly to customers. The brokers charge a small service fee to the mutual funds, which may or may not be passed along to investors via higher expenses. Still, the ease of using your discount broker to purchase mutual funds, plus the simplicity of receiving one consolidated statement with all of your fund holdings, may be worth a small fee.

A Choice When Buying and Selling a Load Fund

It used to be that when you bought a load fund, you had no choice but to pay the broker the load fee—perhaps as much as 8.5 percent of the assets invested. However, **Jack White & Co.,** the discount firm, is providing an alternative.

Jack White has been instrumental in developing a secondary market for load funds. The program works like this: Say you want to buy $10,000 worth of XYZ fund, which carries an 8.5 percent load. You can place an order with Jack White. White, in turn, attempts to find a seller of the fund. If White is successful, he will charge the buyer $200 and give $100 of that to the seller, in addition to the value of the shares.

The deal benefits both the buyer and seller. The buyer's $200 fee compares quite favorably to the $850 fee he or she would have to pay on a $10,000 investment. The seller receives net asset value plus $100—more than if the shares were redeemed through the mutual fund company.

The biggest problem with the system has been matching sellers with buyers. However, White has been developing an electronic quotation system for load funds that is improving the liquidity of the system.

For further information about the program, call Jack White at 800-233-3411.

- Big stock traders may get discounted rates through certain brokerage firms. Fidelity's Spartan deep-discount arm gives discounts to investors with $25,000 or more in securities in an account and who trade at least four times per month.

- You may be able to get discounts on certain investment software by going through your broker.

- Some brokerage firms provide the ability to buy stocks 24 hours a day. Ask your broker if his or her firm has this service.

- Some brokerage firms will periodically run specials on odd-lot or very small purchases.

- If your broker leaves his or her firm, you might be able to finagle a break on commissions if you agree to stay with the old firm. According to *The Wall Street Journal,* in early 1992, **Smith Barney** sent a letter to customers in its White Plains, NY, branch—customers whose brokers had recently left the firm—offering them a 50 percent discount on commissions in order to keep them from jumping along with their brokers. Interestingly, the letter also reminded the customers that termination fees would be levied—a $50 fee, for example, to terminate an IRA—should the customers transfer their accounts.

- No-fee credit or debit cards. Brokerage firms are becoming more like banks in the scope of services they offer. One of these services is no-fee credit or debit cards, and some may carry favorable interest-rate charges. Interested investors should contact their brokers for further information.

- Keep alert for special deals your brokerage firm may run for purchasing certain investments. For example, Charles Schwab ran a special in the fall of 1992. Customers who purchased $10,000 or more face value of bonds in new or existing accounts were eligible for gifts of shares in the Schwab 1000 fund. Bonds in the promotion included Treasuries and STRIPS, as well as certain municipal and corporate bonds. Customers purchasing these bonds received one share in the Schwab 1000 fund for every $10,000 in face value purchased, up to a maximum three shares for a $30,000-or-more purchase.

  Investors should be careful, however, when such inducement is offered. Make sure the freebie is not, in fact, a bribe to entice you to take bad merchandise off the broker's hands. Indeed, it could be that the freebie of the extra shares may be no freebie at all if what you have to buy to qualify is junk. (See Chapter 10 for further insights into when a free lunch is really no free lunch at all.)

- A free lunch—literally. There isn't a full-service broker alive who wouldn't pick up a lunch or dinner tab for a client or even prospective client if he or she felt it could lead to business down the road. If you decide to go the full-service route, don't be shy in taking advantage of a true free lunch from a prospective broker. It gives you a chance to quiz him or her more thoroughly on investment philosophies, commission schedules, track records (always ask for an audited track record from prospective brokers), and services offered by the firm.

Finding a Broker That's Right for You

Knowing what you want out of your broker—the lowest commissions possible, in-depth research capabilities, a friend to lean on, an objective sounding board, etc.—is the first step in finding a broker that's right for you. If it's strictly dollars and cents, a deep discounter may fit the bill. Here are some deep discounters you might want to call:

K. Aufhauser
(800-368-3668)

Pace Securities
(800-221-1660)

Pacific Brokerage
(800-421-8395)

Seaport Brokerage
(800-221-9894)

Spartan
(800-544-5115)

If you want lower commission rates but still would like to receive some of the perks discussed in this chapter, your best bet may be one of the larger, more established discount brokerage firms, such as **Charles Schwab** (800-435-4000), **Fidelity Brokerage** (800-225-1799), and **Quick & Reilly** (800-926-0600). Other discounters to consider include:

Andrew Peck
(800-221-5873)

Burke, Christensen & Lewis Sec.
(800-621-0392)

Olde Discount
(800-872-6533)

R.F. Lafferty
(800-221-8514)

Jack White & Co.
(800-233-3411)

Muriel Siebert & Co.
(800-872-0444)

StockCross
(800-225-6196)

Vanguard Brokerage Service
(800-662-7447)

Waterhouse Securities
(800-765-5185)

Finally, if you want the gamut of services and are willing to pay to get them, try a full-service broker. Prominent names among the national firms include **Merrill Lynch**, **Dean Witter**, **Prudential Securities**, and **A.G. Edwards**. Phone numbers for these firms' local branches are in the Yellow Pages.

Investors also should not overlook regional full-service firms. Regional firms often have special expertise in local companies or certain industry groups. Some top regional brokerage firms include **Chicago Corp.** and **William Blair** in Chicago, **Alex Brown** and **Legg Mason** on the east coast, and **Hambrecht & Quist** on the west coast.

For further information about brokerage firms, specifically discounters and deep discounters, readers should obtain a copy of *Investing at a Discount* (New York Institute of Finance), by Mark Coler of Mercer, Inc. Mr. Coler publishes annual surveys and directories covering the discount brokerage industry, and the book is an excellent reference source when shopping for a broker.

Know Your Rights

Unfortunately, sometimes even the most conscientious effort to find a broker and brokerage firm that's right for you doesn't lead to a happy marriage. Disputes may arise, and sometimes these disputes are over a whole lot of money. I talk to many investors every year concerning problems and alleged unfair treatment at the hands of brokers. Some of the investor pain has been self-inflicted, with the individuals looking for a scapegoat for their poor judgment. However, in a number of instances, individuals were indeed treated unfairly and, in some cases, criminally by their brokers. If this happens to you, what are your rights as an investor?

The first step in handling a dispute is to make sure your account is insulated from broker manipulation. That means that you should never give your broker discretionary power over your account. Granting such power only invites trouble. Maintain full discretion over your account, with only you having the power to enact trades.

Most disputes center around brokers purchasing securities that are deemed unsuitable for the client based on risk tolerances and financial position. Another common complaint is churning, the act by a broker of generating excessive trades in an account in order to reap commissions. If you feel you're the victim of these or any other practices, take it up with your broker first. He or she may see the error of his or her ways and make amends. If you get nowhere with your broker, talk to the branch manager and/or compliance officer. The compliance officer, in particular, may lend a friendly ear since it is his or her job to see that brokers maintain proper relationships with clients as well as abide by the firm's own trading practices.

If you get no satisfaction at this point—and you still believe in your case—you can always sue your broker, especially if you feel that fraud or other acts were committed. However, brokers usually insulate themselves from lawsuits by getting you to give up your ability to sue by signing an arbitration clause. Obviously, brokerage firms want to avoid the possibility of a protracted and expensive court case. You can always refuse to sign the arbitration clause, in which case the brokerage firm may tell you to take a hike. As a practical matter, finding a broker who won't require you to agree to arbitration may be difficult. Nevertheless, there are a lot of brokers who want your business, and you might find one who won't press the arbitration clause.

But let's say you decide that this is the brokerage firm for you because of its many perks and attractive commissions, and you're willing to sign the arbitration clause. At this point, make sure that your options are open in terms of which arbitration organization may hear your case.

More and more investors are taking their complaints to arbitrators. Should you choose to go the arbitration route, your case will be heard by one of five primary organizations that handle arbitration cases: four self-regulatory organizations (SROs)—National Association of Securities Dealers (NASD), New York Stock Exchange, American Stock Exchange, and Chicago Board Options Exchange—or the independent American Arbitration Association (AAA).

In many cases, brokers will try to stipulate that any arbitration cases will be heard by one of the SROs. According to some arbitration experts, SROs are akin to the fox guarding the hen house. The arbitration panels for these four bodies are run by the securities industry, and the panel of arbitrators hearing cases usually includes someone from the securities industry.

Does this mean that these arbitration bodies, just because they are financially supported and run by the securities industry, are always going to side with brokers? Not necessarily. In fact, some multimillion-dollar arbitration awards of recent years have been handed down by SROs. Some of the SRO panels appear to be more friendly to investors than others. Investors are generally seen as having a better chance of receiving an award if their case is heard by the NASD than by the New York Stock Exchange arbitration board. Because it is independent, the American Arbitration Association is the better arena for investors, according to some arbitration experts. It's important to keep your options open by refusing to sign any arbitration agreement that limits the use of the AAA.

The independence of the AAA comes with a price: Arbitration costs may be higher when heard by the AAA, especially for smaller claims. Before deciding on an arbitration board, investors should weigh the costs versus the size of the claim. It may be the case that, based on economics, it makes more sense to arbitrate in front of an SRO.

One plus for arbitration is that the average arbitration case takes about a year, as opposed to anywhere from 2 to 5 years for court litigation.

Once you have decided on arbitration, contact the Securities and Exchange Commission's Consumer Affairs Office (202-272-7440). This office can inform you of your rights and provide information on the arbitration process.

Now, let's say you're ready to go to arbitration. At this point in the process, you may be wondering if retaining a lawyer is worthwhile. According to a study by the General Accounting Office of Congress, investors are 1.6 times more likely to get awards exceeding 60 percent of their claims if they use lawyers. If your claim is in excess of $30,000, a lawyer might be a good idea. Most likely, one will work for a contingency fee—usually one-third of any award. If the claim is below $30,000, a better alternative may be to pay an hourly rate for a lawyer to help map out strategy. Spending a couple of hours and a few hundred dollars on an attorney may be money well spent if it better helps you to prepare your case. The Public Investors Arbitration Bar Association (800-899-9906) should help you locate a securities lawyer in your area.

When entering arbitration, remember that the proceedings are much more loosely structured than in a court case. In some cases arguments can be made through the mail, with the arbitration board ruling after reading both sides' comments. However, the GAO study shows that you are 1.4 times more likely to win when the hearing is face-to-face with arbitrators than through the mail. If a large sum of money is involved, push for a face-to-face hearing.

When presenting your case, documentation is critical. For churning cases, it's a good idea to gain access to other accounts handled by your broker to see if he or she was buying the same securities for them as he or she was buying for you. If the broker was doing similar trading, it weakens the argument that he or she was acting on your instructions. An expert witness may be helpful in pointing out irregular activities by your broker. Remember that your public library has a wealth of information, including back issues of *The Wall Street Journal* and other financial publications, that you may find useful in building a case.

Shorting Your Inheritance

One of the more interesting arbitration cases in recent times involved the nephew of Sam Walton, the founder of Stores. According to *The Wall Street Journal*, the nephew, John J. Robson, was told by his broker that Wal-Mart stock would go down in price. As a hedge against losses, the broker recommended that Robson sell short 403,300 shares of Wal-Mart—the number of shares Robson held in his account—in a strategy called "shorting against the box." Under this strategy, any losses on the drop in price of Wal-Mart would be offset by gains on the short sale.

> However, Wal-Mart stock skyrocketed in price. Thus Robson had a huge loss on the short sale, which meant that he would have to pay millions of dollars to cover his short or be forced to sell a chunk of his Wal-Mart holdings.
>
> Robson filed for arbitration, saying that the short sale was unsuitable and improperly initiated. The NASD arbitration panel agreed, and awarded Robson $9.7 million in damages. "We didn't think there was any way in the world we could lose this," a Paine Webber official was quoted as saying in *The Wall Street Journal*.

Conclusion

What are your chances of winning an arbitration case, and how much might you win? Roughly 60 percent of the claimants win their case, but they receive only around 60 percent of their claim. However, some noteworthy cases have occurred recently that have resulted in awards in the millions of dollars. In one case a former chairman of GTE of Florida won $5.3 million, including $3.5 million in punitive damages.

Punitive damages are a tricky issue in arbitration awards. New York courts have barred panels in that state from granting punitive damages. Thus, most brokerage firm arbitration clauses stipulate that New York arbitration laws will govern the case, even if you live elsewhere. Make sure that you check out this fine print in any arbitration clause and, if possible, retain the freedom to have the case heard under laws of a state other than New York.

5
The Perk of Buying Stocks at a Discount

Executive compensation has become a hot topic in recent years. Do CEOs earn too much money? What is "fair" compensation for a senior executive? What measuring sticks should be used to evaluate the company's performance relative to executive compensation?

Sorry, but I don't have the answers. I don't think anybody really does, as these questions are so subjective that they are almost unanswerable. But what I think is important for our discussion is just how executives really make the big bucks.

If you look at the megacompensations of such corporate honchos as Anthony J. F. O'Reilly of H. J. Heinz (nearly $75 million in compensation in 1991), Leon C. Hirsch of U. S. Surgical ($22.6 million in 1991, $60.7 million in 1992), Richard L. Gelb of Bristol-Myers Squibb ($12.2 million in 1991), Charles Lazarus of Toys 'R Us (more than $64 million in 1992), and Thomas Frist of HCA–Hospital Corp. of America ($127 million in 1992), what is clear is that these men didn't get that rich by just cashing a paycheck each week.

These stratospheric compensations are the result of executive stock options. In 1991, O'Reilly of Heinz exercised stock options worth nearly $72 million; Hirsch, $20.8 million in 1991 and $58.5 million in 1992; Gelb, $9.2 million in 1991; Lazarus, $57.2 million in 1992; and Frist, $125.9 million in 1992. According to a Towers Perrin survey of CEO pay, one-third of the executives in the sample exercised stock options in 1991, for a median gain of nearly $700,000.

Stock options were big news in 1992. With President Clinton winning the White House partly on a "soak the rich" platform, many CEOs decided to exercise stock options in 1992 rather than in succeeding years when higher tax rates will be in effect. The results were some pretty eye-popping announcements. The most impressive was the exercising of stock options by Disney executives Michael D. Eisner and Frank G. Wells, which netted them a pretax profit of more than $187 million.

Stock Options

Stock options give the holders the right to buy stock at a fixed price within a certain time frame. Stock options have become a popular way to compensate a CEO since it ties the manager's pay to stock performance.

For example, in Michael Eisner's case, he was given options to buy 510,000 shares of Disney stock in 1984 at a price of around $57 per share. At that time, Disney was having problems and had just fended off a hostile takeover attempt. In the ensuing years, Disney stock skyrocketed in price, splitting 4-for-1 twice along the way. The stock splits reduced the exercise price on Mr. Eisner's stock options to $3.59 per share. When Eisner decided to exercise some of his options, he purchased Disney at just over $3 per share but turned around and immediately sold it for around $40 per share.

Not a bad deal, you're probably saying. And you're right. Mr. Eisner was literally buying stock at a discount from the market price. Fortunately, even if you're not in the seat of power at some major corporation, a way exists for you to buy stock below market prices.

Buying Stock at a Discount Through DRIPs

Chapter 3 discussed dividend reinvestment plans (DRIPs). These plans permit investors to buy stock directly through companies, bypassing the broker and commissions. Stock is purchased with dividends that are reinvested by the company on the shareholders' behalf for additional shares. Investors may also send cash to purchase shares.

While the commission-free aspect of DRIPs is usually the most publicized benefit of the programs, an attractive wrinkle in nearly 100 programs is the ability to purchase stock at discounts to the market price. These discounts are usually 3 to 5 percent and run as high as 10 percent.

DRIPs with discounts are the closest thing to "stock options for the little guy" that exist in the stock market. The discount allows you to buy, say, a $50 stock for $47.50 if the DRIP has a 5 percent discount. Because of the way the math works, if you sold at the market price, your gain would actually be a little bit more than 5 percent (about 5.3 percent— $2.50 divided by $47.50). In effect, you have an instant profit and a built-in cushion not available to shareholders who buy at the market price.

Discounts in DRIPs are broken down into two categories: DRIPs that offer the discount only on shares purchased with reinvested dividends, and those programs that offer the discount on shares purchased with reinvested dividends and optional cash payments (OCPs). The latter group is much smaller, for reasons we'll discuss shortly.

A comprehensive list of DRIPs with discounts is provided at the end of this section, with addresses and phone numbers given in the perk directory in Chapter 11. Once you have found a company that interests you, join the DRIP using the procedures discussed in Chapter 3. Once enrolled, you can begin investing with the discount.

It is important to consider the following factors when investing at a discount:

- As mentioned in Chapter 1, one of the reasons companies offer discounts in DRIPs is to lure equity capital at a cheaper rate than they'd have to pay by going through an investment bank. Heavy users of capital, such as banks and utilities, often offer discounts, but just because a company offers a discount doesn't make it a great investment. A discount in a DRIP may be an indication that the company is in need of equity capital, which may not be a good sign. Indeed, a number of banks have implemented DRIPs with discounts recently to raise equity capital in order to keep regulators at bay. It's important to focus on quality issues when considering DRIPs with discounts.

- You can't dodge the tax man when it comes to discounts. If you purchase shares at a discount, you must report as income the difference between the cash you invest and the fair market value (full value) of the stock you buy.

- DRIPs differ in the way they determine the price that receives the discount. In some plans, the price is determined using the average of the high and low price for the stock on a 10-day trading period prior to the investment date. For others, it may be the closing price on the investment date. How the price is determined is critical, as it could have an effect on the ultimate size of the discount.

When a Discount Isn't a Discount

Investing at a discount may not always be in your favor, depending on how the company determines the purchase price on which the discount is taken.

For example, let's say the purchase price that receives the discount is based on a five-day average of closing stock prices (this information is given in the plan prospectus). If on the fifth day the stock drops sharply and is trading below the five-day average, it could very well be that the "discounted" price is above the most recent closing market price. In this case, you could actually be buying stock at a higher price than the market.

Conversely, let's say the stock jumps sharply on the last day of the pricing period and is trading well above the five-day average. Under these circumstances, a 3 percent or 5 percent discount could turn into a 15 or 20 percent discount to the most recent closing price.

Forget About the Big Gains— Unless You Have Deep Pockets

Investing at a discount may provide a modest boost to a portfolio, but investors should not have overly big expectations, especially when it comes to a discount on reinvested dividends.

For example, let's say you have 100 shares of American Express, which offers a 3 percent discount on reinvested dividends. American Express's dividend at the time of this writing is $1 per share annually, meaning that you'll have $100 reinvested for you in American Express stock. With the 3 percent discount on reinvested dividends, that $100 will buy $103 worth of stock. In other words, if American Express stock is trading for $22 per share, your reinvested dividends with the discount will purchase 4.68 shares of stock versus 4.55 shares without a discount. Of course every little bit helps, especially over a long period of time. Still, nobody is going to get rich playing the discounts on reinvested dividends unless dividend income is quite significant.

Where the real leverage occurs is in plans that apply the discount to optional cash payments. For instance, South Jersey Industries offers a 3 percent discount on optional cash payments up to $3000 per quarter. If you send the maximum, your $3000 buys approximately $3090 worth of stock each quarter, or an additional $360 per year. And that's only if the optional cash payments are invested quarterly. Let's say you invest in an issue that offers a discount monthly on the OCP, rather than quarterly. Over the course of a year the additional dollar amounts, assuming you have deep pockets to invest the maximum OCP, could be in the thousands.

Arbitraging the Discount

Not many companies offer discounts on optional cash payments, due to the "arbitrage" activity that often occurs. Arbitraging means to buy and sell simultaneously the same investment. Remember, with a discount in a DRIP, you can buy stock cheaper than the market. What investors do is buy the stock at the discount with optional cash payments and sell the same number of shares at the full market price. With a 3 percent or 5 percent discount, this type of trading activity each month can generate huge returns in a portfolio, especially if the individual sets up multiple accounts in which to conduct arbitrage activity.

Maxus Energy offers an interesting example of this type of arbitrage. Maxus started a DRIP in 1991. The firm didn't pay a dividend, but permitted optional cash payments at a 3 percent discount. Maxus also allowed brokerage firms and other large investors to participate in its DRIP. Needless to say, arbitrage activity occurred often in Maxus Energy's program.

An example of this arbitrage activity occurred on November 4, 1991. On that date—five days prior to the beginning of the 10-day pricing period for the November investment of optional cash payments— Maxus Energy topped the Big Board's most active list, with more than 4.5 million shares traded. The amount represented a 1031 percent increase over the average daily trading volume. In the "Abreast of the Market" section of *The Wall Street Journal* on November 5, most of the volume was attributed to two parties swapping a two-million-share block of stock back and forth. "In this case, the trade was apparently made so that one party would be the shareholder of record for the purposes of a stock-purchase plan without holding the block of stock for long," according to the *Journal*.

In effect, the party bought and then immediately sold two million shares in order to be on Maxus Energy's books as a shareholder of record to participate in the DRIP discount.

In Maxus's plan, the upper limit that could be invested via OCP was $0.30 times the number of shares held by the investor. Given these restrictions, the one party, following this swap, had the ability to invest $600,000 (two million shares times $0.30 per share) in optional cash payments in the DRIP to take advantage of the discount. Remember that this $600,000 investment bought stock at a 3 percent discount. In other words, the party could purchase approximately $618,000 of stock for $600,000, providing an instant, risk-free profit of around $18,000. If this transaction were to be repeated 12 times a year, the risk-free profit before taxes would be roughly $216,000. The numbers can be even more impressive if participants are permitted to invest more than the $0.30-per-share limit. Maxus left itself the right to waive this rule and permit investors to exceed the upper limit.

Similar arbitrage activity appears to have taken place in January 1992. On January 6, over 3.3 million shares of Maxus traded, representing a more than 530 percent increase over the average daily trading volume. Not coincidentally, January 6 was the record date in order to participate in Maxus's DRIP program—and take advantage of the 3 percent discount—for the January investment period.

Some interesting arbitrage activity took place more recently in **Texas Utilities** and **NationsBank**. On December 1, 1992, Texas Utilities had volume of nearly 7 million shares, and NationsBank's volume topped 6.6 million.

Both companies offer a 5 percent discount on shares purchased with reinvested dividends. What makes this arbitrage especially noteworthy is that neither Texas Utilities nor NationsBank offers the discount on optional cash payments. Conventional wisdom has been that it doesn't pay to arbitrage the discount on reinvested dividends since the amounts usually are too small. However, while that theory holds for individual investors, it doesn't for large institutional investors, such as mutual funds.

On the day after the big volume occurred, a spokesperson at Texas Utilities attributed the volume to trading by mutual funds. The heavy trading in NationsBank persisted for two more days, with 16 percent of the company's 245 million shares being traded in the three-day period, including 27 million on the third day alone. "We had no idea of the magnitude of trading it would generate," said a NationsBank spokesperson in *The Wall Street Journal*. "It's not anything we wanted to have happen."

Herein lies the rub of such arbitrage trading. On the one hand, some companies welcome and even actively seek institutional participation in their DRIP programs in order to raise large amounts of equity capital. On the other hand, such arbitrage activity shoves individual investors aside and makes small investors nervous because of the volume spikes. The volatile trading caused by arbitrage activity is one reason some companies have eliminated the discount, especially on optional cash payments.

And It Really, Really Works—Just Ask Myron Scholes

A real-life example of how profitable arbitraging the discount in a DRIP can be is provided by an interesting study conducted by Myron Scholes, of the Black-Scholes option-pricing model fame, and Mark Wolfson. The two men decided to see how successful they could be in taking advantage of the discounts offered in DRIPs. They purchased shares in companies that offered discounts on optional cash payments. The study was conducted from 1984 to 1988, with 90 percent of the trading activity occurring in less than two years. Scholes and Wolfson used their own money, upping the ante a bit from your basic academic study.

(Continued)

> Their results were quite impressive. With an investment of $200,000, the two realized a profit of $421,000. This consisted of $163,800 of net discount income, the sum of all gross discounts less transaction costs; $182,600 of return on investment due to a general increase in stock prices; and $74,600 of abnormal return on investment beyond the net discount income. This profit was net of brokerage fees, hedging losses, and other transaction costs.

The following companies offer DRIP discounts. Firms that apply discounts to both optional cash payments and reinvested dividends are in bold.

American Express Co.
3 percent discount on reinvested dividends

American Water Works Co., Inc.
5 percent discount on reinvested dividends

Aquarion Co.
5 percent discount on reinvested dividends

Atmos Energy Corp.
3 percent discount on reinvested dividends

Ball Corp.
5 percent discount on reinvested dividends

Baltimore Bancorp
5 percent discount on optional cash payments

Bancorp Hawaii, Inc.
5 percent discount on reinvested dividends

Bank of Boston Corp.
3 percent discount on reinvested dividends

BankAmerica Corp.
2½ percent discount on reinvested dividends
2½ percent discount on optional cash payments

Bankers First Corp.
5 percent discount on reinvested dividends

5 percent discount on optional cash payments

Bay State Gas Co.
3 percent discount on reinvested dividends
3 percent discount on optional cash payments

BB&T Financial Corp.
5 percent discount on reinvested dividends

Blount, Inc.
5 percent discount on reinvested dividends

BMJ Financial Corp.
5 percent discount on reinvested dividends
5 percent discount on optional cash payments

Boulevard Bancorp, Inc.
5 percent discount on optional cash payments

Burnham Pacific Properties, Inc.
5 percent discount on reinvested dividends

California Real Estate Investment Trust
5 percent discount on reinvested dividends

Central Maine Power Co.
5 percent discount on reinvested dividends

Chase Manhattan Corp.
5 percent discount on reinvested
dividends
3 percent discount on optional cash
payments

Citicorp
3 percent discount on reinvested
dividends
2½ percent discount on optional cash
payments

Colonial Gas Co.
5 percent discount on reinvested
dividends

Connecticut Water Service, Inc.
5 percent discount on reinvested
dividends

CoreStates Financial Corp.
3 percent discount on reinvested
dividends

Crestar Financial Corp.
5 percent discount on reinvested
dividends

E'town Corp.
5 percent discount on reinvested
dividends
5 percent discount on optional cash
payments

Eastern Utilities Associates
5 percent discount on reinvested
dividends

Empire District Electric Co.
5 percent discount on reinvested
dividends

EnergyNorth, Inc.
5 percent discount on reinvested
dividends

F&M National Corp.
5 percent discount on reinvested
dividends

First American Corp.
5 percent discount on reinvested
dividends

First Bank System, Inc.
3 percent discount on reinvested
dividends

First Chicago Corp.
3 percent discount on reinvested
dividends

First Commerce Corp.
5 percent discount on reinvested
dividends

First Eastern Corp.
5 percent discount on reinvested
dividends

First Fidelity Bancorp.
3 percent discount on reinvested
dividends

First Michigan Bank Corp.
5 percent discount on reinvested
dividends

First Midwest Bancorp, Inc.
3 percent discount on reinvested
dividends

First of America Bank Corp.
5 percent discount on reinvested
dividends

First Union Corp.
2 percent discount on reinvested
dividends
2 percent discount on optional cash
payments

Fleet Financial Group, Inc.
5 percent discount on reinvested
dividends
3 percent discount on optional cash
payments

Fleming Companies, Inc.
5 percent discount on reinvested
dividends

General Motors Corp.
3 percent discount on reinvested
dividends
3 percent discount on optional cash
payments

Great Western Financial Corp.
3 percent discount on reinvested
dividends

Health Care REIT, Inc.
4 percent discount on reinvested
dividends

Huntington Bancshares, Inc.
5 percent discount on reinvested
  dividends

Inco, Ltd.
5 percent discount on reinvested
  dividends

Independence Bancorp (PA)
5 percent discount on reinvested
  dividends

Independent Bank Corp. (MI)
5 percent discount on reinvested
  dividends

IRT Property Co.
5 percent discount on reinvested
  dividends

Jefferson Bankshares, Inc.
5 percent discount on reinvested
  dividends

Kennametal, Inc.
5 percent discount on reinvested
  dividends

Lafarge Corp.
5 percent discount on reinvested
  dividends

Maxus Energy Corp.
3 percent discount on optional cash
  payments

Mellon Bank Corp.
3 percent discount on reinvested
  dividends
3 percent discount on optional cash
  payments

Mercantile Bankshares Corp.
5 percent discount on reinvested
  dividends

Meridian Bancorp, Inc.
5 percent discount on reinvested
  dividends

Merry Land & Investment Co., Inc.
5 percent discount on reinvested
  dividends

Morgan, J.P., & Co., Inc.
3 percent discount on reinvested
  dividends

NationsBank Corp.
5 percent discount on reinvested
  dividends

New Plan Realty Trust
5 percent discount on reinvested
  dividends

North Carolina Natural Gas Corp.
5 percent discount on reinvested
  dividends

North Fork Bancorp., Inc.
5 percent discount on optional cash
  payments

NUI Corp.
5 percent discount on reinvested
  dividends

Old National Bancorp (Ind.)
3 percent discount on reinvested
  dividends
2½ percent discount on optional cash
  payments

Pacific Telesis Group
3½ percent discount on reinvested
  dividends
3½ percent discount on optional cash
  payments

Philadelphia Suburban Corp.
5 percent discount on reinvested
  dividends

Piccadilly Cafeterias, Inc.
5 percent discount on reinvested
  dividends

Piedmont Natural Gas Co., Inc.
5 percent discount on reinvested
  dividends

PMC Capital, Inc.
2 percent discount on optional cash
  payments
2 percent discount on reinvested
  dividends

Presidential Realty Corp.
5 percent discount on reinvested
  dividends

Public Service Co. of Colorado
3 percent discount on reinvested
  dividends

Public Service Co. of North Carolina, Inc.
5 percent discount on reinvested dividends

Shawmut National Corp.
3 percent discount on optional cash payments

Signet Banking Corp.
5 percent discount on reinvested dividends

South Jersey Industries, Inc.
3 percent discount on reinvested dividends
3 percent discount on optional cash payments

Southwest Water Co.
5 percent discount on reinvested dividends

Southwestern Electric Service Co.
5 percent discount on reinvested dividends

Suffolk Bancorp
3 percent discount on reinvested dividends
3 percent discount on optional cash payments

Summit Bancorp. (NJ)
3½ percent discount on reinvested dividends
3½ percent discount on optional cash payments

Telephone & Data Systems, Inc.
5 percent discount on reinvested dividends

Texas Utilities Co.
5 percent discount on reinvested dividends

Time Warner, Inc.
5 percent discount on reinvested dividends

Timken Co.
5 percent discount on reinvested dividends

TransCanada PipeLines Ltd.
5 percent discount on reinvested dividends

UGI Corp.
5 percent discount on reinvested dividends

Union Bank
5 percent discount on reinvested dividends

Union Planters Corp.
5 percent discount on reinvested dividends

United Cities Gas Co.
5 percent discount on reinvested dividends

United Water Resources, Inc.
5 percent discount on reinvested dividends
5 percent discount on optional cash payments

UtiliCorp United, Inc.
5 percent discount on reinvested dividends

Washington National Corp.
5 percent discount on reinvested dividends

Westcoast Energy, Inc.
5 percent discount on reinvested dividends

York Financial Corp.
10 percent discount on reinvested dividends

Of these stocks, my preferences are **Morgan, J.P., & Co., Pacific Telesis Group,** and **South Jersey Industries.**

Buying Stocks at a Discount
Through Closed-End Funds

Closed-end funds offer another way to purchase stocks at a discount. Closed-end funds are operated by investment companies in a fashion similar to the popular open-end mutual funds sponsored by **Fidelity, Vanguard, T. Rowe Price, Janus, Twentieth Century,** and others. However, there are a couple of differences between open-end and closed-end funds.

First, an open-end fund continually sells new shares to the public and redeems shares at the fund's net asset value—the market value of the firm's portfolio of stocks minus short-term liabilities. A closed-end fund sells only a certain amount of shares at the initial public offering, just like a stock. Once the shares are sold the fund is "closed," and new money is not accepted. Another difference is that closed-end funds trade on the various exchanges, just like stocks; open-end funds do not.

The fact that closed-end funds trade publicly is key to understanding how investors can use these investments to purchase stocks at a discount. Because closed-end funds trade on the exchanges, the price of these funds is governed by the laws of any market: supply and demand.

Most investors don't think of the stock "market" as a regular marketplace, where products are bought and sold; yet it truly is a market, governed by all of the emotions that drive any purchase decision. In such an environment, some merchandise sells for prices exceeding the sticker price; other merchandise, when there are not enough buyers, ends up on the sale rack.

These same market forces can create unusual pricing in closed-end funds. On the surface, it would appear that a closed-end fund would be priced the same as an open-end fund—the value of all of the stocks in the fund minus short-term liabilities, or in other words the net asset value. However, this often is not the case. Because closed-end funds trade on the stock exchanges, they are subject to the vagaries of all markets. Thus closed-end funds may sell at "premiums," prices above their net asset value, or at "discounts," prices below the net asset value. And sometimes these premiums and discounts may be large, on the order of 20 percent or more.

Does it make sense that investors are sometimes willing to pay more for a basket of stocks than the basket is really worth? Does it make sense to pay $80 for a $50 pair of shoes? Of course not. Yet Wall Street has many adherents to the "Greater Fool" theory, which says that even if I pay too much for something, another fool—a "greater fool"—will take the merchandise off my hands at a still higher price. Sometimes this is exactly what happens. However, at some point no greater fool exists, and the value of the funds comes tumbling down.

The flip side of buying closed-end funds at a premium is buying them at a discount. In other words, paying $20 for a basket of stocks that sell individually for $25. Why would closed-end funds sell at a discount? A number of hypotheses exist that attempt to explain this phenomenon.

Some academicians attribute differences between net asset value and the closed-end fund's price to discrepancies between the market value of the fund's assets and liabilities and the quoted net asset value. For example, some closed-end funds hold fairly illiquid investments. Since the market for these investments may not provide daily prices, assessing the true market value of these investments is difficult. Therefore the stated net asset value, which assumes certain prices for illiquid investments, may actually be overstating their true worth. Hence the discounted selling price.

Another theory holds that since closed-end funds have tax liabilities due to unrealized capital gains, such funds may trade at a discount to reflect the accrued tax liabilities.

Still another theory holds that closed-end funds, due to transaction fees, management expenses, and the prospects of the investment company raising management fees, generally sell at a discount to net asset value to compensate for these fees.

A theory has been expounded that closed-end funds, especially closed-end funds that invest in a single foreign country, do not possess proper diversification and thus expose investors to a higher risk level. To compensate for this higher risk level, the funds trade at a discount.

Whatever the reason, discounts do exist and may represent a potential opportunity. A simple mathematical example demonstrates the power of investing in a closed-end fund selling at a discount.

Let's say you buy a closed-end fund with a net asset value of $35 per share that is trading for $25 per share—a 28 percent discount. Dividends on the fund are paid at the rate of $1.50 per share. That means that the fund, based on the dividends paid on the net asset value of the securities, is yielding 4.3 percent. But because you paid only $25 per share, your yield is a much more substantial 6 percent. And if you reinvest the dividends through the closed-end fund's dividend reinvestment plan—and many closed-end funds have DRIPs— then you are, in effect, buying additional shares at a discount.

One added kicker is that some closed-end funds offer discounts in their DRIPs. Some of these funds apply the discount only if the fund is trading at or above net asset value, so it pays to check with the specific closed-end fund concerning restrictions on discounts in its DRIP. For a listing of closed-end funds with dividend reinvestment plans, investors should refer to my book *Buying Stocks Without a Broker.*

Every specialist in closed-end funds has his or her own methods for buying funds at a discount. Some of these rules include buying a closed-end fund when the discount is 5 percent wider than the fund's average discount tracked over six months. Other fund specialists combine certain rules for purchasing at a discount with a close eye on the fund's expenses.

As discussed in the section on mutual funds in Chapter 3, expenses can kill a fund's performance, and that applies to closed-end funds as well. Keep investments in closed-end funds to those with expenses in the 1 to 1½ percent range, or slightly higher for international closed-end funds. Advisers also suggest that investors concentrate investments in those funds that have provisions to eliminate discounts through buying back shares or converting the fund to an open-end format. In this way, mechanisms to eliminate discounts exist that don't rely solely on market forces.

One final word about closed-end funds is in order. Buying closed-end funds when they are first offered via an initial public offering (IPO) usually leads to short-term losses. The losses stem from a portion of the IPO proceeds going to underwriters for bringing the fund to market. Bottom line: Don't buy a closed-end fund IPO. Take a fresh look after six months to see how the fund has performed and whether it's trading at a discount.

An excellent source of information on closed-end funds is *Herzfeld's Guide to Closed-End Funds,* written by fund expert Thomas Herzfeld and published by McGraw-Hill.

One source of timely information on funds trading at discounts and premiums is *Barron's* (a coupon for four free weeks of *Barron's* is in the coupon section in the back of the book.) Every week, *Barron's* listing of all closed-end funds shows whether funds are trading at discounts or premiums. Figure 5-1 gives a sample of a Barron's closed-end fund listing.

As the table shows, in this particular week **Baker, Fentress & Co.**, a closed-end fund on the New York Stock Exchange, traded at a nearly 17 percent discount from its net asset value. One reason that may account for the discount is that the fund's largest holding by far is Consolidated-Tomoka Land Co., which owns more than 36,000 acres in Florida. Since valuing real estate is an inexact science at best, the discount may reflect the fact that the fund's net asset value may be overstating the real value of the fund's real estate holdings.

Conversely, the **Bergstrom Capital** closed-end fund, which trades on the American Stock Exchange, traded at a 23 percent premium to

Fund Name	Stock Exch	NAV	Market Price	Prem /Disc	52 week Market Return
		Friday, March 12, 1993			
		General Equity Funds			
Adams Express	N	20.85	21⅜	+ 2.5	22.6
Baker Fentress	N	21.45	17⅞	− 16.7	5.7
Bergstrom Capital	A	88.37	109	+ 23.3	− 3.7
Blue Chip Value	N	8.02	8⅛	+ 1.3	13.0
Central Securities	A	15.56	14⅛	− 9.2	48.0
Charles Allmon Tr	N	10.36	9¾	− 5.9	3.1
Engex	A	12.16	9⅞	− 18.8	2.6
Gabelli Equity Tr	N	10.90	11⅜	+ 4.4	13.0
General American	N	26.24	26½	+ 1.0	7.1
Inefficient Mkt	A	11.55	10	− 13.4	− 8.6
Jundt Growth	N	15.05	13⅜	− 11.1	− 7.0
Liberty All-Star	N	10.69	10¾	+ 0.6	13.0
Morgan Gren Sm Cap	N	12.06	11⅝	− 3.6	− 2.4
NAIC Growth	O	N/A	9¾	N/A	20.3
Royce Value Trust	N	13.28	13⅜	+ 0.7	24.7
Salomon Brothers	N	15.50	13⅝	− 12.1	6.8
Source Capital	N	42.80	48	+ 12.1	14.7
Spectra	O	18.34	16½	− 10.0	10.7
Tri-Continental	N	28.64	26	− 9.2	6.5
Z-Seven	O	15.04	16½	+ 9.7	− 18.5
Zweig	N	11.41	13	+ 13.9	8.3
		Specialized Equity Funds			
ASA Limited	N	c31.98	36⅝	+ 14.5	− 14.6
Alliance Glob Env	N	11.32	10	− 11.7	− 14.0
Anchor Gold & Curr	M	N/A	4 9/16	N/A	− 1.3
Central Fd Canada	A	c3.91	3⅝	− 7.3	− 6.2
Counsellors Tandem	N	17.63	15⅜	− 12.8	20.6
Dover Regional Fin	O	7.65	6⅝	− 13.4	61.7
Duff Phelps Ut Inc	N	10.19	11	+ 7.9	17.8
Emerging Mkts Tel	N	14.06	14⅝	+ 4.0	N/A
First Financial	N	16.24	15⅜	− 5.3	78.9
Global Health Sci	N	11.36	10⅜	− 8.7	− 24.7
H&Q Healthcare Inv	N	17.55	17⅞	+ 1.9	− 21.0
H&Q Life Sci Inv	N	12.67	13⅛	+ 3.6	N/A
Patriot Global Dvd	N	14.68	14¾	+ 0.5	N/A

Figure 5.1

the net asset value. This premium may reflect the fund's holdings in a number of popular industry groups. Indeed, the closed-end fund had a huge holding in the biotechnology sector.

When investing in closed-end funds, it's critical to evaluate the possible reasons a fund is selling at a discount or premium. Remember, investigate before investing.

6
Perks for the Active Shareholder

A sermon I've been preaching throughout this book is that shareholders are truly the owners of the corporation and should be treated as such by companies and management. But ownership cuts both ways. Not only should corporations behave properly toward shareholders, but shareholders have the responsibility of behaving like owners. They should care about such things as corporate profitability, management accountability, employee compensation, and community relations.

Why? For starters, such factors directly affect the value of your investment. For example, a company that pays exorbitant wages to top management while profits are deteriorating won't endear itself to Wall Street. Another example would be a utility that has poor relations with the community for a number of reasons, such as a history of poor service or unfavorable hiring practices and employee relations. Such a utility may find regulators less accommodating next time a rate increase is up for review.

An excuse I often hear from shareholders is that they'd like to become more knowledgeable about their companies' businesses and policies, but they don't know how. Fortunately, ways exist to keep on top of your firms' doings, and this chapter explores them. Best of all, by keeping track of the latest developments at your companies, you can pick up some rather interesting perks and freebies.

Annuals, Quarterlies, 10-Ks, 10-Qs

As a shareholder in a publicly traded company, you have certain rights. One of these is the right to be kept informed via financial data that companies are required to send you. These reports, which are sent free of charge, fall into five major types: annual reports, quarterly reports, 10-K reports, 10-Q reports, and proxy statements. Proxies provide their own set of special perks and will be discussed in depth at the end of this chapter.

An annual report is the document sent each year that describes the company's performance for the preceding year. Annual reports come in all shapes and forms, from fancy, high-gloss reports with plenty of color and pizzazz to stripped-down, no-frills reports. An annual report usually contains the following information: a statement from the CEO or chairman discussing the year's performance and expectations for the new year; financial statements, including a balance sheet, income statement, and statement of cash flows; auditor's report; and explanatory information concerning certain accounting treatments. Many companies provide in-depth information concerning their operating segments, while others may devote several pages to their community programs.

Related to an annual report is the accompanying 10-K report. This report explains more thoroughly financial figures and corporate performance. It's a rather drab and formal-looking document, but it's one of the more significant pieces of information you'll receive from your corporations.

Other sources of information are quarterly reports and 10-Qs. Quarterly reports, sent at the end of each quarter, provide information and some financial statistics on the performance for the preceding three-month period. The 10-Qs provide in-depth information on financial performance for the quarter.

I'm not going to lie and say that these reports contain the whole story. Any of you who have actually read these reports—and I'll bet that's a relatively small number—know that they aren't exactly the easiest documents in the world to understand. Companies are skilled in disguising, burying, manipulating, and otherwise obfuscating the information so as to render it virtually incomprehensible in certain instances.

With that said, valid reasons exist for taking the time to read and think about these documents. One reason is that information may be gleaned just by noting the appearance of the annual report. Let's say the annual report is an 80-page, 4-color opus, printed on glossy paper, with a full-page picture of the CEO and other large pictures of top management and board members. It's important to remember that these reports aren't produced and printed for free. Each copy of the average annual report is estimated to cost around $2.60. Multiply that times the thousands or even millions of shareholders—AT&T has well over two million shareholders of record—and the costs can be substantial. These are costs that you, as a shareholder, pay. When thought of in those terms, is it really important that your companies have fancy reports? Could the same information be provided in a less costly package?

Reading an Annual Report

Another reason to look closely at the information is that, surprisingly, you might even learn something. It's quite an event when the average investor finishes reading an annual report and feels that he or she has actually learned something. Nevertheless, while we may have trouble interpreting financial numbers, many of us know a con job when we see one, at least some of the time. That's why reading the CEO's or chairman's statement found in every annual report may be as enlightening as dissecting the numbers.

CEOs and chairmen are experts at putting the company's performance in the best possible light. Rarely will a CEO say that the company's performance stank and that shareholders have the right to lynch management. Instead CEOs blame "a tough economic climate" or a "challenging, competitive environment" for the firm's "underperformance" for the year.

The problem with such sugar coating is that, as a shareholder, you know exactly what the stock market had to say about the company's performance. And make no mistake: the stock market is the best arbiter for judging the actions of management. Executives don't want you to believe this, and many annual reports are sprinkled with language detailing the "unfair treatment" the stock received from Wall Street. Don't buy it. The bottom line is what Wall Street has to say, not what the CEO has to say. If a great gap exists between the thinking of these parties, then it's time to reexamine your investment. Indeed, it's a giant red flag when a CEO's comments in the annual report seem separated from the realities of what's happening to the stock price. Conversely, a company whose CEO treats shareholders intelligently and speaks honestly about the firm and its problems may be a company still worth holding in a portfolio.

"So, Mr. Spider-Man, What Do You Have to Say About the Company's Performance?"

Occasionally, an annual report comes along that is worth treasuring for its uniqueness. The 1991 annual report of **Marvel Entertainment Group** is one such report (see Fig. 6-1).

Marvel, which became a publicly traded company in 1991, has been publishing comic books since 1939 and is responsible for such superhumans as *The Amazing Spider-Man, The Incredible Hulk, Iron Man, Mr. Fantastic, Storm, The Punisher, Wolverine, Captain America, Ghost Rider, The Sensational She-Hulk, Cable,* and *The Mighty Thor.*

What makes the company's first annual report so special is that it looks and reads just like one of the firm's comic books. I must admit it's a bit weird to see *Spider-Man* discussing the company's performance, or *Captain America* talking about product changes and improvements, or *Iron Man* soaring over the company's balance sheet. Nevertheless, the use of the comic-book format enhances the readability of the report, which is definitely a nice perk.

The biggest perk for shareholders, however, is the monetary value that the report may have as a collector's item. Indeed, *The Wall Street Journal* reported that at the company's 1992 shareholder meeting, one shareholder was offered $80 for his copy.

Looking at the Numbers

For those of you who feel up to the challenge, the financial numbers are the next place to stop in your review of an annual report. While I don't want to get too deeply into the financial statements, understanding a few statistics and ratios will make these statements much more valuable for you.

Research and Development Expenditures. This figure is provided on the income statement. Depending on the industry, this information will carry varying degrees of weight. If it's health care, technology, or any other industry where product obsolescence is a real danger, knowing how much your firm spends on research and development is critical. R&D spending should be looked at in two ways: as an absolute trend over the years, and as a percentage of total sales. Ideally, you want to see both R&D outlays and outlays as a percentage of total sales increasing on an annual basis.

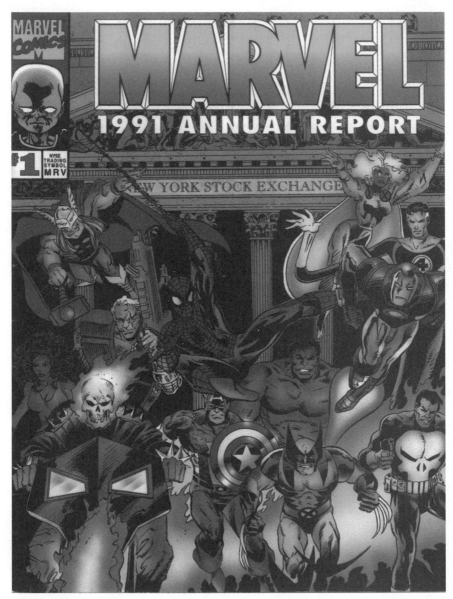

Figure 6.1

Long-Term Debt as a Percentage of Capital. The first step in achieving investment success is finding a company with staying power. High debt levels are a major cause of corporate deaths. Knowing the level of debt is key to discerning a firm's staying power, especially one in a highly cyclical industry such as autos, heavy equipment, chemicals, paper, and other sectors closely tied to the economy. Long-term debt levels are listed in the balance sheet section of an annual report. This number is best examined in conjunction with shareholders' equity. The total capital of the firm is long-term debt plus shareholders' equity. Once you have this figure, divide the amount of long-term debt by the total amount of capital. A percentage greater than 50 percent usually is a red flag.

Dividend Payout Ratio.   This ratio takes the company's dividends paid over the last 12 months, divided by the net income per share earned over the same period. Obviously, if the dividend is equal to net income per share—in other words, a dividend payout ratio of 100 percent—the firm doesn't have any room to expand its dividend, as it is already paying out all of its earnings in the form of dividends. Conversely, a firm with a payout ratio of 30 percent has ample room to expand the dividend at a healthy rate, especially if earnings are rising. This ratio is especially helpful when evaluating income stocks, such as electric utilities.

Current Ratio.   The current ratio is a quick snapshot of the firm's liquidity. The current ratio results from dividing current assets by current liabilities. This figure should be at least 2.0; i.e, current assets should be at least twice current liabilities.

Operating Profit Margin.   A company's revenue level is meaningless if revenues are not turning into profits. The operating profit margin gives investors an idea of how successful the company is in turning sales into profits. To determine this figure, take operating profits—this is found on the income statement—and divide by total sales. Ideally, you want to see this percentage rising or, at the very least, remaining the same on an annual basis. Deterioration in the operating margin signals that expenses may be rising or that prices are under pressure.

There are other statistics that could be considered, but these five are easy to compute and provide a wealth of information concerning the company's health. The New York Stock Exchange provides an "Investor Information Kit" that includes pamphlets on understanding financial statements and a glossary of financial terms. The kit costs only $12 and may be obtained by sending a check to the New York Stock Exchange, P.O. Box 5020, Farmingdale, NY 11736.

Although it's become almost a cliché to mention it in investment books, the footnotes to the financial statements have pertinent information. Unfortunately, much of the information in footnotes discusses what accounting standards were used for evaluating inventories, such as LIFO (last-in-first-out) or FIFO (first-in-first-out), and what method of depreciation was used for property, plant, and equipment. These items do matter, but for the average investor their significance may not be readily understood. However, items such as employee benefits and stock options, related party transactions, and litigation are also discussed in the footnotes. If you want to know, for example, whether the CEO also has a consulting business that is getting paid huge amounts of money by your company; or if your firm is the defendant in a court case that could have a material effect on finances, read this section.

In addition to financial information, annual reports and quarterlies may contain useful shareholder information.

McDonald's, for example, often has a question-and-answer section in its quarterly report discussing such items as how to transfer shares to a child's account, dividend reinvestment plan questions, and record-keeping suggestions. McDonald's occasionally discusses articles on the company that recently appeared in the press and provides a copy of the article to interested shareholders who write the firm. McDonald's also lists various phone numbers, including an investor newsline (708-575-6543), financial media relations (708-575-6150), U.S. franchising inquiries (708-575-6196), and nutrition information center (708-575-FOOD). McDonald's realizes that the stronger its relationship with shareholders, the more *Big Macs* these shareholders will buy.

Another company that believes in keeping shareholders informed—and gaining good PR in the process—is **AMP,** the electronic connectors giant. In the company's 1992 second-quarter report, the firm made available a number of reprints of articles, as well as research information put out by *Value Line* and *Standard & Poor's.*

Discount Coupons and Other Freebies

Companies often use annual and quarterly reports to disseminate discount coupons and other perks for investors. This is especially true for consumer products companies. **Gillette,** for example, had a "money-off" coupon in a quarterly mailing for its *Sensor* razor when it was first introduced. The firm occasionally will enclose discount coupons with dividend checks.

Helene Curtis Industries, maker of shampoos and deodorants, has included coupons for products in its shareholder mailings. Other companies that have periodically included coupons in quarterly and annual reports are **Philip Morris Companies, Colgate-Palmolive, Procter & Gamble, Quaker Oats,** and **Wendy's International.** Investors shouldn't expect huge savings from these coupons. In the case of Colgate-Palmolive, the coupons are usually for $1 off the price of one of its products. Still, the coupons provide a nice kicker to opening the envelope and perusing the quarterly or annual report.

Keep in mind that you don't necessarily have to wait until the company sends you coupons. If you own stock in a consumer products company or fast-food concern, you always have the option of calling the company. Ask for the shareholder relations department, and explain that you're a shareholder who would like to receive a packet of coupons for the company's products. You might get shut out, but you might get lucky, especially if the firm is in the midst of a coupon promotional campaign.

Annual and quarterly reports may also contain other interesting perks and freebies. In Quaker Oats' fiscal 1993 first-quarter report, the firm provided recipes for cookies using its products. In the fiscal 1993 first-quarter report, **Heinz, H.J.** offered to send shareholders *Weight Watchers Slim Ways with Pasta,* a spiral-bound book featuring 150 recipes; an apron; and a coupon for a jar of *Weight Watchers* spaghetti sauce, all for just $13. In the 1991 annual report of **Tambrands,** the maker of *Tampax* tampons, the firm enclosed postcards featuring women of the world. The company invited shareholders to return the postcards to Tambrands with comments on the company, its products, and the annual report.

It Pays to Read the Annual Report—
Literally

Right Start makes reading its annual report a profitable endeavor. The company, founded in 1985, is a leading specialty mail-order concern, offering products for infants and young children.

On page eight of the firm's 1992 annual report—buried at the end of a section with the heading "Impact of Inflation"—is the following paragraph (see Figure 6-2):

> If you have gone this far into the text, you deserve a gift. Take out a crayon, circle this paragraph, and send this page back to Lenny or Stan ["Lenny" is CEO Lenny Targon, and "Stan" is President Stan Fridstein] at The Right Start, Inc. We will send you a $5.00 gift certificate good on any future Right Start Catalog purchase.

How many industrious shareholders found this "buried treasure" and returned the page for the discount? Roughly 40 out of approximately 700 shareholders, according to Mr. Targon.

Impact of Inflation   The impact of inflation on results of operations has not been significant.

If you have gone this far into the text, you deserve a gift. Take out a crayon, circle this paragraph, and send this page back to Lenny or Stan at The Right Start, Inc. We will send you a $5.00 gift certificate good on any future Right Start Catalog purchase.

Figure 6.2

Annual Shareholder Meeting

Another way to keep informed about your company is to attend the annual shareholder meeting. These meetings are often held near the company's headquarters.

Annual meetings provide a forum for management to discuss the company's operations. The meetings are used to vote on various shareholder proposals that have been submitted—I'll show you how to submit a proposal later in this chapter—as well as other business issues. For example, a company undergoing a name change may seek shareholders' approval at the annual meeting. Shareholders may be asked to approve a stock split.

Historically, annual shareholder meetings have been relatively peaceful affairs, with shareholders gathering to take advantage of the free food and/or free gifts—I'll look at some of these gifts shortly—and hear the comments from executives without too much hue and cry. However, in recent years, some annual meetings have taken on the air of a championship heavyweight fight between discontented shareholders and harried top management. Indeed, battles over management compensation, corporate control, the composition of the board of directors, and other issues of corporate governance have transformed these once friendly meetings into rather tense affairs, especially for management.

To be sure, the change from "rubber stamp" shareholders to ones who are more demanding of management is a positive development for investors. Increasing the level of accountability managers have to shareholders ensures that shareholders' best interests are considered. The shareholder meeting, especially the question-and-answer period, is one forum for letting your opinions be known.

Of course it's not always possible to attend the annual shareholder meeting, especially if the company is located a considerable distance from you. Nevertheless, for those times when attending the annual meeting is feasible, investors should consider doing so, and not just to have your voice heard. Many companies provide shareholders who attend the annual meeting with various perks and freebies.

These freebies take many forms. It can be something as simple as free admission to a museum. **Walgreen,** which operates drugstores throughout the country, held its 1993 annual meeting at the Art Institute of Chicago. Registered shareholders of Walgreen attending the annual meeting had the museum's entrance fee waived and were permitted to view the galleries before and after the meeting.

Food is another freebie at the meetings. Usually snacks and drinks are served, and a number of companies offer full lunches or dinners. **National Penn Bancshares,** a Pennsylvania banking concern, provides a family-style dinner for attendees.

Companies may combine the annual meeting with other special events. **V.F. Corp.,** the maker of *Lee* jeans and *Vanity Fair* intimate wear, in the past has given a fashion show consisting of the firm's new lines. Companies may provide tours of their facilities to interested attendees.

Rubbermaid's Annual Meeting
—Shopper's Paradise

Attendees of **Rubbermaid**'s annual meeting get more than just talk from management. They also have the opportunity for a rare shopping experience. The firm, located in Wooster, OH, makes a variety of plastic and rubber products for home and commercial markets. Brand names include *Little Tikes, Rubbermaid, Gott,* and *Con-Tact.* Shareholders who display proper identification of stock ownership—a brokerage or dividend reinvestment plan statement will suffice—receive a free pass to the employee store located near the corporate headquarters. Occasionally the store will run discounts of an additional 20 percent off the already reduced prices. The store is a popular spot for shareholders attending the meeting, although shareholders may shop anytime during the year. The company limits the number of passes to three per year. For further information call 216-264-6464.

Free Gifts

Companies often give attendees of the shareholder meeting a free gift. The types and value of gifts will vary dramatically. **Blockbuster Entertainment,** the operator of video rental stores, gives shareholders a prerecorded videocassette. **Otter Tail Power,** a Minnesota-based utility that serves parts of that state as well as North and South Dakota, has several door prizes for attendees. **Cross, A.T.,** a marketer of fine writing instruments, luggage, and leather products, and **Jostens,** a producer of class rings and other school-related products, usually give one of the firm's products.

Additional companies (several of these are reviewed in Gene Walden's book, *The 100 Best Stocks to Own in America*) that provide perks at the annual shareholder meeting include:

- **International Dairy Queen.** In the past, attendees have been treated to, what else, Dairy Queen products.

- **Abbott Laboratories.** Shareholders attending the annual meeting usually receive lunch as well as a sample gift pack of the firm's consumer products, which include *Selsun Blue* shampoo and *Murine* eye and ear care products.

- **Supervalu.** Shareholders attending the annual meeting of this leading food wholesaler receive a sample gift bag of products "unique to Supervalu."

- **American Brands.** Gift bags with products from various divisions— the company produces cigarettes (*Lucky Strike, Pall Mall, Tareyton*), liquor (*Jim Beam, Old Grandad*), office supplies (*Swingline*), hardware products (*Master Lock* and *Moen*), and golf products (*Titleist* and *Foot-Joy*)—are usually handed out at the annual meeting.

- **Albertson's.** This supermarket chain provides a sample bag containing grocery products.

- **Quaker Oats.** This maker of such products as *Cap'n Crunch* and *Life* cereals, *Quaker Oats* hot cereals, *Aunt Jemima, Rice-A-Roni,* and *Gatorade* has provided product coupons and samples in past years.

- **Hormel, Geo. A.** The company, which produces *Spam* and other meat products, provides shareholders who attend the annual meeting with samples, usually of newer products.

- **McKesson.** This distributor of drug and health-care products and majority stakeholder in *Armor All* car-care products has in the past given attendees a free gift.

- **Deluxe.** This check printer provides a free dinner for attendees.

- **Church & Dwight.** Shareholders in the past have left the annual meeting with samples of the company's product line, which includes *Arm & Hammer* baking soda and other consumer products.

- **General Mills.** Shareholders who attend the annual meeting usually receive samples of some of the company's new products. Consumer brands include *Betty Crocker, Yoplait, Pop Secret, Bisquick,* and *Gold Medal*.

- **Schering-Plough.** Attendees receive a gift bag of samples. Although the company's primary products are prescription drugs, the firm also produces such consumer products as *Coppertone* and *Correctol.*

- **Gillette.** The firm, which produces *Trac II* and *Atra* razor blades, *Daisy* razors, *Braun* shavers, *Right Guard* and *Soft & Dri* deodorants, *White Rain* hair-care products, *Paper Mate* and *Flair* writing instruments, and *Oral-B* dental products, gives attendees products from each of the divisions.

- **ConAgra.** Attendees receive a free lunch consisting entirely of ConAgra products such as *Country Pride* chicken and turkey products, *Banquet* and *Healthy Choice* frozen meals, and *Armour* meat products.

- **Stanhome.** Shareholders who attend the annual meeting of this producer of giftware and *Precious Moments* collectibles receive a gift bag of company products.

- **Alberto Culver.** Product samples—the company's brand names include *Alberto VO5, Static Guard,* and *Get Set*—are available, as well as a company tour.

- **Universal Foods.** A new product sample is usually provided by this leading producer of frozen foods and flavorings.

- **Kellogg.** Hospitality kits, with product samples and coupons, are usually distributed.

- **Borden.** A shopping bag containing several items has been given in the past. Borden has a broad product line, with such brands as *Creamette, Prince, Cracker Jack, Elmer's* glue, and *Meadow Gold.*

- **Dean Foods.** Gift boxes containing the firm's dairy and specialty food products are distributed.

- **Pfizer.** This health-care and consumer products company gives a gift bag, usually with a new consumer product. Its stable of consumer brands includes *Ben-Gay, Visine, Plax,* and *Barbasol.*

- **Newell.** This consumer products firm, which markets *Anchor Hocking* cookware and *Sanford* and *Stuart Hall* office supplies, has periodically distributed samples of new products.

- **Hershey Foods.** A sample of the company's food and chocolate items is provided.

- **Anheuser-Busch Cos.** Attendees are treated to beer and *Eagle* snack foods at the conclusion of the annual meeting.

- **Disney, Walt.** Attendees of the annual meeting have received passes to *Disneyland.*

- **UST.** A grab bag is provided consisting of such products as *Skoal* smokeless tobacco and key chains with the company emblem.

- **Sara Lee.** Attendees receive a bag of products and coupons. Popular brand names include *Ball Park, Sara Lee, Hanes, L'eggs, Sheer Energy, Playtex,* and *Kiwi.*

- **Smucker, J.M.** Gift packages consisting of three or four new products, fruit spreads, etc., are distributed.

- **Loctite.** This specialty-chemical concern has distributed such products as its *Super Glue* adhesive at past annual meetings.

- **Procter & Gamble.** In the past this producer of such products as *Bounce, Cascade, Cheer, Crest, Zest, Charmin, Pampers, Head & Shoulders, Pepto-Bismol, Vicks, Duncan Hines,* and *Folgers* has provided product samples as well as snacks and refreshments.

- **Philip Morris Companies.** Shareholders who attend Philip Morris' annual meeting receive a gift package of products from the company's extensive line, which include cigarettes as well as *Kraft* cheeses, *Jell-O* desserts, *Birds Eye* frozen foods, *Oscar Mayer* meats, *Maxwell House* coffee, *Jacobs Suchard* chocolates, and *Miller* beer.

What's in It for the Company?

Why the show of generosity? Free advertising is one reason. Companies know that the more products you try, the more likely you are to buy the products next time you visit a store. Companies also know that if they shower you with free food and gifts at the annual meeting, you may be less apt to interrogate managers on the company's performance.

One final freebie that may be obtained by attending the annual shareholder meeting is a tax write-off. Now, I'm not suggesting that the IRS will let you get away with buying one share in Hawaiian Electric Industries in order to write off your vacation to Hawaii every year. But there may be instances when at least part of the costs incurred in attending the annual meeting may be included among miscellaneous deductions and subject to the 2 percent rule. For example, if you attend an annual meeting six hours away, you may be able to deduct your travel costs as well as your hotel stay, provided that most of the time spent on the trip pertained to business involving your investment. For complete details on when expenses incurred to attend shareholder meetings may be deducted, consult your tax adviser.

Check with the Companies

Companies reserve the right to change freebie policies at any time. If a firm is going through a downsizing, or other cost-cutting programs, perks that were offered one year may not be offered the next. Check with companies to see what shareholder goodies, if any, are on the annual meeting agenda.

Attend the Annual Meeting—Find a Spouse

Betty Rogers of Chicago was looking for more than just a free meal or a key chain when she attended annual shareholder meetings in 1987. She was looking for a husband. According to an article in the *Chicago Tribune,* Ms. Rogers, then in her 50s, had been single for nine years after a divorce. She was tired of being alone, and she made 1987 her year to find a mate. Rogers embarked on several paths in order to meet her goal. Figuring that eligible men attend annual shareholder meetings, she had a broker buy one share in 25 Chicago-area companies. That one share was her ticket to attend 25 annual shareholder meetings. Was Ms. Rogers' perseverance rewarded? Through a mutual friend, she met Lyman Jeffreys later that year and eventually married him.

Shareholder Activism—The Perk of Power

A new era of shareholder activism is infiltrating corporate America. Many reasons exist for the rise in activism. The increasing concentration of stock ownership in the hands of institutional investors has allowed them to wield considerable influence on management. Traditionally, the thinking was that if a big pension fund didn't like the way a company was being managed, the pension fund manager would vote with his or her feet by selling the stock. However, with pension funds now so big in size, as well as the growth of "index investing"—investment in a basket of stocks that mirrors the S&P 500, for example—institutional investors are more reluctant to sell stock and more inclined to work to change the corporation.

Another reason for the increased shareholder activism is that a major stick that had been used to reform management—takeovers and leveraged buyouts—has decreased in importance. Whether you agreed or disagreed with the merger mania of the 1980's, the takeover activity did have a huge influence on corporate management, especially managers of companies that had been perceived as laggards. However, the decline of merger activity has lessened the pressure managers otherwise would have felt to perform better. The result is that management has become more insular, forcing active shareholders to become the new agents for change.

The realization that the 1990s probably won't be like the roaring 1980s is no doubt causing shareholders to take a more active approach to improving their companies. In the 1980s, when stock returns averaged approximately 18 percent annually and some years saw returns of 25 and 30 percent, stockholders became a lazy bunch. After all, why be an active participant in corporate governance matters when your portfolio is rising at a rapid rate. Who cares?

But with the likelihood of a return to more traditional stock returns of 10 to 11 percent, the ability to generate improved corporate performance by challenging current managers may mean the difference between having a profitable portfolio and one that performs poorly.

The threat of shareholder litigation, specifically aimed at the stewards for the shareholders—the board of directors—has put a fire under directors to become less the mouthpiece for management and more the ombudsman for shareholders. This has led to increased activism directed toward directors, especially outside directors.

The mechanisms that allow shareholders to have greater say in the company are becoming more widely known and less restrictive. For example, groups such as the United Shareholders Association have been quite active in representing the rights of shareholders, and the success of shareholder activist groups in some high-profile situations has helped to energize the movement.

Look Out, Management—Here Comes the USA

If you're a CEO or a member of the board of directors of a corporation, a phone call from the United Shareholders Association (USA) is about as cheery as hearing that Mike Wallace of *60 Minutes* is in the reception area with a camera crew.

USA, a nonprofit advocacy group founded by T. Boone Pickens in 1986, has become a gadfly of corporate America in recent years. Each year the company prepares its *Shareholder 1000* report. The report looks at the top 1000 companies based on market capitalization and rates them on such factors as stock performance, shareholder rights, executive compensation, and executive stock ownership. The company then targets firms that rank poorly and attempts to effect change through measures, subtle or otherwise.

The organization has had a fairly high degree of success in recent years in lobbying for change on a variety of issues. One notable victory occurred at the end of December 1992 when Westinghouse Electric dismantled some of its antitakeover defenses and agreed to elect all directors annually instead of staggering their terms. Staggered terms make it more difficult to oust a majority of directors in a single year.

Membership to USA is $50 and up, depending on the scope of information you would like to receive from the organization. The membership fee may be tax-deductible, so consult with your tax adviser on this issue. For information, write the USA Foundation for Research and Education; 1667 K Street, NW; Suite 770; Washington, DC 20006 (202-393-4600).

Power for the Individual Investor

You're probably saying that this shareholder activism is all well and good, but what perk can I get out of all of this? If you define "perk" as something that has value but doesn't cost you anything, the perk of shareholder power may be the most valuable perk you have. Individual investors do have the ability to have their voices heard and to influence managers directly and indirectly. Investors who choose not to exercise this perk of power, especially if they're dissatisfied with the company's performance, are shortchanging themselves.

Call the Company

One avenue for getting your voice heard is by picking up the telephone and calling the company. Your chance of talking with the chairman or CEO is probably slight, as there are plenty of gatekeepers. If you can't get through to top management, notify the shareholder relations department of your beef and request that someone from the company return your call. If you don't like calling, pick up a pen and write a letter. Of course, your letter may go right into the waste can. But management is becoming more sensitive to opinions of shareholders, especially if your opinion is echoed by other shareholders. And the cost of making a phone call or writing a letter is insignificant. What do you have to lose?

A letter I wrote to the head of **Bristol-Myers Squibb** in 1992, following what I felt was a negative change in the company's dividend reinvestment plan, generated a phone call from a company spokesperson inquiring about my beef. Sure, he may have just been giving me lip service. Still, it didn't cost me anything, and at least I fulfilled my responsibility of being an active owner.

Power of the Press

Another avenue to pursue is to take your case to the press. The press loves to jump on a good story about top management shirking their responsibility to shareholders. If you can state your case clearly, without emotion, and back it up with specifics and performance statistics, you may be able to get a reporter to look a bit more closely into the situation.

All business media are providing more coverage of shareholder activism, and some are even taking a watchdog role. *Barron's* has traditionally been the eyes and ears of individual investors and thus may be a good place to send your letter. *Forbes* magazine is another. Sending a copy of your letter to the business editor of the company's hometown newspaper may help you find a sympathetic ear. Chances are, many shareholders of the company live in the area, and they may have been expressing similar concerns. If you're a member of United Shareholders Association, be sure to send a copy of the letter to its headquarters.

Will your letter do any good? It's a long shot. Nevertheless there's little cost to you and, with a little luck, the rewards could be substantial.

Voting Your Proxy—Weapon of Shareholder Activism

With stock ownership also comes voting power on corporate issues. Under SEC regulations, corporations are required to have certain items approved by shareholders, such as the election of the board of directors. The way to cast your vote is by using a proxy.

Proxy materials consist of a proxy card and a multipage proxy statement. The proxy statement contains information concerning the board of directors and executive compensation. It also includes the date, time, and location of the pending annual meeting; proposals that have been submitted by shareholders for a vote; and information concerning when and where to send such proposals to be considered for vote at the following year's annual meeting.

The proxy card lists the specific items to be voted on at the share-holder meeting and provides spaces for shareholders to cast their vote. If a shareholder does not plan to attend the annual meeting, he or she can return the proxy card so that his or her vote will be counted.

Shareholders can vote their proxies in a variety of ways to show their feelings. A popular tactic of some shareholder activists has been a vote of "no confidence"—in effect, withholding votes from directors. This is one way an investor can express his or her dissatisfaction with the company and board. Of course, you can vote against management proposals and for certain shareholder proposals. Shareholders are permitted to include written comments on the proxy card, providing yet another avenue to have management hear your concerns.

Most investors probably never look at proxy materials, nor vote the proxy card. Yet at least scanning the materials provides a wealth of information that a shareholder is not likely to get in any other report. For example, proxy statements usually give detailed information about each person on the board of directors. The statements go in-depth concerning executive compensation. With executive compensation being a lightning rod of the shareholder activist community, proxy statements are taking on even greater importance.

Using Proxy Information to Pick Stocks

Most investors pick stocks using fundamental information such as earnings growth, dividends, financial strength, and industry prospects. Others use technical indicators such as stock price action, relative strength, volume indicators, and sentiment readings. Still others use a combination of fundamental and technical analysis. However, few investors use data found in proxy materials. Yet this information provides valuable insights into the inner workings of the company, especially on matters of corporate governance.

Shareholders of corporations automatically receive their companies' proxy material. Nonshareholders, for a fee, may obtain proxy information by contacting the SEC. Inside the proxy statement are answers to many questions that provide a nice supplement to fundamental and technical analysis. For example:

- *How many outside directors does the company have?* A board with an abundance of outside directors should have greater autonomy than a board comprised primarily of executives of the corporation.

(Continued)

> - *Do the board members have staggered terms, or is the entire board reelected each year?* Staggered terms make it difficult to effect wholesale changes in the board's composition.
> - *Do the current executives have hefty "golden parachutes"?* Golden parachutes may make an acquisition much more costly for an acquirer, which can help to keep poor managers in power.
> - *Does the firm have various "poison pills" that hinder a takeover by an unfriendly party?* Such takeover deterrents benefit entrenched management.
> - *Are the positions of chairman and CEO held by the same person?* While one person holding both jobs is not necessarily bad, it may inhibit accountability to shareholders. From the standpoint of checks and balances, it might be better to have the jobs held by two people.
> - *How does compensation among top executives relate to the performance of the stock?* Are executives getting rich at the expense of shareholders? How closely is compensation linked with the performance of the stock?
>
>   With information being everything when it comes to choosing investments, the data contained in a proxy statement is information investors can't afford to be without.

Shareholder activists have found the proxy to be a powerful weapon in bringing about change. Shareholder activists have been more aggressive in recent years in getting shareholder proposals placed in the proxy material. Historically, these proposals have primarily been concerned with the social behavior of companies, such as affirmative action policies, charitable contributions, or company divestitures as a result of dealings in, say, South Africa. However, many shareholder proposals in recent years have focused on corporate governance issues: executive compensation, board elections and functions, and shareholder rights.

Who can submit shareholder proposals to be placed on a proxy for voting? Surprisingly, nearly any investor, even an investor with a relatively small holding, has the opportunity to at least have his or her proposal considered. The rules for filing a shareholder proposal are fairly straightforward:

- You must have held at least $1000 worth of stock for a year, as of the date of the company's annual meeting.

- Your proposal, along with a supporting statement, must be sent to the company by the deadline listed in the proxy statement. For example, in proxy materials highlighting the 1993 shareholder meeting will be information, including deadlines, regarding the submission of shareholder proposals for inclusion in the 1994 proxy statement.

- Your proposal can cover a variety of topics, but it cannot meddle in what is called "ordinary business operations" of the company. What constitutes "ordinary business operations" is open to interpretation, but it is usually the escape clause that companies use to disallow proposals. Members of United Shareholders Association can seek guidance from the organization on the proper wording of a shareholder proposal to increase the chances that it will appear on the proxy statement.

Once your shareholder proposal has been accepted, you can either pat yourself on the back and relax or start the process of getting other shareholders to rally around your cause. Previously, soliciting backing for a proxy proposal was quite difficult. SEC regulations mandated that in order to talk to more than 10 other shareholders you first had to file a formal proxy statement with the agency. This stringent requirement limited discussion between corporate shareholders. However, at the end of 1992, the SEC changed its rules on shareholder communications, making it easier to solicit backing for shareholder proposals. Granted, soliciting support for your proposal could be a time-consuming and expensive proposition. However, at least you have the option of doing so without the previous restrictions. If nothing else, you're now freer to communicate your beefs to big institutional shareholders, who are in a better position to act as agents for change.

Jack (or Ed) of All Trades

Sears, Roebuck & Co. has been the "poster child" for shareholder activism in recent years. The giant retailer created many unhappy shareholders through most of the 1980s, due to what one shareholder labeled "a poor mix of business and a lack of accountability to owners."

Sears was a perfect place for shareholder activists to flex their muscles. Perhaps the firm's biggest offense was the lack of accountability by its top executive, Edward Brennan. At one time in his

---

(Continued)

career, Brennan simultaneously held five jobs. He was Chairman of the Board and CEO. He was CEO of the company's merchandising operations—its largest division. He was head of the board's nominating committee, meaning he had a huge say as to whom was picked for the board of directors. He was also a trustee of the employee stock plan, which gave him the power to influence the voting of the 25 percent of Sears stock held by the plan. In effect Edward Brennan, given his various jobs, was accountable only to Edward Brennan.

Given Sears's relative underperformance and the unique position of "jack of all trades" Brennan, the company became a favorite target of shareholder activists.

How successful have these activists been in effecting change at Sears? They themselves claim that Sears's major restructuring of recent years is due in part to the arm-twisting of activist shareholders.

Conclusion

A few final words on proxies are in order. First, proxies aren't reserved exclusively for stock investments. Mutual funds are required to send proxy material to fund holders. Mutual fund proxies usually cover such issues as management expenses and investment policies. Take the time to read the proxy material and to vote.

If you are shareholder of record, proxy material will be sent to you. If you hold the stock in "street name" at the brokerage firm, the material will be sent to the broker, and it's up to the brokerage firm to forward the proxy materials to you. Make sure that the broker passes along all proxies, as well as annual and quarterly reports, in a timely fashion.

7

Company Tours, Museums, and Other (Surprisingly) Fascinating Freebies

Most shareholders have never seen what goes on in the factories and plants in which they have ownership. Of course, geography may present some roadblocks. However, it seems that more and more the problem is due to corporate policies prohibiting tours.

It seems ludicrous that a shareholder is forbidden from seeing the inner workings of the corporation firsthand. However, companies have valid reasons for prohibiting tours.

One reason is liability. In these days when a hangnail on corporate property can lead to a lawsuit, companies are reluctant to leave themselves vulnerable to litigation. Another reason is that firms have increasingly become protective of their manufacturing methods and equipment and don't welcome unfamiliar eyes spying on their operations. A third reason is that tours cost money, and companies are not always willing to pay for such "goodwill" gestures.

That's not to say that the company tour is dead. A number of companies still offer tours for shareholders and the public, and these tours represent an especially interesting freebie. Related freebies are the corporate museums that have been established to promote education about companies and their industries.

Granted, the benefits from taking a company tour or visiting a corporate museum may be less significant, in dollar terms, than other perks discussed in this book. Nevertheless, it's difficult to place a monetary value on the benefits derived from seeing commerce at work. Seeing how an everyday product is produced and packaged for the masses provides a new appreciation of the industrial ingenuity that went into building our country's finest corporations. Oftentimes, the biggest beneficiaries of company tours and museums are children and young adults, who experience the sense of discovery of seeing how products are made. At the very least, company tours and museums represent a pleasant and educational, not to mention cheap, diversion during a family vacation.

In doing research for this chapter, I visited a number of well-known corporations that offer tours and museums. Here are my observations.

Chocolate Town, USA

I grew up about 20 minutes from Hershey, PA. Of course "Chocolate Town, USA," as Hershey is called, is home to **Hershey Foods,** the nation's largest producer of chocolate and, surprisingly, its second-largest producer of pasta.

Hershey holds fond childhood memories for me. One of those memories is of taking the tour through the chocolate factory and being bombarded by the omnipresent aroma of chocolate. That was my first contact with company tours, and it was an extremely pleasant one.

I've visited Hershey through the years, but I hadn't taken a plant tour in some time. Thus, when making plans for my visit, I was a bit disappointed to learn that the company no longer give tours at its Hershey manufacturing plant (it still does at its Oakdale, CA facility, however). Instead the company now has *Chocolate World,* a facility that provides visitors with a motorized tour through the world of chocolate making.

Approximately 1.8 million guests visit *Chocolate World* each year. When I entered the facility, I immediately smelled the chocolate—surprising since chocolate is not produced in *Chocolate World.* I soon discovered that to give visitors the total chocolate experience, the smell of chocolate is pumped into the building.

At the beginning of the *Chocolate World* tour, you are greeted by a series of placards discussing the history of Hershey Foods and its founder, Milton Hershey.

Born in central Pennsylvania in 1857, Milton Hershey was your classic entrepreneur. He attended school through the fourth grade but quit at his father's behest to become a printer's apprentice. Realizing that printing was not his calling, he went on to become an apprentice to a candy maker and opened his first candy shop at the age of 18. The business failed after six years, as did other ventures in the years thereafter. However, Hershey was learning all along what it takes to make great candy. He put that knowledge to work in 1886 when he began the business that established his reputation as a candy maker: the Lancaster Caramel Company. It was at this company that he soon began to develop products that would be the forerunners to his most popular products: *Hershey's* milk chocolate bar, *Hershey's* milk chocolate bar with almonds, and *Hershey's* cocoa.

Hershey sold Lancaster Caramel in 1900 for $1 million but retained the rights to manufacture chocolate. He returned to his birthplace and located a chocolate manufacturing operation in the heart of Pennsylvania's dairy country, where he could obtain the large supplies of fresh milk needed to make fine milk chocolate. The new plant opened in 1905, and the rest, as they say, is history.

Milton Hershey's legacy lives on not only in his chocolate but also in what he gave back to the community. In 1909 he established what is now called the Milton Hershey School. The school, situated on a 10,000-acre estate, houses and provides education for nearly 1200 children whose family lives have been disrupted. Through the Hershey Trust Company—established to provide for the school's future—the school owns over 42 percent of Hershey Foods common stock and controls nearly 77 percent of voting shares (that's why you should take any takeover talk surrounding Hershey—and such talk appears occasionally in the business press—with a grain of salt). There is also the Milton S. Hershey Medical Center of Pennsylvania State University, which was made possible by a $50 million grant from the Hershey Trust Co.

After you have read about the history of the company, a series of monitors provides you with the "Cocoa Bean Story." You learn, for example, that the growth cycle of cocoa trees is continuous; that cocoa beans really are white but darken when exposed to light outside the pod. Once you've completed the cocoa bean story, you're ready to embark on the tour ride. The ride, which reminded me of *Walt Disney World*'s "It's a Small World," shows how chocolate is made, from the cocoa bean to the finished product. You learn that the three most important ingredients of chocolate are sugar, milk, and cocoa beans and that cocoa beans from different parts of the world have different tastes. You discover how chocolate liquor is made and see how chocolate is "conched" and "rolled." You'll also see how products are packaged without ever being touched by human hands. That goes for *Hershey's Kisses,* which can be produced at the rate of nearly 33 million *per day*! At the end of the ride you even get some free samples—I received three *Hershey's Kisses.*

There's more than just the tour at *Chocolate World.* The facility holds gift shops and food stands. The center is also the best place to get information about other Hershey attractions.

Particulars: *Chocolate World—400 Park Blvd., Hershey, PA—is free to the public and usually open daily from 9 a.m. to 4:45 p.m. Times may vary during the winter months and on holidays. For further information call 717-534-4900. Other attractions include Hershey Gardens, Hershey Museum, ZooAmerica, Hershey Bears minor league hockey team, Hersheypark amusement park, and Hersheypark arena. And, yes, the streetlights really are shaped like* Hershey's Kisses.

Born to Be Wild

Most people pass through York, PA, never knowing that the town is home to an American classic—the **Harley-Davidson** motorcycle.

Milwaukee, WI, is actually the headquarters for Harley-Davidson. However, the company's only assembly plant is in York.

I must confess that I've never ridden a Harley; I don't even have a tattoo. Nevertheless, it's hard not to be drawn to the story of this company. Founded in 1903, Harley-Davidson has survived foreign competition, poor management, quality lapses in its bikes, and rocky finances to become an American institution. This firm, once on the brink of bankruptcy, now reigns as the only U.S. manufacturer of motorcycles and a model for manufacturing ingenuity and skillful product marketing.

It is the latter quality—the successful marketing of the Harley "mystique"—that gives the tour much of its appeal. If there's one thing Harley understands, it's the importance of being close to your customer, of making him or her feel that a Harley is not just a bike, but truly a lifestyle. The tour is just one more way the company helps to cement this relationship with its market.

The assembly plant sits on almost 300 acres and employs roughly 2000 people. The tour begins in the Rodney C. Gott Museum. Here you learn the history of the company. The firm was founded by 18-year-old Bill Harley in Milwaukee in 1903. Bill, together with the Davidson brothers, built an engine that was strapped to a bicycle. The first "Harley" went 6 miles per hour. The boys built three bikes in 1903: one is in the Milwaukee headquarters, one is in the Smithsonian, and the third bike has never been found. By 1906 the boys were in full production of their motorized bikes, making 50 that year. Today, the company makes approximately 350 motorcycles per day.

The museum is interesting in that it traces the development of the Harley over the course of 90 years, showing all of the model changes and various technological advances. Bikes of special interest include one the late Malcolm Forbes—a Harley enthusiast with 45 bikes in his collection—gave to Elizabeth Taylor; bikes the company made for the war effort; and a miniature replica of a Harley made by the jeweler Cartier and valued at $45,000.

After completing the museum tour, the group is taken to the first of the plant's two assembly lines. What is impressive about the tour is that you truly get a feel for the manufacturing process, being only a few feet from workers who are stamping out parts and assembling the bikes.

What I noticed was the plant's cleanliness and the many workers sporting Harley T-shirts and hats.

A tour highlight is seeing how every motorcycle is "test-driven" in the plant. The plant has a treadmill-like device on which new bikes are tested at various speeds.

At the tour's conclusion, you are led into a room containing all of Harley's new models for that year. Feel free to sit on the bikes and take pictures if you wish.

Particulars: *The plant is located at 1425 Eden Rd., York, PA. The tour lasts about 1½ hours and is free to the public. The plant and museum tour starts at 10:00 a.m and 2:00 p.m., Monday–Friday. The museum tour only is available Monday–Saturday at certain times of the day. Call 717-848-1177 for information about times. Children must be 12 years of age to go on the plant tour. Preschedule groups of 20 or more. No cameras are permitted on the plant tour. Other nearby attractions include the city of Baltimore (about one hour's drive) and Harrisburg (about 30 minutes' drive), the capital of Pennsylvania.*

Good Things Come in Small Packages

In a city where a pastrami on rye costs about as much as a summer house, it's always a special treat to find something in New York that costs nothing and delivers plenty. **The Forbes Magazine Galleries,** located in the Forbes Building on Fifth Avenue in New York, is such a find.

The galleries are proof that good things come in small packages. The entire galleries are snugly situated in the lobby of the building. The galleries, which contain memorabilia collected by the late Malcolm Forbes (*Forbes* magazine remains privately held), are divided into five sections: "Ships Ahoy," "On Parade," "Trophies," "Presidential Papers," and "Fabergé."

(Continued)

"Ships Ahoy" contains hundreds of toy boats Forbes collected during his lifetime. The boats, some dating back to the late 1800s, include models of yachts, warships, riverboats, and ocean liners. One of the boats on display is a replica of the *Lusitania* that Forbes purchased in 1983 for $28,600—at the time, a world's record for a toy. Of all the boats my favorite was *Titanic* soap, a bar of soap shaped liked the *Titanic* and carrying the words, "Guaranteed to sink."

"On Parade" is a collection of Forbes's miniature soldiers, cowboys, knights, GIs, and other military personnel. The complete collection contains more than 100,000 pieces, with 12,000 housed in the New York gallery.

"Trophies" contains some 175 athletic trophies, athletic memorabilia, and war medals. A chunk of the *Hindenburg* is on display in this section.

"Presidential Papers" was my favorite. The gallery has selections from the total collection of 3000 American historical documents. One of the more interesting pieces on display was an expense report, submitted by Paul Revere to the Boston patriots' Committee of Correspondence in 1774, asking to be paid for his ride from Boston to New York to tell allies about the Boston Tea Party. (John Hancock paid the voucher out of his own pocket, then applied to the committee for reimbursement.) The display includes a letter from John Adams complaining bitterly that his role in the American Revolution was overshadowed by the likes of Washington and Franklin.

Lincoln's opera glasses used on the night he was shot are on display, as is Herbert Hoover's terse reflection on his Presidency: "Herbert Hoover, once of Washington, DC, now fortunately elsewhere." But best of all is a 1950 letter from Harry Truman to *Washington Post* music critic Paul Hume after Hume had criticized Truman's daughter Margaret's musical talents: " Some day I hope to meet you. When that happens, you'll need a new nose, a lot of beef steak for black eyes, and perhaps a supporter below."

The last section of the gallery is devoted to Forbes's collection of Fabergé eggs and other jewelry of distinction. For lovers of "objets de luxe," as the pamphlet says, this section is of special interest.

Particulars: *The Forbes Magazine Galleries, located at 62 Fifth Avenue in the lobby of the Forbes Building, are free and open to the public. Hours are 10:00 a.m. to 4:00 p.m., Tuesday through Saturday. Thursday is reserved for group tours. The galleries are closed on Sunday, Monday, and all legal holidays. For information call 212-206-5548.*

Foam Home

The suds capital of the world. The home of superior foam. The town that Busch built.

St. Louis is home to **Anheuser-Busch Cos.**, the nation's largest brewer.

During a time when it seems harder to find companies willing to give tours, Anheuser-Busch is an anomaly. The firm provides tours at 10 of its U.S. facilities, including the brewery I visited at its headquarters in this Missouri city on the banks of the Mississippi.

Since some 400,000 visitors each year tour the facilities, Anheuser-Busch has one of the more organized tour programs. As you enter the Anheuser-Busch complex, which is just outside the downtown area, you see signs for tour parking. The parking lot is adjacent to a large building that houses a gift shop filled with T-shirts, mugs, and other gift items. The area also includes exhibits providing a history of beer and the company. I was surprised to learn that as early as 3000 B.C. beer was known to the Egyptians, who believed that it had been invented by the gods. (I have friends who still believe this.) Beer came to St. Louis via the immigration of Germans, with their beer-making wisdom, to this city in the 1840s. The company started as a small brewery in 1852 and gradually grew into the brewing giant that it is today.

I found the information concerning Prohibition especially interesting. Imagine having your product declared illegal virtually overnight! Faced with the unwelcome prospect of making an illegal product, Anheuser-Busch diversified into other areas. This diversification is one reason that today the firm is the nation's second largest commercial baker.

After you have perused the gift shop, stein collection, and information exhibits, it's time to take the tour. The first stop is the Clydesdale stable. The first Clydesdale horse came to the company in 1933 when August Busch, Jr., gave one as a gift to his father to celebrate the repeal of Prohibition. All of us have probably seen Clydesdales on television. But up close, these are truly impressive animals. The horses stand approximately six feet tall and weigh 2300 pounds. The company's Clydesdales travel 90,000 miles annually to shows and parades throughout the country.

After viewing the stables, visitors take a motorized trolley bus to the packaging plant. The tour normally goes into the brew house, but on the day of my tour this area was closed due to construction. In the packaging plant, visitors are treated to a six-minute video explaining the brewing process. After the video, visitors are guided to a viewing area overlooking one of the packaging areas. Seeing thousands of bottles of beer speeding by—the company produces over 80 million barrels of beer per year—is a remarkable sight.

The tour then proceeds to the aging facility. Here you see the huge tanks, filled with beechwood chips and beer, used for the slow process of beechwood aging.

The tour ends in the hospitality area, where free samples of the company's beers are available (limit two). For teetotalers like myself, soft drinks also are available.

Particulars: *The tour of the plant—located at 13th and Lynch St., St. Louis, MO—takes one hour and 15 minutes. It's free and open to the public. Tours are available year-round, Monday–Saturday, 9:00 a.m. to 4:00 p.m. For further information call 314-577-2333. After taking the tour, make the short drive downtown and see the city's riverfront district near the Arch.*

Stop the Presses!

All manufacturing plants have special smells. Hershey smells of chocolate, Anheuser-Busch of hops and barley.

And newspapers smell like printer's ink.

Having worked at newspapers, I've always been drawn to the smell of ink, the racing of printing presses, the banter of newsrooms, and the general hustle and bustle that accompanies a business where a new product is produced every day without fail. That's one of the reasons I visited the **Tribune Company's** printing and shipping facility in Chicago.

The Tribune Company is a media and entertainment conglomerate. The company publishes the *Chicago Tribune* and a host of smaller newspapers. In addition the firm owns broadcasting operations, including *WGN* in Chicago and *WPIX* in New York City. The Tribune Company is also the owner of the Chicago Cubs baseball team.

My trip took me to the printing and shipping facility for the *Chicago Tribune*. The facility, dubbed the "Freedom Center," is next to the Chicago River, a couple of miles west of the famed "Magnificent Mile" shopping area in downtown Chicago. The building, completed in 1982, sits on a 21-acre site with 697,000 square feet of production space—the largest offset printing facility under one roof in the world.

The tour begins with a nine-minute film covering the history of the *Chicago Tribune*. You learn that the newspaper has been published continuously since 1847 and ranks today as one of the country's top five newspapers. Following the movie, you proceed to the newsprint storage area. This huge area is 70 feet tall and can store 26,000 rolls of paper. Two shipments of paper come each day by boxcar to the facility. Each roll weighs one ton and contains seven miles of paper. The company uses approximately 240,000 rolls of newsprint in an average year. The newspaper is generally composed of at least 55 percent recycled newsprint. The paper rolls are moved via a cranelike device with giant "suction cups" that drop down on the rolls and carry them to their proper areas.

From the newsprint area you move into full view of the printing presses. The Freedom Center houses 10 offset presses containing 9 printing units each. Each press, operating at maximum speed, runs at 25 miles per hour, and can print 70,000 newspapers per hour. The presses are approximately three stories high and are mounted on their own foundations so that vibrations won't disturb the main foundation of the building. The presses are fed by four 8000-gallon tanks of ink.

After viewing the presses, my tour moved to the plate room, where we saw how plates, which make the printed images for the presses, are "burned." If you're not familiar with offset printing technology, this department should be of special interest.

From there the tour leads to the packaging area. This area is 80,000 square feet and contains 2000 skids of preprinted sections, each skid weighing one ton. You see the Sunday paper, with its various sections, being put together—a process that takes a full 10 days.

At tour's end, visitors are given a Freedom Center button as well as a newspaper containing 20 famous front pages of the newspaper. Some of the events commemorated include the first man on the moon (FLY U.S. FLAG ON THE MOON) and the end of Prohibition (14-YEAR DRY ERA ENDS TODAY).

Particulars: *The Freedom Center is located at 777 W. Chicago Ave. The tour is free, but reservations are required. Approximately 30,000 visitors take the tour annually. For tour times and other information, call 312-222-2116.*

Sound in Motion

Most companies are built on a simple idea. For Paul Galvin, that idea was to build and install a better and cheaper car radio. Galvin coined the name **Motorola** for the radio since he thought this best exemplified his notion of sound ("ola," as in Victrola) in motion ("Motor," as in a motor for a car). These and other facts may be discovered at the Motorola Museum of Electronics, located in Schaumburg, IL, a suburb of Chicago (see Fig. 7-1).

The Motorola Museum is a relatively new freebie, opened in September

Figure 7.1

1991. A tour through the museum is really a walk through the history of communications and electronics.

You start your tour with an eight-minute video on the company shown in the museum's auditorium. In the museum, you'll see a bunch of "firsts": the first radios built for the auto and home, the first push-button radio, the first portable radio, the first two-way radio system, the first walkie-talkies, one of the first televisions, the first television remote control (1956), the first color television (it carried a $1000 price tag), the first pagers, and the first cellular phones. You'll see how semiconductors are made and used. And you'll experience a new vehicle highway system, currently being tested, that can guide a car to any designation using an on-board computer.

Particulars: *The Motorola Museum of Electronics is located at 1297 East Algonquin Road, Schaumburg, IL. The museum is free and open to the public by appointment, its hours being 9:00 a.m. to 4:30 p.m., Monday–Friday, To preregister, call 708-576-8620. Make sure that you treat yourself after the museum to a stop at the Lord & Taylor Clearance Center, located about 10 minutes away in the Town & Country mall in Arlington Heights, IL. Lord & Taylor, which is owned by May Department Stores (May offers a dividend reinvestment plan and is listed in the perk directory), specializes in upscale men's and women's clothing. The Clearance Center has a good selection of quality men's and women's clothing at drastically reduced* *prices. I shop there frequently and am rarely disappointed. Call 708-259-4211 for hours and travel directions.*

Other Corporate Tours, Museums, and Exhibits

Here are additional companies offering tours, exhibits, and museums for the public:

- **Ben & Jerry's Homemade**—Rt. 100, Waterbury, VT. Come see how *Cherry Garcia* and *Chocolate Chip Cookie Dough* are made at what is Vermont's biggest tourist attraction (250,000 visitors in 1992). Tours are offered seven days a week from 9:00 a.m. to 5:00 p.m. Call for extended summer hours. The cost is $1 for adults—half of the admission fee is donated to charity—and children under 12 are free. The tour starts with a 12-minute slide and video show and ends with free samples taken right off the production line. For further information about the tour, which lasts about a half hour, call 802-244-5641. After visiting the plant, take a trip to see how apple cider and chocolate are made, New England-style, at Cold Hollow Cider Mill and Vermont Chocolate Factory, both located a short distance away.

- **Lincoln National's** Lincoln Museum—1300 S. Clinton, Fort Wayne, IN. The headquarters of this insurance firm is home to the world's largest private collection of memorabilia devoted to Abraham Lincoln. The museum houses 60 exhibits as well as a library of 20,000 volumes on Lincoln. Approximately 19,000 guests visited the museum in 1992. The museum is free to the public and open Monday–Friday, 9:00 a.m. to 5:00 p.m.; Saturday 10:00 a.m. to 5:00 p.m.; and Sunday 1:00 p.m. to 5:00 p.m. Groups over 10 must make reservations. For further information call 219-455-3864.

- **World of Coca-Cola**—55 Martin Luther King Jr. Drive, Atlanta, GA. Started in 1990, this exhibit is home to over 1000 Coke-related artifacts. Those of you with a nostalgic bent will revel in an old-fashioned soda fountain set up in its own room. A special treat is the taste-testing of 36 flavors of beverages sold by Coca-Cola around the globe. Movies explaining the history of Coca-Cola are interspersed with world events within the same time frame. You may tour the facilities at your own pace.

    The exhibit costs $2.50 for adults 55 or younger; $2 for those over 55; $1.50 for children 6 to 12 years old; and is free for children under 6. The exhibit is open Monday–Saturday 10:00 a.m. to 8:30 p.m.;

Sunday 12:00 p.m. to 5:00 p.m. For further information call 404-676-5151. Other nearby attractions are the Underground Atlanta shopping area and Fulton County Stadium, home of the Falcons and Braves.

- **Boise Cascade**—100 Second St., International Falls, MN. The tour of this paper giant includes a look at one of the world's largest machines (it produces fine white paper) as well as a bleach plant with a capacity of 900 tons per day. The tour lasts about 1 hour and 15 minutes, and guests receive as souvenirs a full-color guidebook describing the operation as well as a ream of wrapping paper. No cameras and no children under 10 years old are allowed. Tours are offered three times daily at 8:30 a.m., 11:00 a.m., and 1:30 p.m.—Monday–Friday from June 1 through August 31. For further information call 218-285-5011.

- **McDonald's** Museum—400 Lee St., Des Plaines, IL. Ray Kroc's first franchised fast-food outlet serves as the home to the museum. The restaurant is preserved just as it was in 1955, vintage cars and all. Visitors see a short video about the company, as well as other memorabilia. The museum, which is free to the public, is open from April through October. Call 708-297-5022 for daily hours.

- **Boeing**—3003 West Casino Rd., Everett, WA. Boeing's Everett plant ranges over the equivalent of 57 football fields. The plant has to be that big since this is where the firm puts together some of its giant 747 planes. The 1½- to 2-hour tour takes you along catwalks overseeing the assembly area. Tours are given daily, 9:00 a.m. and 1:00 p.m., Monday–Friday. For reservations for groups of 10 or more, call 206-266-9974. There's a lot of walking and steep climbing. No cameras are allowed. The tour is free and open to adults and children over 10. For further information call 206-342-4801.

- **Corning** Glass Center—located on Centerway, Corning, NY. The Corning Glass Center is really several tours in one. The Center houses the Steuben factory, where visitors see artists creating crystal works of art. The Center also includes the Hall of Science and Industry, which has on display one of the largest pieces of glass ever poured. The museum has a variety of hands-on exhibits demonstrating various properties of glass. A glass museum is also part of the Center. The museum houses Tiffany glass created in 1905, a piece of carved glass from the Ch'ien Lung dynasty in the 18th century, and a perfume bottle made 2000 years ago, as well as a glass harmonica made by Benjamin Franklin. The Center also includes a variety of shops selling glass items and Corning cookware and dishes. Admission is $6 for adults, $5 for seniors, $4 for children 6 to 17, and children under 6 free. The maximum charge per family is $14. The Center is open seven days a week, 9:00 a.m. to 5:00 p.m.; in July and August, it is open until 8:00 p.m. Call 607-974-2000. The Center is located in the Finger Lakes region of New York, which is home to various vineyards. Also the Baseball Hall of Fame in Cooperstown, NY, is a 2½-hour drive.

- **Wal-Mart**—105 North Main St., Bentonville, AR. Started in May 1990 to accommodate the many tourists who came to this small town to see the birthplace of a retailing legend, The Wal-Mart Visitors Center is housed in the first store to share Sam Walton's name. The center includes a reproduction of Walton's first office, as well as various memorabilia. The center is open daily 9:00 a.m. to 5:00 p.m. except on Sunday, and admission is free. Call 501-273-1329 for further information.

- **New York Stock Exchange, Chicago Board Options Exchange, Chicago Mercantile Exchange.** Have you ever been curious to see how your stock, options, and futures trades are conducted? After seeing the mayhem in the pits, you may wonder how you ever had your order filled correctly. Tours are provided by the major financial exchanges. For information on the NYSE, 20 Broadway, NY, call 212-656-5167; for the CBOE, 400 South LaSalle and Van Buren, Chicago, IL, 312-786-7492; and for the CME, 30 South Wacker, Chicago, IL, 312-930-1000.

But Is It Art?

Corporate America is one of the largest holders of art, sculptures, antiques, and other artifacts in the country. And the diversity of the holdings is especially interesting.

   CIGNA, the Philadelphia insurance company, has a museum with some 9000 pieces on display, including the nation's largest collection of antique fire-fighting equipment.

   The Campbell Museum, housed in the headquarters of **Campbell Soup** in Camden, NJ, is a museum about—what else?—soup bowls. The majority of soup tureens on display were made in western Europe in the 18th century. "No other part of the dinner service has lent itself to the unusual and bizarre in form and design as have tureens," according to the company's pamphlet. Some of the museum's pieces include tureens shaped like boars' and cows' heads.

(Continued)

Wells Fargo, the West Coast banking giant, has a number of museums displaying western memorabilia, including the legendary Wells Fargo stage wagons. Visitors can take a simulated ride in one.

Some of the museums take on a local flavor. **Hartford Steam Boiler Inspection & Insurance** in Hartford, CT, has collections of early 19th- and 20th-century Connecticut antiques, paintings, and furniture. **National Bancorp of Alaska** has a collection of over 8000 artifacts, sculptures, and paintings emphasizing history of the area and native Alaskan arts.

A good resource for information on corporate art holdings is the *International Directory of Corporate Art Collections,* published by International Art Alliance and *ARTnews* magazine. The book, which sells for $109.95, can be obtained by calling 212-398-1690.

Occasionally, a corporation's (or more likely its chairman's) passion for art can get the firm in hot water with shareholders. Such was the case with **Occidental Petroleum** and its longtime chairman, Armand Hammer.

Occidental constructed the Armand Hammer Museum of Art and Cultural Center, which opened in 1990, next door to its headquarters. What angered OXY shareholders was that over $90 million of corporate funds went into the museum's construction and endowment fund. These outlays became the subject of shareholder suits claiming that the corporation should not be funding what was, in effect, a private project. The lawsuits were settled shortly before Hammer's death at the end of 1990.

Conclusion

This chapter has provided a sampling of the interesting travel freebies available from corporate America. To find out if a company of interest offers a tour, contact the firm's public relations office.

8
Socially Responsible Investing

The Feel-Good Perk for Investors

As this book has shown, investor perks come in all shapes and sizes: shareholder discounts on corporate products and services, gifts and meals at the annual meeting, free research material from your broker, and commission-free investing via dividend reinvestment plans.

A less obvious, but no less significant, perk for some investors is the satisfaction derived from investing in companies that share their beliefs and ideologies concerning the environment, affirmative action, education, and family matters. This form of investing falls under the acronym of SRI—Socially Responsible Investing.

What Is SRI?

Socially responsible investing is investing in companies that meet certain criteria based on a variety of social screens. Early socially responsible investors, such as churches and other religious organizations, focused primarily on avoiding investments in "sin" companies— tobacco, gambling, and alcohol firms.

Today, socially responsible investors examine a broader range of issues:

- Does the company pollute the environment?
- Does the firm do business in South Africa or Northern Ireland?
- Does the company make weapons or do business with the military?
- Is the firm involved in nuclear power?
- What is the company's employment record concerning women and minorities?
- What is the firm's stance on gay rights and abortion?
- Does the company test its products on animals?
- What does the firm give back to the community?
- Is on-site child care and elder care available for employees?

SRI has grown in popularity over the last decade. By the end of this century, it's estimated that well over $1 trillion will be invested in a socially responsible manner. One reason given for the growth in SRI is that the "flower children" of the '60s, who are now at stages in their careers where they are accumulating wealth, are investing their money in what they feel is a socially responsible manner. In effect, they are replacing the peace sign with the dollar sign in order to effect change in society.

Don't Tell *Me* What's Socially Responsible Behavior

Not everyone is a believer in SRI. Wall Street traditionalists believe that P-E ratios, earnings, and balance sheets—not whether the company offers baby-sitting services—are the important criteria when evaluating a company. When you hamstring the investment process with qualitative factors that eliminate a big universe of stocks from consideration, you destine your portfolio to mediocre performance, or so some on Wall Street feel. Better to invest in a tobacco firm or defense contractor that triples in price, and use your profits to change the world, than to buy a do-gooder firm that loses money for you.

Another problem that many investors have with socially responsible investing, and that really makes it a greased pig of an issue, is: Who's to decide what is "socially responsible" behavior? Your notion of socially responsible behavior may not be mine.

Adding to the slipperiness of SRI are the many instances when the same company fares both well and badly based on SRI criteria. For example, Kraft/General Foods donates food each year to food banks and does charity work aimed at eliminating child hunger. But Kraft/General Foods' owner is cigarette maker **Philip Morris Cos.** Another example is **Hershey Foods,** which has an outstanding record of charitable work and community involvement but also supplied candy bars for soldiers in Desert Storm. And what about **WMX Technologies,** whose business it is to clean up the earth—admirable under SRI criteria. But what dims WMX Technologies' shine for those who look at socially responsible behavior are the firm's run-ins with environmental regulators.

As one last example, some SRI followers avoid investments in treasury securities since this is money that's used by the nation's military and intelligence organizations. But isn't this also money that funds "Head Start" and entitlement programs?

Good for Business

SRI backers give plenty of reasons for investing with your heart. One is that acting in a socially responsible manner makes good business sense. Socially responsible companies, so say SRI boosters, generally have lower employee turnover, fewer problems with regulators, higher employee morale, and greater productivity.

Another way companies benefit from backing specific social causes is through the positive public relations it often generates. **Ben & Jerry's Homemade** ice cream provides an excellent example of using a social agenda as a PR tool.

Ben & Jerry's "Caring Capitalism"

No firm gets more mileage out of advancing social causes than **Ben & Jerry's Homemade,** the maker of such super-premium ice cream flavors as *Rainforest Crunch, Blueberry Cheesecake, Cherry Garcia,* and *Chocolate Chip Cookie Dough.* The firm donates 7½ percent of pretax profits to charity through the Ben & Jerry's Foundation. Causes supported are divided into three groups: the environment, children, and disabled groups. The firm also has an Employee Community Fund, which uses revenue obtained from the $1 fee charged to tour the company's headquarters in Waterbury, VT.

(Continued)

What sets the firm apart from other philanthropic efforts is how the company exploits this "caring capitalism," a term credited to Ben Cohen and Jerry Greenfield, the company's founders. The firm ties certain social programs closely to various products. For instance, *Peace Pops*—chocolate-covered ice cream on a stick—promote world peace. The firm introduced the *Harlem Blues Berries* flavor to mark the opening of a Harlem franchise owned partly by a local nonprofit program aiding the homeless.

The firm's social agenda also includes its relationship with employees. The company limits the pay for top executives to no more than seven times the pay of the lowest-compensated worker with at least one year at the company.

How has Wall Street reacted to Ben & Jerry's heightened social awareness? The stock has soared since trading at a split-adjusted price of under $5 in 1987. Of course you could make the argument that what whets Wall Street's appetite for the ice cream maker isn't so much the company's socially responsible behavior as its fantastic earnings growth in recent years.

Pick Your Perk

My purpose for including this chapter on SRI isn't to defend or refute socially responsible investing. What I want to demonstrate is that if you have a particular cause or social issue about which you feel strongly, and if you want to link this cause to your investment program, there's probably a company that meets your criteria. Want to invest in a company that gives generously to children's causes? There are literally hundreds from which to choose. Looking for a firm that deals only with union shops? No problem. Have a special interest in preserving national parks or the rain forest? There are companies that share your views.

Be Patrick Ewing's Boss

Although this chapter discusses socially responsible investing, the concept of "affinity" investing can assume a variety of forms. For instance, perhaps you've always dreamed about owning a professional sports team. Fortunately, a "poor man's" way exists for individual investors to own a piece of certain professional baseball, basketball, and hockey teams.

For example, if you hold shares in **Paramount Communications** you own a piece, albeit a very small one, of Patrick Ewing and the New York Knicks basketball team, as well as the New York Rangers hockey team.

Paramount Communications is not the only publicly traded firm that owns a professional sports team. The purest play among publicly traded firms is the **Boston Celtics Limited Partnership,** whose sole asset is the Boston Celtics basketball team. Other publicly traded firms with interests in professional sports include **Anheuser-Busch Cos.** (St. Louis Cardinals), **Ackerly Communications** (Seattle Supersonics), **Tribune Company** (Chicago Cubs), **Southwestern Bell** (part owner of the San Antonio Spurs), **Coors, Adolph** (Colorado Rockies), and **Turner Broadcasting** (Atlanta Hawks and Atlanta Braves).

An unusual member of this fraternity is **Disney, Walt,** which is the proud owner of the Anaheim Mighty Ducks, a new NHL hockey franchise. The Mighty Ducks play their home games at The Pond in Anaheim. Shareholders who don't make it to The Pond can get all the latest news about their Mighty Ducks by calling the Mighty Ducks' "hotline": 800-HOCKEY-4.

The best way to maximize the feel-good perk of investing in companies, whether it be for socially responsible reasons or otherwise, is for you to decide what is important to you and then focus on those companies that share your interests. Perhaps you feel a strong national defense is important to maintaining peace—an opinion that's at odds with most SRI purists—and you also feel strongly about corporate America taking a more active involvement in education in the country. I'm sure there are companies that are involved in defense work but also give time and money to further educational causes.

The other approach to take is to find a company and then determine if the firm's social agenda, or lack of one, disqualifies it from consideration.

How can you find out about a firm's community involvement, philanthropic activities, or employment programs? Call the company's public relations department. Also, corporate annual reports contain information on social and community achievements.

Other sources of information on socially responsible firms are directories that cover corporate giving. A good one to check is the *Taft Corporate Giving Directory.* Ask for it at your library.

Books on the subject include *The Social Investment Almanac* (Henry Holt), by Peter Kinder, Steven Lydenberg, and Amy Domini (this group is responsible for the Domini 400 Social Index, a stock index comprised of socially responsible companies); *Investing from the Heart* (Crown), by Jack Brill and Alan Reder; *Investing with Your Conscience* (Wiley), by John Harrington; and *Companies with a Conscience* (Carol), by Mary Scott and Howard Rothman.

The Clean Yield

An excellent newsletter covering socially responsible investing is *The Clean Yield* (802-533-7178). Below are companies with an "all-around" top *Clean Yield* social rating based on charitable giving, community relations, employee relations, environmental responsibility, affirmative action, world citizenship, and product quality:

- Affiliated Publications, Inc.
- Apple Computer, Inc.
- Ben & Jerry's Homemade, Inc.
- Church & Dwight Co., Inc.
- Edwards, A.G., Inc.
- Federal Express Corp.
- Federal National Mortgage Association
- Fuller, H.B., Co.
- Giant Food, Inc.
- Hechinger Co.
- Heinz, H.J., Co.
- Hershey Foods Corp.
- Lillian Vernon Corp.
- Liz Claiborne, Inc.
- Maytag Corp.
- McCormick & Co., Inc.
- Miller, Herman, Inc.
- Pitney Bowes, Inc.
- Progressive Corp.
- Southwest Airlines Co.
- Spec's Music, Inc.
- Stride Rite Corp.

Strategic Giving

Community and charitable groups look to corporate America to support their causes. However, as many nonprofit groups are discovering, the corporate philanthropic well, while not dry, is not as full as it once was. Major cutbacks at some of the country's biggest companies have had a big impact on corporate giving. **General Motors,** for example, gave $86 million in 1991, but that amount declined in 1992. Overall, corporate giving has been relatively flat, at about $6 billion since 1990.

Tight purse strings have caused firms to change their strategy concerning philanthropy. Previously, many companies used a shotgun approach, spraying small amounts of money to many organizations. A tighter belt has caused firms to focus their giving on a few key areas. This "strategic giving" has led to what has been called "enlightened self-interest," that is, the ability of companies to benefit from their charitable contributions beyond just the sheer satisfaction of knowing they've done a good deed. Companies now examine more closely what good PR can be had from being linked to a particular social cause. Certainly Ben & Jerry's knows that *Rainforest Crunch,* by any other name, probably wouldn't sell as much ice cream.

Companies increasingly look at how they may be able to benefit directly as a by-product of giving to a charitable, educational, or community organization. For example, a company may be more willing to provide funds for a job training program for inner-city youths if it believes that these better-equipped youths could someday be its employees. Why do you think corporate America is taking a leadership position in improving the nation's educational system? Because it needs a better "product" from schools if corporations are to compete successfully in the global markets of tomorrow.

I realize this sounds cynical. But I don't see any inherent evil in a company benefiting from doing good. In fact, such "win-win" relationships between charitable and social organizations and companies make charitable "investments" more likely to occur. As a result, charitable and community groups are making their programs more attractive for corporate investment.

The remainder of this chapter first covers specific companies whose charitable programs forward various social programs, then looks at mutual funds that invest in socially responsible firms. At the end of the chapter I'll show you how to establish your own private charitable foundation—all it takes is a phone call and $10,000—with the help of Fidelity Investments.

Stocks for All Causes

SRI investing covers a multitude of areas, including:

- Environment
- South Africa
- Weapons
- Fair employment/Family rights
- Nuclear power
- Tobacco
- Labor relations
- Alcohol
- Animal testing
- Gambling
- Northern Ireland
- Gay rights
- Abortion/Contraception

Of course many more topics fall under the heading of socially responsible investing, such as children and education. Let's look at some of these issues and see which companies stand out for their social programs.

The Environment

Companies that clean up the environment offer attractive investments for socially responsible investors. There are many ways to play the "green" market. You could invest in companies that produce environmental instruments used to measure and monitor water and air quality. **Hewlett-Packard** and **Thermo Instrument Systems** are two prominent players in this market. You could invest in a company that specializes in recycling, such as **Wellman.** You could invest in **Air Products & Chemicals,** which manufactures scrubbers used on utility smokestacks to lower emissions. You could invest in companies that help improve water quality, such as **Betz Laboratories** and **Nalco Chemical.** Of course, big pollution-control firms such as **Browning-Ferris Industries** and **WMX Technolgies** have appeal, although neither company has a spotless track record with regulators.

Another approach to "green" investing is to focus on companies with stellar environmental records. For example, **Southwest Water** is a perennial winner of the Plant of the Year Award from the California Water Pollution Control Association. Given California's progressive approach toward the environment, this award is especially significant. Another example is **AT&T.** When the U.S. Environmental Protection Agency asked manufacturers to reduce toxic emissions voluntarily, AT&T claims it was the first company to meet both 1992 and 1995 goals, cutting by two-thirds its emissions of 17 chemicals. (The company's annual report is also printed on recycled paper.)

Companies that were not always looked upon favorably by environmentalists but have been cleaning up their act represent potential investments. **McDonald's** was not favored by "green" investors when it used plastic foam containers for its sandwiches. McDonald's subsequently switched to paper wrappers.

One final way to invest responsibly in the green market is to focus on companies that have made the environment and related issues favorite charitable programs. For example:

- **WD-40,** the maker of the all-purpose lubricant, sponsors a "Preserve Our Parks" program.
- **Lillian Vernon,** the direct-mail marketer of specialty products, doesn't sell furs or ivory products.
- **TECO Energy,** the holding company for Tampa Electric utility, has taken a special interest in preserving the manatee, a large, plant-eating mammal found in tropical waters.

Fair Employment/Family Rights

This issue has become popular for SRI investors, especially with the rise of women in the work force. Fair employment covers a multitude of areas, from corporate hiring practices and employee compensation to pro-family policies such as on-site child- and elder-care facilities.

AT&T has been active in establishing family programs. For example, AT&T funds a program that provides for volunteers to visit employees' elderly family members. The firm also provides company referral services for AT&T-funded child-care centers.

St. Paul Companies operates an electronic-mail system that allows its child-care center staff to send messages about the children to their parents during the day.

Stride Rite, the shoe company, has been a leader in corporate child-care, elder-care, and family-leave policies. The firm is also strong in the philanthropic arena, annually giving 5 percent of pretax profits to charity.

Related to the fair employment issue are company hiring and advancement practices, especially for women and minorities. One leader in this area is **Spec's Music,** which operates a chain of specialty stores selling prerecorded music and videos. At the time of this writing, women make up more than half of the board of directors.

Another way to view the issue of fair employment and labor relations is by focusing on companies sensitive to organized labor. One interesting company in this regard is **American Income Holding.** The firm, which is union-organized, sells life and term insurance primarily to union and credit union members. Women comprise roughly two-thirds of middle and top management. An interesting wrinkle to its insurance policies is that if a union employee with a policy is on strike, American Income Holding will waive policy premium payments for up to a year, and up to three months if the individual has been laid off.

Education/Children's Causes

Improving the educational system and the quality of a child's life in this country have become major priorities of corporate America. Many companies have pet educational and children's programs they support with time and money:

- In 1991, **AT&T** donated computer equipment valued at $22 million to colleges and universities. The AT&T Foundation's "AT&T Teachers of Tomorrow" program helps prepare teachers for urban schools. In 1991, the foundation awarded nearly $4 million to enhance the libraries at 41 member colleges of the United Negro College Fund.

- The **Sears-Roebuck Foundation** has made education a cornerstone program. The company provided more than $1 million to 700 private colleges and universities through its Teaching Excellence and Campus Leadership Awards program, and through grants to the United Negro College Fund and the Hispanic Association of Colleges and Universities.

- **John Nuveen,** the Chicago-based manager of tax-exempt funds, pays college tuition for all children of full-time employees with more than five years' service (employees have to pay tax on the benefit).

- **Blockbuster Entertainment,** via its "KidPrint" program, provides free videotaping of children for emergency identification purposes. The company also provides free videos on important health and welfare issues.

- **American Express** sponsors "academies" in inner-city schools to teach students about finance, travel, and tourism. Students in these academies are guaranteed jobs upon graduation.

- **Apple Computer** has donated computers to low-income and disabled students.

- **BellSouth** has awarded grants of nearly $18 million over the last five years to various educational projects.

- In 1992, **Bankers Trust,** the New York bank, gave a share of its stock to each of about 800 African-American high school students participating in "Act-So," an NAACP-sponsored academic competition.

- **Cooper Industries** provides educational grants to vocational-educational programs in communities where the company has plants.

- **Exxon** donates millions of dollars to further math education among children.

- **Mattel** has taken a special interest in helping learning-disabled children to read.

- **PepsiCo** contributes to programs aimed at dropout prevention in high schools in Dallas and Detroit.

- **Perkin-Elmer,** an electronics instrument manufacturer, encourages adults in communities around its Norwalk, CT, headquarters to become foster parents.

- **Time Warner** employees tutor individuals using company magazines, such as *Time, Money, Fortune,* and *Sports Illustrated.*

- **Xerox** sponsors programs in which employees work with educators in Texas, Virginia, and New York to help improve the quality of teaching and student management in schools.

- **McDonald's** has joined with the American Library Association in the ALA's 1993 national reading program. The ALA sent all 16,000 U.S. public libraries a kit, compliments of McDonald's, with a librarian's guide and materials for 100 children including posters, bookmarks, certificates, stickers, and reading logs.

Community Relations/Charitable Donations

Corporations give back to the community in a variety of ways:

- **The Allstate Foundation** has donated to various community revitalization programs, including The National Center for Neighborhood Enterprise, a national organization that helps community leaders attack the problems of residents in low-income neighborhoods.

- **Stride Rite** has been active in a variety of inner-city programs.

- **American Federal Bank** in Greenville, SC, contributes nearly 3 per-

cent of pretax profits to community programs, including United
Way and March of Dimes as well as local programs.

- In 1991, **AT&T** gave $26 million to nonprofit organizations through
  payroll deductions and employee-matching gift programs.

As you can see, corporate America sponsors a wealth of charitable
and social programs. If you have a particular pet cause and want the
feel-good perk of investing with your conscience, you should be able
to find a corporate kindred spirit.

SRI Mutual Funds

Mutual fund investors may invest in socially responsible companies
via one of the many SRI mutual funds.

If you're a backer of environmental causes, "green" funds may interest
you. Some of the more prominent green funds include **Kemper
Environmental Services Fund** (800-621-1048), **Fidelity Select-
Environmental** (800-544-8888), **Oppenheimer Global Environmental**
(800-525-7048), and **John Hancock Freedom Environmental A** (800-225-
5291). Remember that when you focus investments in one particular
area, you limit diversification. Also keep in mind that environmental
stocks have had extended periods of rather volatile price performance.

If you desire a more diversified mutual fund that invests in firms that
pass several SRI screens, consider **Calvert Social Investment Managed
Growth** (800-368-2748), **Dreyfus Third Century** (800-782-6620), **New
Alternatives** (516-466-0808), **Parnassus** (800-999-3505), and **Pax World**
(800-767-1729).

When considering any mutual fund, it's always a good idea to check
the fund's record in *Morningstar,* a mutual fund rating service.
Morningstar is available in most libraries.

Wall Street Has a
Conscience?

Suppose you'd like to advance your social agenda not only through what
investment you buy, but also through how you buy that investment?
Muriel Siebert & Co. (800-872-0444), a brokerage firm headed by the
first woman member of the New York Stock Exchange, gives to charity
half of the gross commissions that investors pay for stocks or bonds from
certain new issues. The Siebert Entrepreneurial Philanthropic Plan gave
away $300,000 in 1991 and $1 million in 1992.

If you like the sound of this program, don't be afraid to try to strike a similar deal with your broker.

Start Your Own Private Foundation

Historically, only the very wealthy have established private foundations. However, **Fidelity Investments** is now bringing the notion of the private foundation to the masses.

The **Fidelity Charitable Gift Fund** provides an interesting way to start your own private foundation. The Charitable Gift Fund works like a no-load mutual fund. Individuals deposit money into the Charitable Gift Fund (minimum initial investment $10,000, $2500 thereafter), with the funds invested in three investment pools—growth, equity income, and interest income—managed by Fidelity. The investor chooses how the money is divided among the pools.

Because the fund is a charity in the eyes of the IRS, the money that's invested grows tax-free. Investors have the ability to earmark their investments for the charities of their choice, with Fidelity handling the distribution and paperwork. Investors receive a tax deduction in the year in which the contribution to the fund is made. There's no fee to establish the account. The only catch is that money invested in the fund cannot be taken back by the investor. For further information contact Fidelity at 800-682-4438.

9
Financial Perks Off Wall Street

Corporate America is a bountiful source for many investor perks and freebies. However, for the knowledgeable and resourceful individual, several sources of financial perks and freebies exist off Wall Street.

Bank Freebies

The banking industry is in hot pursuit of your money. It used to be that the local bank was the only game in town, but times have changed. With the development of brokerage cash management accounts—which offer many banklike services—individuals no longer need a checking or savings account at the local bank. Banks know this and have been scrambling for ways to keep your money in their vaults. This competition has spawned a number of bank perks and freebies, some well publicized by the banks, others provided on a request-only basis. These perks include:

- *Special services for senior citizens.* My bank, Mercantile National Bank of Indiana, has a program for people 50 and over called "Pathfinders Club." The program provides such services as free checking with a minimum daily balance of $100 or more, no fees on ATM transactions, cashier's checks, money orders, traveler's checks, and personalized checks. If your bank doesn't offer special services, talk to the manager about implementing a similar program. If he or she balks, find a new bank.

- *Fee waivers/lower rates on loans.* Banks are sensitive about losing customers and are making exceptions when it comes to certain fees. A bank may give you a break on fees if you have direct deposit for your paychecks or dividends. Checking fees may be waived if you're willing to forgo receiving canceled checks. Banks may waive monthly fees if you maintain a minimum balance in the account, and you may be able to negotiate the minimum. Banks may waive fees on a second account established for a child or spouse. Some banks will waive the fees on credit cards and traveler's checks to good customers.

  If you're a good customer—for instance, you're a business owner and your company does its banking where you also have personal bank accounts—don't settle for the same rate on a personal loan that other customers are paying. Negotiate for a more favorable rate. Remember: Your bank isn't likely to tell you about these fee waivers. In fact, your bank may not tell you much of anything about its services, especially the ones that save you money. I was doing business at my bank for years before I realized the bank offered a NOW account that would pay interest on my checking account. Don't expect the bank to tell you what's in your best interest when it comes to your money. Ask about their services. If you don't like what you hear, go elsewhere.

- *ATM perks.* If you use the Automated Teller Machine often, it pays to shop for a bank that doesn't charge you a fee to use other banks' ATM machines. Fees on ATM usage can add up quickly, so make sure you know the costs. Also, pay attention to the perks your bank dispenses at its ATM. **CoreStates Financial** in Pennsylvania dispenses ATM receipts printed with coupons for the Philadelphia Zoo.

- *Checks.* Two direct mailers of checks are **Current** (800-426-0822) and **Checks in the Mail** (800-733-4443). These two outfits print checks at rates that are usually well below what you'd pay by going through your bank.

- *Perks for new accounts.* The increased competition in the banking field has brought a new word to the vocabulary of bank executives: *marketing.* When the local bank was a virtual monopoly, a bank's idea of marketing was a toaster. However, with bankers' turf being invaded not only by the likes of Merrill Lynch and Charles Schwab but also GE and GM with their credit cards, marketing has become key to a bank's survival. Consequently, banks are responding with innovative marketing strategies in order to win new accounts.

  Wachovia Bank has offered a $50 credit to new credit card customers at its branches in North Carolina. **LaSalle Talman Bank** in Chicago has offered a "Good Neighbor" certificate of deposit, which provides the holder with a market rate of return, with Talman making a contribution to the holder's favorite charity based on the value of the CD. **NationsBank** offers holders of its NationsBank "Start Card" rebates ranging from 1 to 6 percent on purchases. The rebate is set aside in an annuity for retirement—a "spend-your-way-to-a-retirement-nest-egg" approach.

With competition heating up in the banking industry, your leverage has increased with your banker. Don't be afraid to use it.

Credit Card Perks

There are no free lunches in the credit card field if you carry a balance from month to month. Oh sure, there are those credit cards that will pay you a modest rebate on goods purchased above a certain level. But that's small consolation when you're being charged interest of 15 percent or more. The best credit card perk of all is the saved interest that comes by not carrying a monthly balance.

Nevertheless, for those of you who insist on using credit cards as, well, a source of credit, some credit cards are better than others. The previously mentioned **Wachovia Bank** (800-241-7990) offers a very competitive rate on its charge cards. Also, **Signet Banking** (800-952-3388) offers very low rates that are adjustable each year. The bottom line to remember is that, if you tend to carry a monthly balance, focus on the credit card with the lowest possible interest rate.

If you don't carry a balance and are not concerned about the monthly interest rate, then the perks available to you open up substantially. It's foolish these days to pay an annual fee on a credit card. Many cards charge no annual fees. GM's *MasterCard* is one.

And just because your current card carries an annual fee, that doesn't mean you can't dodge it with some negotiation. I once threatened to cancel a *MasterCard,* and the *MasterCard* people agreed to waive the annual fee if I kept the card. Try this with your current card company if it still charges you an annual fee.

Given the competition among credit card issuers, look for more bells and whistles to accompany credit cards. GE's *Rewards MasterCard* (800-GE-REWARD), for example, gives a $10 GE Rewards Check for every $500 purchase. These checks may be used to purchase goods at any participating merchant or service company within 75 days after issuance. The card also entitles users to rebates on GE appliances. GM's card provides rebates that can be used toward the purchase of GM cars and trucks.

The point is that the credit card you may have been using for all of these years may not be the one that now provides you with the best rate, perks, and service. Find out what's available. And remember: No perk is worth paying 15 percent interest charges. Before you search for special perks and discounts, pay off your balance.

"Low-Load" Insurance

"Low-load" insurance products are still relatively new. However, given that insurance products can carry stiff commissions, low-load insurance potentially can provide big savings for individuals.

Of course, low-load products may not be for everyone. However, if you feel that the service you're receiving isn't worth the hefty premiums you're paying, take a look at what some low-load insurers are offering. Three sellers of no-load and low-load policies are **USAA** (800-531-8000), **John Alden Financial** (305-470-3767), and **Ameritas** (800-552-3553).

Unclaimed $$$

Believe it or not, billions of dollars in assets are unclaimed in this country. The abandoned assets result from dormant checking and savings accounts, uncashed money orders and dividend checks, unclaimed insurance benefits, forgotten safekeeping depository contents, and unclaimed security deposits. The funds are often left by individuals who die and fail to account for the funds in their wills.

Under state laws, holders of unclaimed property such as banks, insurance companies, mutual funds, and brokerage firms have to try to find the rightful owners. If they can't, usually within a five-year period, the funds are turned over to the states' abandoned-property divisions. It is up to these divisions to try to track down the rightful owners. The departments do this by posting notices in papers and by public-service announcements.

Various procedures and forms need to be followed and filed in order to claim assets. The turnaround time for claiming an asset may vary. However, states attempt to expedite claims in a timely manner when sufficient ownership documentation is provided. According to the National Association of Unclaimed Property Administrators (NAUPA), some of the most common reasons for delays in claim processing are:

- Claim form is not signed by claimant, or signature is not notarized.
- No identification is presented by claimant.
- No supporting proof of ownership is filed with the claim.
- There is insufficient information available to verify property ownership.

If you believe you may be entitled to assets either you or a relative has left unclaimed, contact the state agency responsible for its administration (see Fig. 9-1). Include your name, social security number, social security number of person whose property you're claiming, and all addresses where you or the individual have lived in the state.

Figure 9.1

ALABAMA	CONNECTICUT
Unclaimed Property Division	**Office of the Treasurer**
PO Box 327580	**Unclaimed Property Division**
Montgomery, AL 36132-7580	**55 Elm St.**
	Hartford, CT 06106
ALASKA	DELAWARE
Department of Revenue	**Unclaimed Property Division**
Unclaimed Property	**PO Box 8931**
111 W. 8th, Rm. 106	**Wilmington, DE 19899**
Juneau, AK 99801	
	DISTRICT OF COLUMBIA
ARIZONA	**Unclaimed Property Division**
Department of Revenue	**300 Indiana NW, Rm. 5008**
Unclaimed Property	**Washington, DC 20001**
1600 W. Monroe	
Phoenix, AZ 85007	FLORIDA
	Abandoned Property Section
	State Capitol
ARKANSAS	**Tallahassee, FL 32399-0350**
Auditor of State	
Unclaimed Property Division	GEORGIA
230 State Capitol	**Unclaimed Property Section**
Little Rock, AR 72201	**270 Washington St., #405**
	Atlanta, GA 30334
CALIFORNIA	HAWAII
Unclaimed Property Division	**Unclaimed Property Section**
PO Box 942850	**PO Box 150**
Sacramento, CA 94250-5873	**Honolulu, HI 96810**
COLORADO	IDAHO
Unclaimed Property Division	**Unclaimed Property Division**
1560 Broadway, #630	**PO Box 36**
Denver, CO 80202	**Boise, ID 83722-2240**

Figure 9.1 (Continued)

ILLINOIS
Unclaimed Property Division
Dept. of Financial Institutions
500 Iles Park Pl.
Springfield, IL 62718

INDIANA
Unclaimed Property Division
219 State House
Indianapolis, IN 46204-2794

IOWA
Treasurer of State Unclaimed
  Property Division
Hoover Bldg.
Des Moines, IA 50319

KANSAS
Unclaimed Property Division
900 Jackson, #201
Topeka, KS 66612-1235

KENTUCKY
Abandoned Property Unit
Revenue Cabinet, Sta. 62
Frankfort, KY 40620

LOUISIANA
Unclaimed Property Section
PO Box 91010
Baton Rouge, LA 70821-9010

MAINE
Treasury Department
Abandoned Property Division
State Office Bldg., Sta. 39
Augusta, ME 04333

MARYLAND
Unclaimed Property Section
301 W. Preston St.
Baltimore, MD 21201-2385

MASSACHUSETTS
Abandoned Property Division
1 Ashburton Pl., 12th Fl.
Boston, MA 02108

MICHIGAN
Department of Treasury
Escheats Division
Lansing, MI 48922

MINNESOTA
Minnesota Commerce Dept.
Unclaimed Property Section
133 E. 7th St.
St. Paul, MN 55101

MISSISSIPPI
Unclaimed Property Division
PO Box 138
Jackson, MS 39205

MISSOURI
Unclaimed Property Section
PO Box 1272
Jefferson City, MO 65102

MONTANA
Dept. of Revenue
Abandoned Property Section
Mitchell Building
Helena, MT 59620

NEBRASKA
Unclaimed Property Division
PO Box 94788
Lincoln, NE 68509

(Continued)

Figure 9.1 (Continued)

NEVADA

Unclaimed Property Division
State Mail Room
Las Vegas, NV 89158

OHIO

Unclaimed Funds Division
77 South High St.
Columbus, OH 43266-0545

NEW HAMPSHIRE

Treasury Department
Abandoned Property Division
25 Capitol St., Rm. 121
Concord, NH 03301

OKLAHOMA

Oklahoma Tax Commission
Unclaimed Property Section
2501 Lincoln Blvd.
Oklahoma City, OK 73194-0010

NEW JERSEY

Department of Treasurer
Property Administration
CN 214
Trenton, NJ 08646

OREGON

Division of State Lands
Unclaimed Property Section
775 Summer St., NE
Salem, OR 97310-1337

NEW MEXICO

Unclaimed Property Unit
PO Box 630
Santa Fe, NM 87504

PENNSYLVANIA

Abandoned/Unclaimed Property
2850 Turnpike Industrial Drive
Middletown, PA 17057

NEW YORK

Office of Unclaimed Funds
9th Fl.,
Alfred E. Smith Bldg.
Albany, NY 12236

RHODE ISLAND

Unclaimed Property Division
PO Box 1435
Providence, RI 02901

NORTH CAROLINA

Escheat/Unclaimed Property
325 N. Salisbury St.
Raleigh, NC 27603-1388

SOUTH CAROLINA

South Carolina Tax Commission
Unclaimed Property Section
PO Box 125
Columbia, SC 29214

NORTH DAKOTA

State Land Department
Unclaimed Property Division
PO Box 5523
Bismarck, ND 58502-5523

SOUTH DAKOTA

Unclaimed Property Division
500 E. Capitol
Pierre, SD 57501

Figure 9.1 (Continued)

TENNESSEE

Unclaimed Property Division
11th Fl.
Andrew Jackson Bldg.
Nashville, TN 37243-0242

TEXAS

Texas Treasury Department
Unclaimed Property Division
Box 12019
Austin, TX 78711-2019

UTAH

State Treasurer's Office
Unclaimed Property Division
341 S. Main, 5th Floor
Salt Lake City, UT 84111

VERMONT

State Treasurer's Office
Abandoned Property Division
133 State Street
Montpelier, VT 05633-6200

VIRGINIA

Department of Treasury
Division of Unclaimed Property
PO Box 3-R
Richmond, VA 23207

WASHINGTON

Dept. of Revenue
Unclaimed Property Section
PO Box 448
Olympia, WA 98507

WEST VIRGINIA

State Treasurer's Office
Unclaimed Property Division
Capitol Complex
Charleston, WV 25305

WISCONSIN

State Treasurer's Office
Unclaimed Property Division
PO Box 2114
Madison, WI 53701

WYOMING

Wyoming State Treasurer
Escheat Section
State Capitol
Cheyenne, WY 82002

ONTARIO, CANADA

Office of Public Trustee
145 Queen Street West
Toronto, Ontario
M5H 2N8

That Old Stock Certificate May Be Worth Big Money

If you're rummaging around in your attic and come across stock certificates, don't throw them out with that old baseball glove and leisure suit.

Those stock certificates may be worth big bucks.

(Continued)

If you find old certificates, how do you know if they're worth anything? A good place to start is Standard & Poor's reference books at the library. It may be the case that the company is still publicly traded. If the firm is not listed, check the subsidiary section of the S&P books. It may be that the firm was acquired by another company. If you strike gold here, notify the parent company about the certificates.

If you can't find anything on your own, one source for information on obsolete securities is R.M. Smythe, 26 Broadway, New York, NY 10004 (212-943-1880). Smythe, for a $50 fee, will evaluate the certificate to determine if it has any value. Send a Xerox copy of the certificate along with your check to the company. You should hear back within a month.

And even if your certificates were issued by a now-defunct company, they still may have value as a collector's item. For example, Playboy's original Playmate certificate may be worth as much as $300 to collectors; an original certificate of Standard Oil Co., signed by John D. Rockefeller, perhaps $11,000 or more.

Tax Refund for European Travelers

If you've traveled overseas, you've no doubt come across the huge value-added tax (VAT) on goods and services in many European countries. These VATs can be as high as 25 percent. Most people complain, pay the tax, and forget about it. However, as a foreign citizen, you are entitled to a refund on this tax.

Procedures for requesting VAT refunds should be investigated at the time of purchase. In order to reclaim the tax, keep all receipts of your purchases. In many cases a VAT form is completed at the time of purchase. When you are leaving the country, present your VAT forms to customs officials, who should assist you in reclaiming the taxes. I've been told that the time to process claims varies between countries, so leave yourself plenty of time prior to your flight.

Free Credit Check

The credit-reporting industry has come under much scrutiny in recent years due to incorrect information and the renting of data to direct mailers. In order to repair their public image, credit verification services have made themselves more accessible to consumers. **TRW** has gone the extra step of making available a free copy of your credit report once a year. To obtain a free report, write TRW Consumer Assistance, P.O. Box 2350, Chatsworth, CA, 91313. Include your full name, middle initial, your spouse's full name, birth dates, social security numbers, current and previous addresses if you have moved in the last five years, and proof of your current address (a copy of your driver's license will do).

If you'd like a consolidated document with information from all the major credit services, a merged file is available through **Credco** (800-443-9342) for $24.

Social Security Check

So you want to know where all that money goes that you pay in FICA taxes? Individuals have the ability to check on their social security earnings by obtaining free information from the Social Security Administration.

To get the ball rolling, obtain a copy of the "Request for Earnings and Benefits Statement" from Social Security (800-772-1213). When you receive the statement, fill it out and return it to the agency. In about two months or less, you should receive a printout detailing such things as how much you've paid into the system and what you can expect to receive when you start drawing social security.

Make sure the report reflects your complete work history. Mistakes may have been made, so it's up to you to verify the information. If you find an error, notify your local Social Security office.

Free Financial Information and Economic Data

Want to be the first person on your block to get the latest unemployment statistics? Have an interest in knowing what the latest consumer price index is saying—before it hits the papers? Want to know what federal job opportunities are available? This information is available free or for a nominal charge via financial publications and databases available to the public.

One of these sources is the Labor Department's Electronic Bulletin Board. Information can be accessed via a phone number (202-219-4784) and downloaded to your computer via a modem. The bulletin board contains such information as consumer and producer prices, real earnings, employment and unemployment statistics, job safety and health regulations, job training and other department grants, and wage-hour, pension, and other enforcement actions. A nationwide listing of federal job opportunities is also available. For further information about the bulletin board, call 202-219-7343.

Another database filled with economic information is offered by the Department of Commerce's Electronic Bulletin Board. The bulletin board releases information put out by the Census Bureau, Federal Reserve Board, Bureau of Economic Analysis, and Bureau of Labor Statistics. The annual fee is $35, plus small "per-minute" charges to access the information. For further information call 202-482-1986.

Want more financial data? The Federal Reserve Banks of St. Louis (314-621-1824), Minneapolis (612-340-2489), and Dallas (214-922-5199) have databases that can be accessed at these phone numbers for the price of the phone connection.

If you don't own a computer, most of these bulletin boards will provide hard copies of the statistical information upon request.

Another source of free or nearly free financial information is the government's Consumer Information Center. The Center publishes a catalog four times a year that lists all of the brochures and pamphlets available. The catalog is free and may be obtained by writing Consumer Information Catalog, Pueblo, CO 81009.

Many nongovernment and private sector organizations offer free financial publications. Keep in mind that free material from a mutual fund organization or insurance firm will likely be a subtle or not-so-subtle sales pitch. The information may be biased toward a particular financial product or strategy.

Even so, information from these sources may be worth having. Many associations representing insurance agents, financial planners, mutual fund companies, and brokerage firms provide free financial information.

One association that provides a wealth of information is the American Association of Retired Persons. One AARP publication is **A Single Person's Guide to Retirement Planning.** For information about this and other AARP guides—many of which are available free of charge—write AARP Fulfillment; 601 E Street, NW; Washington, DC 20049.

Further Advice on How to Save a Buck

This chapter has barely scratched the surface of the many perks and freebies off Wall Street. The "cheap-is-chic" lifestyle of the '90s has spawned a number of books and newsletters providing ways to save or stretch a buck:

Books

- *1,001 Ways to Cut Your Expenses* (Dell), by Jonathan Pond
- *Living Cheap: The Survival Guide of the Nineties* (Ropubco), by Larry Roth
- *The Tightwad Gazette* (Villard), by Amy Dacyczyn

Newsletters

- *The Banker's Secret Bulletin* (quarterly; $19.95 per year; 914-758-1400)
- *Skinflint News* (monthly; $9.95 per year; 813-785-7759)
- *Cheapskate Monthly* (monthly; $12.95 per year; 310-630-8845)
- *Living Cheap News* (10 issues; $12 per year; 408-257-1680)
- *The Penny Pincher* (monthly; $12 per year; 516-724 1868)
- *The Tightwad Gazette* (monthly; $12 per year; 207-524-7962)

Each of the newsletters provides a free sample copy. Call for details.

10

When a Free Lunch Isn't a Free Lunch

This book has discussed several ways to get a "free lunch" on Wall Street. But what about those times when a "free lunch" is really no free lunch at all? This chapter highlights some common misconceptions in the market and shows why investment deals that seem too good to be true usually are.

Stock Splits

Stock splits aren't a bad thing by any means, and some market pundits argue that splits really are a favorable development for a stock.

In reality, investors shouldn't care if their stocks split. Stock splits do not affect a company's earnings prospects nor its financial position, nor does a split enhance the value of a portfolio. Stock splits merely take an investor's current holdings and divide them according to the terms of the split. In a 2-for-1 split, investors who had 100 shares of stock will have 200 shares. However, the price is cut in half as well. A $20 stock that splits 2-for-1 now trades at $10. The total value of the investor's portfolio is unchanged.

Why Do Companies Split Their Stock?

Companies split their stock for a variety of reasons. They may want to increase market liquidity or to bring in more individual investors as shareholders. It may be that a company believes that a stock-split announcement will boost its stock momentarily—and studies indicate some short-term strength following split announcements—in which case company executives may want to exercise their stock options.

It may sound a bit cynical, but it is possible that the large number of stock splits in 1992 was due, in part, to executives wanting to boost their stock with split news before exercising options. Executives wanted to exercise stock options in 1992 because they expected higher tax rates under the Clinton administration. Thus, they wanted to push taxable income into 1992.

Companies also may announce stock splits to provide support to the stock price. A stock that has had a good run but has begun to decline may be a candidate for a stock split, especially if the company plans to enter the equity markets to raise capital.

Why Do Investors Like Splits?

If the value of the shares doesn't change following a split, why do investors get so excited about stock splits? Perhaps psychology is involved. Investors may feel better when they hold a larger number of shares, even if the dollar value remains the same.

Investors may react favorably to a stock split simply because a stock that had been too expensive to buy is now more affordable.

As I have noted, there is evidence to suggest that stocks rise following split announcements, at least for a short period of time. One rationale for this phenomenon is that companies often announce stock splits along with dividend increases. The improved price action may be a response to the positive signal the company is sending through its dividend increase.

Some studies indicate that stock splits themselves give positive signals to investors, which may account for some of the near-term price rise. Some analysts believe that a stock split is a signal by management that a jump in earnings is coming and the firm is undervalued. Others believe that stock splits, since they usually occur after a big move in a stock, generally confirm the bullish trend.

A study by the New York Stock Exchange provides an interesting link between stock splits and stock performance. According to the study, stocks that have split increase in price 2½ times faster than nonsplitting shares in the seven years surrounding a split. Most of the gains occur within three years of the split.

Cause or Effect?

From this study, it would appear that stock splits are, indeed, a plus for investors. However, it's important to differentiate between cause and effect when looking at these studies. Are stock splits actually enhancing the stock's performance, or are splits more common in issues with excellent earnings momentum and price rises? Companies with strong earnings momentum will be more highly regarded by investors and show decent price movement. Such price movement may lead to stock splits. But earnings growth, not the fact that the stock is splitting, is the key to discerning stock market winners.

In fact, some analysts argue that stock splits may have a negative effect on stock. Remember that, with each split, more shares come into the market. A rising supply of stock can dampen the price in much the same way as an oversupply of any commodity without a similar increase in demand will adversely affect the price.

Another potential negative is that transaction costs usually rise following a stock split. Since brokerage commissions are influenced by the number of shares traded, a $10,000 investment to purchase 200 shares of a stock that has split 2-for-1 will likely generate a higher commission than the same $10,000 investment for 100 shares.

Stocks often perform sluggishly following a split. One study indicates that while stocks tend to head higher following a stock-split announcement, they tend to level off 3 to 6 months after the split.

Many hypotheses have been given for this action. One says that volume often falls after a split, since volume usually had been higher on the split news. As traders take their short-term profits, the buying volume dries up, driving the stock price lower.

Reverse Stock Splits

One situation where a stock split is definitely bad news for investors is when companies enact "reverse" stock splits. For example, a company undergoing a 1-for-5 reverse stock split will exchange one share for every five shares held by an investor. If the investor had 100 shares, he or she will have 20 shares after the reverse stock split.

Why would companies undergo reverse stock splits? One reason is that a reverse stock split automatically raises the price of a share. In our example, a $2 stock prior to the 1-for-5 reverse stock split becomes a $10 stock after the split. Higher-priced stocks are perceived to be of higher quality than lower-priced stocks. Pension funds and other institutional investors may not be permitted to invest in such low-priced stocks, so companies undergo reverse splits to expand the potential market for their shares.

Another reason that companies undergo reverse stock splits is to escape the purview of regulators, who have cracked down on penny-stock scams. A stock trading for $1 may come under closer scrutiny by regulators than one trading for $10. Therefore, the company undergoes a 1-for-10 reverse stock split and becomes a $10 stock.

Stock prices generally react negatively to a reverse stock split announcement, and the stock usually underperforms for a long time after the reverse split.

What's an Investor to Do?

Don't focus on an issue merely because the company splits its stock frequently. Also, all things being equal, it is better to buy a stock that is splitting sometime after the split than during the presplit price run-up.

If You Still Want to Buy Stock Split Candidates, Some Key Factors to Consider

There is no exact formula for picking a stock-split issue. Nevertheless, for investors who want to invest in stocks in anticipation of splits, common characteristics can be identified:

- A stock split usually occurs after a stock has made a big move.
- Companies that split their stock often have histories of stock splits or stock dividends.
- More than half of all stock splits occur in stocks priced $20 to $49, with a median price of $42.
- Industrial issues represent the majority of stock splits of any size.
- Firms that split their stock often were tracked beforehand by fewer analysts than other companies of similar size.
- Stock splits occur most often in the second quarter, apparently after having been approved at annual meetings.

- Stock splits often are accompanied by dividend hikes, so look for a stock split during the quarter in which the company usually boosts its dividend.

Readers who would like a current list of stock-split candidates should send a note with the code words "Stock Splits," along with a business-size, self-addressed stamped envelope, to me at the address given at the end of Chapter 2.

Stock Splits and the Dow

While it's debatable whether stock splits really matter when it comes to individual stocks, there is no doubt that stock splits have a powerful impact on the performance of the Dow Jones Industrial Average.

To see how splits in Dow components affect the average, it is important to know how the Dow Jones Industrial Average is calculated. Each day, the gains and losses of the 30 Dow stocks are added up and divided by the Dow's "divisor," currently 0.45160. For example, suppose that each of the Dow components increases by $1 for the day. The gain in the Dow will be 1, times the 30 components, divided by 0.45160 or 66.43 points.

Each dollar increase is given the same weight, regardless of what percentage gain occurred in the individual stock. In other words, the Dow is a price-weighted average; higher-priced issues have more weight in the average.

Since higher-priced stocks have more of an impact on the average, the Dow Jones Industrial Average's complexion changes when one or several of its higher-priced components split. This situation occurred in 1992 when three high-priced components—Coca-Cola; Disney, Walt; and Merck & Co.—split 2-for-1, 4-for-1, and 3-for-1, respectively.

Prior to the split, these three issues exerted a big influence on the performance of the average due to their high prices. However, when these three stocks split in May of 1992, their influence on the Dow Industrials weakened considerably.

Stock splits also boost the volatility of the average, since a split adjusts the divisor downward. For example, a 10-point move in the Dow Industrial components translates into a 22.14 move in the Dow Jones Industrial Average (10 divided by 0.45160). If the divisor were to fall to, say, 0.4200 because of a stock split, that same 10-point move would mean a 23.81 move on the DJIA.

High-Yielding Stocks

The stock market is the best arbiter of future dividend cuts I've ever seen. Yet many investors think they can second-guess the market when it comes to a stock that's offering a too-good-to-be-true yield.

Income investors, pay attention to this statement: *There are no free lunches when it comes to chasing yields.* A stock's yield takes into account the likelihood that the dividend will be maintained, and a high yield indicates that Wall Street believes a dividend cut or omission is likely.

How do you know if a yield is too good to be true? Compare the stock's yield to the yield on the S&P 500, which is reported weekly in *Barron's*. Compare the yield to fixed-income investments, such as Treasury bills, CDs, and money markets. Compare the yield to other stocks in its industry group. Is it several percentage points higher? A stock that is nearing a dividend cut usually is behaving as if the dividend cut had already occurred. In other words, stocks reflect pending bad news. If a stock you are considering has a high yield and has been vastly underperforming the market, chances are that Wall Street is expecting a dividend cut.

Being greedy rarely pays when it comes to investing for yields. High yield means high risk. Period.

Special Dividends

I wish I had a dollar for every time an investor called me thinking he or she had found the ultimate free lunch in a stock that was paying a special dividend to shareholders. Special dividends have cooled in popularity, but they were quite common during the '80s as a way of protecting a company from an unwanted takeover. Basically, a company that felt it was among the hunted would load up on debt (this made the firm less attractive to a prospective suitor) and pay shareholders a "special" dividend. These dividends could be several dollars a share.

For example, **Sealed Air,** a producer of packaging materials, paid a special dividend of $40 per share in 1989. At the time, I can remember receiving phone calls from investors who wanted a piece of this deal. The callers didn't understand exactly what was happening. They believed that if they purchased the stock, they would be entitled to the $40 special dividend. Free money, they thought.

What they failed to understand is that following the special dividend, the stock price dropped by the amount of the special dividend. In other words, let's say a stock is trading for $60 per share and pays a special dividend of $40 per share. Following the payout of the special dividend, the stock price will fall to $20—*not* stay at $60 per share as some investors had figured.

Special dividends bring up a little-understood point about dividends in general. Although you may not know it, every time your stock pays a dividend, the stock price reflects the payout and adjusts downward. The reason you may not be aware of this is that, in many instances, the quarterly dividend represents a very small part of the overall stock price. Nevertheless, a dividend payout has a downward effect on a stock price. With large special dividends, this downward effect is accentuated. Special dividends aren't a free lunch. You don't get anything extra and, in most cases, you will be left holding stock in a company that has increased its debt to a dangerous level.

New Issues

Initial public offerings (IPOs), or new issues, are often portrayed as a free lunch. IPOs occur when a privately held company goes public and sells stock for the first time.

Many investors get excited about new issues, since it is not uncommon, especially during frothy market periods, for new issues to jump sharply immediately after they start trading.

Unfortunately, the best IPOs are reserved for institutional investors and other big customers of the underwriting syndicate. Shares in popular IPOs are fully subscribed and are rarely available to small investors.

Because the most attractive IPOs never find their way to small investors, you should think twice anytime a broker calls you touting a "hot" new issue. Chances are, the new issue is merchandise that has already been passed over by the bigger players. A new issue that is being mass-marketed to individual investors is usually not an IPO that you want to own, even if up-front commissions aren't charged.

Companies choose to go public during the most frothy market periods, when they can get the highest price for their shares. Therefore you may be paying a substantial premium for buying a new issue during periods when many new companies are coming to market. As a rule, you'll be better off passing on a new issue and taking a fresh look six months or so down the road. By that time the shares will have developed a trading history, which may be helpful in assessing volatility. You may even be able to buy the shares below their initial offering price.

Another point to remember is to avoid buying the initial public offering of a closed-end fund. As mentioned in Chapter 5, studies show that closed-end-fund IPOs usually perform poorly for buyers in the short term. Part of the reason is that, even though these funds are often sold without a brokerage fee to investors, the underwriter's fee usually comes out of the pool of assets brought in by the offering. This automatically reduces the fund's value. It is better to wait for at least six months and reexamine the closed-end fund to see if it's trading at a discount to the net asset value.

Beware of Those Financial Projections Made by Your Insurance Salesperson

If you've ever bought whole life insurance, annuities, and other insurance products, your insurance salesperson has probably run projections for you on his or her computer. Invariably these projections, which show that you will accumulate staggering amounts of money over the life of the investment, seem like a free lunch.

To be sure, compounding is a powerful force, and a long-term investment strategy in stocks, bonds, insurance, or any investment can pay handsomely. Nevertheless, the future payout, depending on the expected returns used in the projections, may be greatly exaggerated.

For example, let's say you plan to purchase a whole life policy from an insurance salesperson. If it's an independent broker, the salesperson may run projections on several different policies.

At that point, it's critical that you ask the salesperson a few key questions. First, what future rate of return is he or she using to come up with the projections? Usually, the salesperson will use the most recent year or five-year period. However, those projected returns, especially if the projected annual return is based on performance generated during the '80s, may overstate the actual returns to be received in the future. Keep in mind that since 1926 the average annual return on stocks has been roughly 10 to 11 percent, and portfolios with a mixture of stocks and bonds have returned less than 10 percent. Using annual returns of 15 percent or more over a period of many years may provide a distorted picture of what you can expect to earn over the life of the policy.

Make sure the projected annual returns that the salesperson uses make sense. Have projections run at rates more in line with historical returns, say 10 percent or so for stock investments (all this requires is for the salesperson to change the expected return in the spreadsheet). Also, keep in mind that higher returns carry higher risk. An insurance firm that has been paying 20 percent on its various policies in recent years may not be better, in risk-adjusted terms, than an insurance firm paying 12 percent. Make sure you know where the annuity or whole life policy invests your money and evaluate if the risk level is acceptable to you.

Those "PERCS" May Not Be Perks After All

PERCS—Preferred Equity Redemption Cumulative Stock—have become popular in recent years. PERCS represent a kind of convertible preferred stock, combining a yield that is often twice the level of the common stock with upside potential.

High yield with growth potential—sounds like the ultimate free lunch. The problem with PERCS is that you have limited upside potential but unlimited downside risk.

Let's look at an example to see how PERCS work. **Tandy** issued PERCS in February of 1992. At that time the PERCS were yielding 7.2 percent, well above the yield on the common. Tandy is obligated to terminate the PERCS three years after issue (the three-year life of PERCS is standard). The potential problem has to do with the price PERCS holders receive at termination. In the case of the Tandy PERCS, the termination or conversion price after three years is $39.50; that is, the maximum value that the PERCS will return is $39.50, regardless of how high the Tandy common shares go. At the time of the termination, if Tandy stock is trading at, say, $45 per share, PERCS holders will get 0.87 share (the equivalent of $39.50) of stock for each PERCS they hold. However, let's say that Tandy stock drops to $19 per share at the time of termination. PERCS holders will receive one share of common stock for each PERCS.

As you can see, PERCS holders share in only part of common stock's potential gains but in all of the losses. In effect, by receiving the higher yield on PERCS, holders are exposing themselves to all of the downside risk of the common without all of the upside potential. Of course if your primary interest is income, this is a tradeoff you perhaps are willing to make. Keep in mind, however, that, although you may have bought the PERCS for income, if you hold the security to termination you'll wind up with common stock in a company that could have poor prospects and a much lower yield than the PERCS. For this reason, consider PERCS issued only by firms whose common stock you find attractive.

Beware of Any Investment That's "Guaranteed"

Many investments are sold with the word "guaranteed." Guaranteed Investment Contracts (GICs) are one such investment.

GICs are contracts sold by insurance companies that "guarantee" a certain return. The contracts are backed by bonds and a pledge by the insurance company that if the GICs don't produce the desired return, the insurer will make up the difference.

As you can imagine, any investment that claims it's guaranteed gets investors' attention, and GICs quickly became a popular vehicle for corporate employee pension plans. Unfortunately, a pledge or promise of payment is a far cry from a guarantee, and the value of some GICs fell sharply when a number of major insurers ran into financial troubles and could not produce the promised return on their GICs.

Interestingly, GICs are still quite prevalent in many retirement plans. Fortunately, companies have become a bit more selective in investing in GICs. Investors should consider GICs sold only by financially sound insurance companies.

Another type of investment carrying "guarantees" comes from the growing number of funds that promise to return at least your principal after a stated amount of time, often 10 years. On the surface, these funds seem like a can't-miss deal—a guarantee of at least your principal back, and the chance for upside gains.

When evaluating such funds, it's critical to consider several factors. A fund that invests cautiously to meet some baseline obligation may have a big opportunity cost attached to it in the form of lost gains. Forgoing big returns to assure a minimum return may appeal to the most conservative investor, but merely running in place is not the path to market riches.

If you find such a fund appealing, you can provide the same guarantee yourself by investing your money the way such funds do—and pocketing the management expenses and load charges. The way a fund guarantees the return of at least your principal is by investing a portion of the money in zero coupon bonds. Zero coupon bonds are purchased at a discount from face value and return the face value at maturity.

For example, a zero coupon bond paying an implicit yield of 7 percent annually doubles in 10 years. In other words, a 10-year zero coupon bond, with a face value at maturity of $1000 and yielding 7 percent, will cost approximately $500 to purchase. Now, let's say that you start with an investment pool of $1000. You can guarantee yourself that at the end of 10 years you will have at least your initial investment of $1000 by taking half of the money and buying one 10-year zero coupon bond yielding 7 percent. At the end of 10 years that bond will be worth $1000. With the remaining $500 you can buy stocks, options, or any other investment carrying a higher degree of return but also more risk. Even if you lose your entire investment in these securities, you'll be bailed out by the zero coupon investment, which will bring $1000 at maturity.

Of course there are opportunity costs to consider, such as foregone interest. Also, one dollar today is worth more than one dollar 10 years from now, due to the effects of inflation. Still, it's an interesting approach for investors who want to speculate with some of their funds but would still like to guarantee having at least the original investment at the end of the investment period.

Risk-Free Government Securities

The concept of risk is essential in evaluating any fixed-income investment, especially so-called "risk-free" government securities.

Three types of risk should be considered when looking at fixed-income investments. The first is default risk—the risk that the issuer of the bond will go out of business. The second is interest rate risk—the risk that fluctuations in interest rates will affect the value of the bond prior to maturity. Interest rate risk plays an important role if you sell a fixed-income investment before maturity. The third risk for fixed-income investments is reinvestment risk; that is, the risk that the interest that is earned from fixed-income investments will be reinvested at lower rates. Of course there is also liquidity risk—the risk that you won't get out of an investment without taking a beating, due to a thinly traded market—as well as call risk—the retirement of an issue prior to the scheduled maturity—but these risks are usually minor considerations in the government securities market.

Most investors regard government securities as being risk-free investments. After all, the government does guarantee the return of the principal and interest on its securities. However, while government securities don't have default risk, they may be exposed to interest rate and reinvestment risk.

For example, let's say you've purchased long-term government securities and are forced to sell before maturity. Depending on interest rate movements, you may take a beating on the sale. Likewise, let's say that you buy a 30-year government security. If interest rates drop, you will be reinvesting the interest at lower rates. This reinvestment risk could affect the bond's realized yield to maturity.

Since government securities are often thought of as risk-free investments, some mutual funds exploit this misconception by using "government securities" in their name. However, it pays to do your homework on the fund's composition before investing in a fund that you may think invests strictly in government securities. Indeed, as long as the fund has at least 65 percent of its assets in government securities, it can call itself a government securities fund. However, that guideline leaves the door open for government securities funds to have a major portion of assets—up to 35 percent—in riskier investments, and it's not uncommon for some "government securities" funds to invest in junk or near-junk bonds. Don't take at face value any fund claiming to invest in "government securities." Obtain a prospectus of the fund, which spells out its holdings and investment policy.

Conclusion

This chapter has taken a brief look at some common misconceptions and misinformation concerning popular investment vehicles and strategies. Each year investors are faced with an ever-increasing menu of complicated and confusing investment alternatives purporting to be a free lunch. But remember, when it comes to investment results, return and risk are joined at the hip. You can't have higher returns without higher risk, no matter how good the deal may sound.

11

Directory of Corporate Perks, Freebies, and Giveaways

We've covered a lot of ground in the first 10 chapters of the book, and you may be having trouble remembering which company offers what perk and/or discount. This chapter provides a directory of all the corporate perks, freebies, and giveaways discussed in the book.

Each directory listing has the company name, stock symbol (NYSE—New York Stock Exchange; ASE—American Stock Exchange; NASDAQ—NASDAQ Market), address, and phone number. In addition, various perks are listed. Some of the more common perks include:

- *DRIP.* This company has a dividend reinvestment plan. DRIPs were discussed in Chapter 3.

- *Discounts in DRIPs.* A number of companies provide discounts on stock purchased through DRIPs. In most cases the discounts, which usually range from 3 to 5 percent, apply only to reinvested dividends, but some companies also apply the discount to shares purchased with optional cash payments (OCPs).

- *Certificate safekeeping services.* Many companies offer certificate safekeeping services to DRIP participants. This reduces the risk that certificates will be lost or stolen.

- *Electronic deposit of dividends.* This service allows investors to have their dividends deposited directly into their bank accounts, thus eliminating lost or delayed dividend checks.

Additional perks that apply specifically to the company are listed as well.

Stay With Quality

One point I've made throughout the book that bears repeating is this: Focus on quality stocks when you invest. Don't take a big position in a lousy stock just because the company offers a good perk. If you like the perk but don't like the stock, limit your investment to just a share or two. In most cases, that's enough to qualify for the perk. To give you guidance on investment quality, I've highlighted, with an arrow (▶), issues that I feel are most attractive for long-term investment.

Remember that companies frequently change perk policies, and corporate America's cost-cutting penchant in recent years has taken its toll on a number of shareholder perks. Be sure to check with companies of interest concerning their perks and the number of shares needed to qualify.

▶ **Abbott Laboratories (NYSE:ABT)**
1 Abbott Park Road
Abbott Park, IL 60064-3500
(708) 937-6100

Perks:
- DRIP
- Certificate safekeeping services
- Shareholders who attend the annual meeting usually receive lunch as well as a sample gift pack of the firm's consumer products

AFLAC, Inc. (NYSE:AFL)
1932 Wynnton Road
Columbus, GA 31999
(800) 235-2667

Perks:
- DRIP
- Certificate safekeeping services

▶ **Air Products & Chemicals, Inc.**
(NYSE:APD)
7201 Hamilton Blvd.
Allentown, PA 18195-1501
(215) 481-4911

Perks:
- DRIP
- Certificate safekeeping services

▶ **Alberto-Culver Co. (NYSE:ACVA)**
2525 Armitage Ave.
Melrose Park, IL 60160
(708) 450-3000

Perks:
- Shareholders who attend the annual meeting usually receive product samples (the firm manufactures *Alberto VO5* and *Static Guard*) as well as a company tour

▶ **Albertson's, Inc. (NYSE:ABS)**
250 East Parkcenter Boulevard
Boise, ID 83706
(208) 385-6200

Perks:
- Shareholders who attend the annual meeting usually receive a sample bag of grocery products

Allegheny Power System, Inc.
(NYSE:AYP)
12 E. 49th St.
New York, NY 10017
(212) 752-2121

Perks:
- DRIP
- Certificate safekeeping services
- Electronic deposit of dividends

AlliedSignal, Inc.
(NYSE:ALD)
101 Columbia Road
Morristown, NJ 07962
(201) 455-2127

Perks:
- DRIP
- Certificate safekeeping services

Aluminum Co. of America
(NYSE:AA)
1501 Alcoa Bldg.
Pittsburgh, PA 15219
(412) 553-4545

Perks:
- DRIP
- Certificate safekeeping services
- Electronic deposit of dividends

▶ **American Brands, Inc.**
(NYSE:AMB)
1700 East Putnam Ave.
Old Greenwich, CT 06870
(203) 698-5000

Perks:
- DRIP
- Electronic deposit of dividends
- Shareholders who attend the annual meeting usually receive a

gift bag of products from the company's various divisions (the firm markets liquors, office supplies, and hardware products)

▶ **American Cyanamid Co. (NYSE:ACY) One Cyanamid Plaza Wayne, NJ 07470 (201) 831-3586**

Perks:
- DRIP

American Electric Power Co., Inc. (NYSE:AEP) One Riverside Plaza Columbus, OH 43215 (614) 223-1000

Perks:
- DRIP
- Certificate safekeeping services

American Express Co. (NYSE:AXP) 200 Vesey St. New York, NY 10285 (212) 640-5693

Perks:
- DRIP
- 3 percent discount on reinvested dividends
- Certificate safekeeping services
- Electronic deposit of dividends

American General Corp. (NYSE:AGC) 2929 Allen Parkway Houston, TX 77019 (800) 446-2617 (713) 522-1111

Perks:
- DRIP
- Certificate safekeeping services
- Electronic deposit of dividends

American Greetings Corp. (NASDAQ:AGREA) 10500 American Road Cleveland, OH 44144 (216) 737-5742 (216) 252-7300

Perks:
- DRIP
- Certificate safekeeping services
- Electronic deposit of dividends

▶ **American Home Products Corp. (NYSE:AHP) 685 Third Ave. New York, NY 10017-4085 (212) 878-5000 (800) 647-4273**

Perks:
- DRIP
- Certificate safekeeping services

American Recreation Centers, Inc. (NASDAQ:AMRC) 11171 Sun Center Drive, Suite 120 Rancho Cordova, CA 95670 (916) 852-8005 (916) 852-8329

Perks:
- DRIP
- First-time purchases of stock may be made directly from company
- Certificate safekeeping services
- Shareholders of 500 or more shares join the Distinguished Shareholder Club, which entitle them to five free games of bowling per day at any of the firm's bowling centers
- Distinguished Shareholder Club members also receive a 20 percent discount on products in the company's Right Start children's catalog

▶ **American Telephone & Telegraph Co. (NYSE:T) 32 Avenue of the Americas New York, NY 10013-2412 (212) 387-5400 (800) 348-8288**

Perks:
- DRIP
- Certificate safekeeping services
- Electronic deposit of dividends

▶ **American Water Works Co., Inc. (NYSE:AWK)**
1025 Laurel Oak Road
Voorhees, NJ 08043
(617) 575-2900

Perks:
- DRIP
- 5 percent discount on reinvested dividends

▶ **Ameritech Corp. (NYSE:AIT)**
30 South Wacker Drive
Chicago, IL 60606
(312) 750-5353 (800) 233-1342

Perks:
- DRIP
- Certificate safekeeping services
- Electronic deposit of dividends

▶ **Amoco Corp. (NYSE:AN)**
200 East Randolph Drive
Chicago, IL 60601
(312) 856-6111 (800) 638-5672
(800) 446-2617

Perks:
- DRIP
- Certificate safekeeping services
- Electronic deposit of dividends

▶ **AMP, Inc. (NYSE:AMP)**
470 Friendship Road
Harrisburg, PA 17111
(717) 780-4869

Perks:
- DRIP
- Certificate safekeeping services
- The company periodically makes available to shareholders reprints of articles and research information about the firm

AmSouth Bancorp. (NYSE:ASO)
1901 Fifth Avenue North
Birmingham, AL 35203
(205) 583-4439

Perks:
- DRIP
- Electronic deposit of dividends

▶ **Anheuser-Busch Companies, Inc. (NYSE:BUD)**
1 Busch Place
St. Louis, MO 63118
(314) 577-3342

Perks:
- DRIP
- Shareholders receive 15 percent discount at the company's amusement and theme parks: *Busch Gardens, Sea World, Sesame Park, Adventure Island, Water Country USA, Cypress Gardens*
- Shareholders who attend the annual meeting are usually treated to beer and *Eagle* snack foods
- Company tour

Aquarion Co. (NYSE:WTR)
835 Main St.
Bridgeport, CT 06601
(203) 335-2333

Perks:
- DRIP
- 5 percent discount on reinvested dividends

ARCO Chemical Co. (NYSE:RCM)
3801 West Chester Pike
Newtown Square, PA 19073-2387
(215) 359-2000

Perks:
- DRIP
- Certificate safekeeping services

**Arrow Financial Corp.
(NASDAQ:AROW)**
250 Glen St.
Glens Falls, NY 12801
(518) 745-1000

Perks:
- DRIP
- First-time purchases of stock may be made directly from the company

ASARCO, Inc. (NYSE:AR)
180 Maiden Lane
New York, NY 10038
(212) 510-2000 (800) 524-4458

Perks:
- DRIP
- Certificate safekeeping services

Atlanta Gas Light Co. (NYSE:ATG)
235 Peachtree St. N.E.
Atlanta, GA 30303
(404) 584-4000

Perks:
- DRIP
- Certificate safekeeping services
- Electronic deposit of dividends

Atlantic Energy, Inc. (NYSE:ATE)
PO Box 1334
6801 Black Horse Pike
Pleasantville, NJ 08232
(609) 645-4506

Perks:
- DRIP
- Electronic deposit of dividends
- First-time purchases of stock may be made directly from the company

▶ **Atlantic Richfield Co. (NYSE:ARC)**
515 South Flower St.
Los Angeles, CA 90071-2256
(213) 486-3511

Perks:
- DRIP
- Electronic deposit of dividends

▶ **Atmos Energy Corp. (NYSE:ATO)**
Suite 1800, 3 Lincoln Centre
5430 LBJ Freeway
Dallas, TX 75240
(214) 934-9227

Perks:
- DRIP
- IRA option in DRIP
- 3 percent discount on reinvested dividends
- First-time purchases may be made directly through the company
- Certificate safekeeping services
- Electronic deposit of dividends

▶ **Avnet, Inc. (NYSE:AVT)**
80 Cutter Mill Rd.
Great Neck, NY 11021
(516) 466-7000 (800) 524-4458

Perks:
- DRIP
- Electronic deposit of dividends

Avon Products, Inc. (NYSE:AVP)
9 West 57 St.
New York, NY 10019
(212) 546-6015

Perks:
- DRIP
- Certificate safekeeping services
- Electronic deposit of dividends

Baker Hughes, Inc. (NYSE:BHI)
3900 Essex Lane
Houston, TX 77027
(713) 439-8600 (212) 791-6422

Perks:
- DRIP
- Certificate safekeeping services

Ball Corp. (NYSE:BLL)
345 South High St.
Muncie, IN 47307-0407
(317) 747-6100 (800) 446-2617

Perks:
- DRIP
- 5 percent discount on reinvested dividends
- Electronic deposit of dividends

Baltimore Bancorp (NYSE:BBB)
120 E. Baltimore St.
Baltimore, MD 21202
(410) 576-4490

Perks:
- DRIP
- 5 percent discount on optional cash payments
- Certificate safekeeping services

Baltimore Gas and Electric Co.
(NYSE:BGE)
39 W. Lexington St.
Baltimore, MD 21201
(410) 783-5920

Perks:
- DRIP
- Electronic deposit of dividends

▶ **Banc One Corp. (NYSE:ONE)**
100 East Broad Street
Columbus, OH 43271
(614) 248-5944 (800) 753-7107

Perks:
- DRIP
- Certificate safekeeping services

▶ **Bancorp Hawaii, Inc.**
(NYSE:BOH)
130 Merchant St.
Honolulu, HI 96813
(808) 537-8111

Perks:
- DRIP
- 5 percent discount on reinvested dividends
- Electronic deposit of dividends
- Residents of Hawaii may purchase initial shares directly from the firm

Bank of Boston Corp.
(NYSE:BKB)
100 Federal St.
Boston, MA 02110
(617) 575-2900

Perks:
- DRIP
- 3 percent discount on reinvested dividends
- Certificate safekeeping services

BankAmerica Corp.
(NYSE:BAC)
Bank of America Center
San Francisco, CA 94104
(415) 622-2091

Perks:
- DRIP
- $2\frac{1}{2}$ percent discount on reinvested dividends
- $2\frac{1}{2}$ percent discount on optional cash payments

Bankers First Corp.
(NASDAQ:BNKF)
One 10th Street
Riverfront Office Building,
Suite 700
Augusta, GA 30901
(212) 791-6422 (706) 849-3305

Perks:
- DRIP
- 5 percent discount on reinvested dividends
- 5 percent discount on optional cash payments

Bankers Trust New York Corp.
(NYSE:BT)
280 Park Ave.
New York, NY 10017
(800) 547-9794 (212) 250-2500

Perks:
- DRIP

▶ **Bard, C.R., Inc. (NYSE:BCR)**
730 Central Ave.
Murray Hill, NJ 07974
(908) 277-8000 (212) 791-6422

Perks:
- DRIP
- Electronic deposit of dividends

Barnett Banks, Inc. (NYSE:BBI)
50 North Laura St.
Jacksonville, FL 32202
(904) 791-7720

Perks:
- DRIP
- Certificate safekeeping services
- Electronic deposit of dividends

▶ **Bausch & Lomb, Inc. (NYSE:BOL)**
Shareholder Relations
PO Box 54, 1 Lincoln First Sq.
Rochester, NY 14601-0054
(716) 338-6025 (800) 442-2001

Perks:
- DRIP
- Certificate safekeeping services

▶ **Baxter International, Inc.**
(NYSE:BAX)
One Baxter Parkway
Deerfield, IL 60015
(708) 948-2000 (212) 791-6422

Perks:
- DRIP
- Electronic deposit of dividends

Bay State Gas Co. (NYSE:BGC)
300 Fiberg Parkway
Westborough, MA 01581
(508) 836-7000

Perks:
- DRIP
- 3 percent discount on reinvested dividends
- 3 percent discount on optional cash payments

- Certificate safekeeping services
- Electronic deposit of dividends

BB&T Financial Corp.
(NASDAQ:BBTF)
PO Box 1847
Wilson, NC 27894-1847
(919) 399-4291

Perks:
- DRIP
- 5 percent discount on reinvested dividends
- Certificate safekeeping services
- Electronic deposit of dividends

BCE, Inc. (NYSE:BCE)
2000 McGill College Ave., Suite 2100
Montreal, Quebec H3A 3H7 Canada
(514) 499-7000 (514) 982-7666

Perks:
- DRIP
- Electronic deposit of dividends

▶ **Bell Atlantic Corp. (NYSE:BEL)**
1717 Arch St.
Philadelphia, PA 19103
(215) 963-6000 (800) 631-2355

Perks:
- DRIP
- Certificate safekeeping services
- Electronic deposit of dividends

▶ **BellSouth Corp. (NYSE:BLS)**
1155 Peachtree St., N.E.
Atlanta, GA 30367
(404) 249-2000 (800) 631-6001

Perks:
- DRIP
- Certificate safekeeping services

▶ **Bemis Co., Inc. (NYSE:BMS)**
222 S. 9th St., Suite 2300
Minneapolis, MN 55402-4099
(612) 376-3000

Perks:
- DRIP
- Certificate safekeeping services

▶ **Ben & Jerry's Homemade, Inc.**
   (NASDAQ:BJICA)
   Duxtown Common Plaza
   Junction of Rts. 2 and 100
   Waterbury, VT 05676
   (802) 244-6957

Perks:
- Company tour
- Contributes 7½ percent of pre-tax profits to various charitable organizations

Beneficial Corp. (NYSE:BNL)
400 Bellevue Parkway
Wilmington, DE 19809
(302) 798-0800

Perks:
- DRIP
- Certificate safekeeping services

Black Hills Corp. (NYSE:BKH)
625 Ninth Street
Rapid City, SD 57701
(605) 348-1700

Perks:
- DRIP
- Electronic deposit of dividends

▶ **Block, H & R, Inc. (NYSE:HRB)**
   4410 Main St.
   Kansas City, MO 64111
   (816) 753-6900

Perks:
- DRIP
- Certificate safekeeping services

Blockbuster Entertainment Corp.
 (NYSE:BV)
1 Blockbuster Plaza
Fort Lauderdale, FL 33301
(305) 524-8200

Perks:
- Shareholders who attend the annual meeting usually receive a free prerecorded videocassette

Blount, Inc. (ASE:BLT.A)
4520 Executive Park Drive
Montgomery, AL 36116-1602
(205) 244-4000

Perks:
- DRIP
- 5 percent discount on reinvested dividends

BMJ Financial Corp.
 (NASDAQ:BMJF)
243 Route 130
PO Box 1001
Bordentown, NJ 08505
(609) 298-5500

Perks:
- DRIP
- 5 percent discount on reinvested dividends
- 5 percent discount on optional cash payments

Boatmen's Bancshares, Inc.
 (NASDAQ:BOAT)
800 Market St.
St. Louis, MO 63101
(314) 466-6000

Perks:
- DRIP
- Electronic deposit of dividends

▶ **Bob Evans Farms, Inc.**
   (NASDAQ:BOBE)
   3776 South High Street
   PO Box 07863
   Columbus, OH 43207
   (614) 491-2225

Perks:
- DRIP

- Certificate safekeeping services
- Electronic deposit of dividends

Boeing Co. (NYSE:BA)
7755 E. Marginal Way South
Seattle, WA 98108
(206) 655-1976

Perks:
- Company tour of 747 assembly plant in Everett, WA

Boise Cascade Corp. (NYSE:BCC)
One Jefferson Square
Boise, ID 83728
(208) 384-7590

Perks:
- DRIP
- Certificate safekeeping services
- Electronic deposit of dividends
- Company tour

Borden, Inc. (NYSE:BN)
277 Park Ave.
New York, NY 10172
(212) 573-4000

Perks:
- DRIP
- Electronic deposit of dividends
- Shareholders who attend the annual meeting usually receive a shopping bag containing Borden products (brand names include *Creamette, Prince, Cracker Jack, Elmer's* glue, and *Meadow Gold*)

Boulevard Bancorp, Inc.
(NASDAQ:BLVD)
410 N. Michigan Avenue
Chicago, IL 60611
(312) 836-6500 (312) 427-2953

Perks:
- DRIP
- 5 percent discount on optional cash payments

▶ **Bristol-Myers Squibb Co.**
(NYSE:BMY)
345 Park Ave.
New York, NY 10154
(212) 546-4000 (800) 356-2026

Perks:
- DRIP
- Certificate safekeeping services
- Electronic deposit of dividends

British Petroleum Co. Plc (NYSE:BP)
200 Public Square
Cleveland, OH 44114-2375
(216) 586-4141 (800) 428-4237

Perks:
- DRIP

▶ **Brooklyn Union Gas Co. (NYSE:BU)**
1 Metrotech Center
Brooklyn, NY 11201
(718) 403-3334

Perks:
- DRIP
- Certificate safekeeping services
- Electronic deposit of dividends

▶ **Brown-Forman Corp. (NYSE:BF.B)**
850 Dixie Highway
Louisville, KY 40210
(502) 585-1100

Perks:
- DRIP
- Electronic deposit of dividends
- Brown-Forman has traditionally provided shareholders with a 50 percent discount on certain *Lenox* holiday china as well as 50 percent off on *Hartmann* luggage

▶ **Browning-Ferris Industries, Inc.**
(NYSE:BFI)
Browning-Ferris Bldg.
757 N Eldridge, PO Box 3151
Houston, TX 77253
(713) 870-8100

Perks:
- DRIP
- Certificate safekeeping services

**Burnham Pacific Properties, Inc.
(NYSE: BPP)**
610 West Ash St., Suite 2001
San Diego, CA 92101
(619) 232-2001

Perks:
- DRIP
- 5 percent discount on reinvested dividends

**California Real Estate Investment
Trust (NYSE:CT)**
705 University Ave. #A
Sacramento, CA 95825
(916) 929-5433

Perks:
- DRIP
- 5 percent discount on reinvested dividends

▶ **Campbell Soup Co. (NYSE:CPB)**
Campbell Place
Camden, NJ 08103-1799
(609) 342-4800

Perks:
- DRIP
- Certificate safekeeping services
- Company museum featuring soup tureens made primarily in western Europe in the 18th century

Capital Holding Corp. (NYSE:CPH)
400 W. Market Street
Louisville, KY 40202
(502) 560-2992

Perks:
- DRIP
- Certificate safekeeping services

Carolina Power & Light Co. (NYSE:CPL)
411 Fayetteville St.
Raleigh, NC 27601-1748
(919) 546-6111 (919) 546-7844

Perks:
- DRIP
- Certificate safekeeping services
- Electronic deposit of dividends
- Customers of the utility may purchase initial shares directly from the firm

▶ **CBS, Inc. (NYSE:CBS)**
51 W. 52nd St.
New York, NY 10019
(212) 791-6422 (212) 975-4321

Perks:
- DRIP

Centerior Energy Corp. (NYSE:CX)
Shareowner Services
PO Box 94661
Cleveland, OH 44101
(216) 447-3100 (800) 433-7794

Perks:
- DRIP
- IRA option in DRIP
- Certificate safekeeping services
- Customers may make initial purchase of stock directly from the company

▶ **Central Fidelity Banks, Inc.
(NASDAQ:CFBS)**
1021 East Cary St.
Richmond, VA 23219
(804) 697-6942

Perks:
- DRIP

**Central Louisiana Electric Co., Inc.
(NYSE:CNL)**
2030 Donahue Ferry Rd.
Pineville, LA 71360-5226
(318) 484-7400

Perks:
- DRIP
- Certificate safekeeping services
- Electronic deposit of dividends

Central Maine Power Co. (NYSE:CTP)
Edison Drive
Augusta, ME 04336
(207) 623-3521

Perks:
- DRIP
- 5 percent discount on reinvested dividends
- Certificate safekeeping services
- Electronic deposit of dividends
- Residents of Maine may make initial purchase of stock directly from the firm

Central Vermont Public Service Corp. (NYSE:CV)
77 Grove St.
Rutland, VT 05701
(802) 773-2711

Perks:
- DRIP
- Certificate safekeeping services
- First-time purchases of stock may be made directly from the company for residents in less than half the states

Chase Manhattan Corp. (NYSE:CMB)
1 Chase Manhattan Plaza, 9th Floor
New York, NY 10081
(800) 526-0801

Perks:
- DRIP
- 5 percent discount on reinvested dividends
- 3 percent discount on optional cash payments
- Certificate safekeeping services

▶ **Chevron Corp. (NYSE:CHV)**
225 Bush St., Room 236
San Francisco, CA 94104
(415) 894-7700

Perks:
- DRIP
- Electronic deposit of dividends

Chrysler Corp. (NYSE:C)
12000 Chrysler Drive
Highland Park, MI 48288
(313) 956-5741

Perks:
- DRIP
- Certificate safekeeping services

▶ **Church & Dwight Co., Inc. (NYSE:CHD)**
469 North Harrison St.
Princeton, NJ 08543-5297
(609) 683-5900

Perks:
- DRIP
- Product samples provided at shareholder meeting

▶ **CIGNA Corp. (NYSE:CI)**
1601 Chestnut Street
Philadelphia, PA 19192
(215) 761-1000

Perks:
- DRIP
- Certificate safekeeping services
- Electronic deposit of dividends
- Company museum with 9000 pieces on display, including the nation's largest collection of antique fire-fighting equipment

CILCORP, Inc. (NYSE:CER)
Shareholder Records
300 Hamilton Blvd., Suite 300
Peoria, IL 61602
(800) 622-5514 (800) 322-3569

Perks:
- DRIP
- Electronic deposit of dividends

▶ **Cincinnati Bell, Inc. (NYSE:CSN)**
  201 E. 4th St.
  Cincinnati, OH 45202
  (800) 321-1355 (513) 397-9900

Perks:
- DRIP
- Certificate safekeeping services
- Electronic deposit of dividends

CIPSCO, Inc. (NYSE:CIP)
607 East Adams St.
Springfield, IL 62739
(217) 525-5317

Perks:
- DRIP
- Certificate safekeeping services
- Electronic deposit of dividends

Citicorp (NYSE:CCI)
404 Sette Drive
Paramus, NJ 07652
(800) 422-2066 (800) 342-6690

Perks:
- DRIP
- 3 percent discount on reinvested dividends
- 2½ percent discount on optional cash payments
- Certificate safekeeping services

Citizens First Bancorp, Inc.
(ASE:CFB)
208 Harristown Road
Glen Rock, NJ 07452-3306
(201) 445-3400

Perks:
- DRIP
- First-time purchases of stock may be made directly from the company

▶ **Citizens Utilities Co. "A" and "B"**
  (NYSE:CZNA/CZNB)
  High Ridge Park
  Stamford, CT 06905
  (203) 329-8800

Perks:
- The company's unique dividend policy gives shareholders the option of receiving either stock dividends or cash dividends

▶ **Clorox Co. (NYSE:CLX)**
  1221 Broadway
  Oakland, CA 94612
  (510) 271-7000

Perks:
- DRIP
- Certificate safekeeping services

▶ **Coca-Cola Co. (NYSE:KO)**
  1 Coca-Cola Plaza, N.W.
  Atlanta, GA 30313
  (404) 676-2121 (800) 446-2617

Perks:
- DRIP
- Certificate safekeeping services
- Electronic deposit of dividends
- Company museum

▶ **Colgate-Palmolive Co. (NYSE:CL)**
  300 Park Ave.
  New York, NY 10022
  (212) 310-2000

Perks:
- DRIP
- Certificate safekeeping services
- Electronic deposit of dividends
- New shareholders receive product discount coupons valued at about $15. Company also periodically includes discount coupons in shareholder mailings

Colonial Gas Co. (NASDAQ:CGES)
40 Market Street
Lowell, MA 01852
(508) 458-3171 (800) 442-2001

Perks:
- DRIP
- 5 percent discount on reinvested dividends
- Certificate safekeeping services

Comerica, Inc. (NYSE:CMA)
Attn: Stock Transfer Dept.
211 West Fort St.
Detroit, MI 48275-1093
(313) 222-3300 (800) 468-9716
(800) 327-5965

Perks:
- DRIP
- Electronic deposit of dividends

▶ **Communications Satellite Corp. (NYSE:CQ)**
950 L'Enfant Plaza, S.W.
Washington, DC 20024
(202) 863-6200

Perks:
- DRIP

▶ **ConAgra, Inc. (NYSE:CAG)**
One ConAgra Drive
Omaha, NE 68102-5001
(402) 595-4000

Perks:
- DRIP
- Certificate safekeeping services
- Shareholders receive a meal at annual meeting consisting of ConAgra products

Connecticut Energy Corp. (NYSE:CNE)
880 Broad St.
PO Box 1540
Bridgeport, CT 06604
(203) 382-8111

Perks:
- DRIP
- IRA option in DRIP
- Certificate safekeeping services
- Electronic deposit of dividends
- Customers of the utility may purchase initial shares directly from the firm

Connecticut Natural Gas Corp. (NYSE:CTG)
100 Columbus Blvd.
Hartford, CT 06103-2805
(203) 727-3203 (212) 613-7143

Perks:
- DRIP
- Certificate safekeeping services

Connecticut Water Service, Inc. (NASDAQ:CTWS)
93 West Main St.
Clinton, CT 06413
(203) 669-8636 (800) 426-5523

Perks:
- DRIP
- 5 percent discount on reinvested dividends

▶ **Consolidated Edison Co. of New York, Inc. (NYSE:ED)**
30 Flatbush Avenue
Brooklyn, NY 11217
(800) 221-6664 (800) 522-5522

Perks:
- DRIP
- Electronic deposit of dividends

▶ **Consolidated Natural Gas Co. (NYSE:CNG)**
625 Liberty Ave.
Pittsburgh, PA 15222-3199
(412) 227-1125 (412) 227-1485
(800) 542-7792

Perks:
- DRIP
- Certificate safekeeping services
- Electronic deposit of dividends

▶ **Consolidated Rail Corp.**
  (NYSE:CRR)
  2001 Market Street
  Philadelphia, PA 19101-1419
  (215) 209-4000

Perks:
- DRIP
- Certificate safekeeping services

Consumers Water Co.
 (NASDAQ:CONW)
Three Canal Plaza
PO Box 599
Portland, ME 04112
(800) 292-2925 (207) 773-6438

Perks:
- DRIP
- Electronic deposit of dividends

Cooper Industries, Inc. (NYSE:CBE)
1001 Fannin Street, Suite 4000
Houston, TX 77002
(713) 739-5400

Perks:
- DRIP

CoreStates Financial Corp.
 (NASDAQ:CSFN)
Centre Square West
1500 Market St.
Philadelphia, PA 19102-2104
(215) 973-3100 (800) 446-2617

Perks:
- DRIP
- 3 percent discount on reinvested dividends
- Certificate safekeeping services
- Electronic deposit of dividends

▶ **Corning, Inc. (NYSE:GLW)**
  Houghton Park
  Corning, NY 14831
  (607) 974-9000

Perks:
- DRIP
- Electronic deposit of dividends
- Company tour and museum

▶ **CPC International, Inc.**
  (NYSE:CPC)
  International Plaza
  PO Box 8000
  Englewood Cliffs, NJ 07632-9976
  (201) 894-4000

Perks:
- DRIP
- Certificate safekeeping services

▶ **Crane Co. (NYSE:CR)**
  100 First Stamford Place
  Stamford, CT 06902
  (203) 363-7300 (212) 587-6617

Perks:
- DRIP
- Certificate safekeeping services

Crestar Financial Corp.
 (NASDAQ:CRFC)
919 East Main Street
Richmond, VA 23219
(804) 782-5769

Perks:
- DRIP
- 5 percent discount on reinvested dividends
- Electronic deposit of dividends

▶ **Crompton & Knowles Corp.**
  (NYSE:CNK)
  One Station Place-Metro Center
  Stamford, CT 06902
  (203) 353-5400

Perks:
- DRIP
- Certificate safekeeping services

Cross, A.T., Co. (ASE:ATX.A)
One Albion Rd.
Lincoln, RI 02865
(401) 333-1200

Perks:
- Shareholders usually receive a gift at the annual meeting

▶ **CSX Corp. (NYSE:CSX)**
901 East Cary Street
Richmond, VA 23219
(800) 521-5571 (804) 782-1400

Perks:
- DRIP
- Electronic deposit of dividends
- Shareholders receive discounts on stays at the company's exclusive Greenbrier resort in West Virginia

Dana Corp. (NYSE:DCN)
4500 Door Street
Toledo, OH 43615
(419) 535-4633

Perks:
- DRIP
- Electronic deposit of dividends

▶ **Dauphin Deposit Corp.**
(NASDAQ:DAPN)
213 Market Street
Harrisburg, PA 17108
(800) 458-0348

Perks:
- DRIP

▶ **Dayton Hudson Corp. (NYSE:DH)**
Attn: Investor Relations Dept.
777 Nicollet Mall
Minneapolis, MN 55402
(612) 370-6732 (212) 791-6422

Perks:
- DRIP
- Certificate safekeeping services

▶ **Dean Foods Co. (NYSE:DF)**
3600 North River Road
Franklin Park, IL 60131
(708) 678-1680

Perks:
- DRIP
- Electronic deposit of dividends
- Shareholders who attend the annual meeting usually receive a gift box of the company's dairy and specialty products

Delta Air Lines, Inc. (NYSE:DAL)
Hartsfield Atlanta Int'l Airport
Atlanta, GA 30320
(404) 715-2600

Perks:
- DRIP
- Certificate safekeeping services

▶ **Dexter Corp. (NYSE:DEX)**
1 Elm Street
Windsor Locks, CT 06096
(203) 282-3509 (203) 627-9051
(800) 288-9541

Perks:
- DRIP

▶ **Dial Corp. (NYSE:DL)**
1850 N. Central
Phoenix, AZ 85077-1424
(800) 453-2235

Perks:
- DRIP
- First-time purchasers may be made directly from the company

▶ **Disney, Walt, Co. (NYSE:DIS)**
500 South Buena Vista St.
Burbank, CA 91521
(818) 560-1000 (818) 505-7040

Perks:

- Electronic deposit of dividends
- Shareholders receive 20 percent discount ($10 value) on membership in the Magic Kingdom Gold Card Program (membership fee for shareholders is $39). Gold Card members receive discounts on Disney merchandise, hotel accommodations, and theme park tickets
- In the past, shareholders attending annual meeting have received free passes to *Disneyland*

Dominion Resources, Inc. (NYSE:D)
901 East Byrd St.
Richmond, VA 23219
(804) 775-5700

Perks:

- DRIP
- Certificate safekeeping services
- Customers of the utility may purchase initial shares directly from the firm

Donaldson Co., Inc. (NYSE:DCI)
PO Box 1299
Minneapolis, MN 55440
(612) 887-3131 (800) 468-9716

Perks:

- DRIP
- Certificate safekeeping services

▶ **Donnelley, R. R., & Sons Co.**
  (NYSE:DNY)
  77 W. Wacker Drive
  Chicago, IL 60601
  (312) 326-8000

  Perks:

  - DRIP
  - Certificate safekeeping services

▶ **Dow Chemical Co. (NYSE:DOW)**
  2030 Dow Center
  Midland, MI 48674
  (517) 636-1000

Perks:

- DRIP
- Certificate safekeeping services
- Electronic deposit of dividends

▶ **Dow Jones & Co., Inc. (NYSE:DJ)**
  200 Liberty St.
  New York, NY 10281
  (212) 416-2000 (212) 406-5475

  Perks:

  - DRIP
  - Electronic deposit of dividends

Du Pont, E.I., de Nemours & Co.
 (NYSE:DD)
Attn: Stockholder Relations
1007 Market St.
Wilmington, DE 19898
(302) 774-0195 (800) 526-0801

Perks:

- DRIP
- Certificate safekeeping services

▶ **Duke Power Co. (NYSE:DUK)**
  422 S. Church
  Charlotte, NC 28242
  (704) 373-4011

  Perks:

  - DRIP
  - Electronic deposit of dividends
  - Customers of the utility may purchase initial shares directly from the firm

E-Systems, Inc. (NYSE:ESY)
6250 LBJ Freeway
Dallas, TX 75240
(214) 661-1000

Perks:

- DRIP
- Electronic deposit of dividends

E'town Corp. (NYSE:ETW)
600 South Ave.
Westfield, NJ 07090
(908) 654-1234

Perks:
- DRIP
- 5 percent discount on reinvested dividends
- 5 percent discount on optional cash payments

Eastern Utilities Associates (NYSE:EUA)
1 Liberty Square
PO Box 233
Boston, MA 02107
(617) 357-9590

Perks:
- DRIP
- 5 percent discount on reinvested dividends
- Certificate safekeeping services

Eastman Kodak Co. (NYSE:EK)
343 State St.
Rochester, NY 14650
(716) 724-4000 (800) 253-6057

Perks:
- DRIP
- Certificate safekeeping services
- Electronic deposit of dividends

Ecolab, Inc. (NYSE:ECL)
370 N. Wabasha
St. Paul, MN 55102
(612) 293-2233

Perks:
- DRIP
- Certificate safekeeping services

EG&G, Inc. (NYSE:EGG)
45 William St.
Wellesley, MA 02181-4078
(617) 237-5100

Perks:
- DRIP
- Certificate safekeeping services

▶ **Emerson Electric Co.**
  (NYSE:EMR)
8000 W. Florissant Ave.
St. Louis, MO 63136
(314) 553-2000 (314) 553-2197

Perks:
- DRIP
- Certificate safekeeping services

Empire District Electric Co.
  (NYSE:EDE)
602 Joplin Street
Joplin, MO 64801
(417) 623-4700

Perks:
- DRIP
- 5 percent discount on reinvested dividends
- Electronic deposit of dividends

Energen Corp. (NYSE:EGN)
2101 Sixth Ave. North
Birmingham, AL 35203
(205) 326-8421 (800) 654-3206

Perks:
- DRIP
- Electronic deposit of dividends

EnergyNorth, Inc. (NASDAQ:ENNI)
PO Box 329
1260 Elm St.
Manchester, NH 03105
(603) 625-4000

Perks:
- DRIP
- 5 percent discount on reinvested dividends
- Electronic deposit of dividends

▶ **Equifax, Inc. (NYSE:EFX)**
  1600 Peachtree St.
  Atlanta, GA 30302
  (404) 885-8000

Perks:
- DRIP
- Certificate safekeeping services
- Electronic deposit of dividends

**Equitable Resources, Inc.
(NYSE:EQT)
420 Boulevard of the Allies
Pittsburgh, PA 15219
(412) 553-5877**

Perks:
- DRIP
- Electronic deposit of dividends

**Ethyl Corp. (NYSE:EY)
330 South Fourth St.
Richmond, VA 23219
(804) 788-5000**

Perks:
- DRIP

▶ **Exxon Corp. (NYSE:XON)
225 E. John Carpenter Freeway
Irving, TX 75062
(214) 444-1000 (800) 252-1800**

Perks:
- DRIP
- IRA option in DRIP
- Certificate safekeeping services
- Electronic deposit of dividends
- First-time purchases of stock may be made directly from the company

**F & M National Corp.
(NASDAQ:FMNT)
PO Box 2800
Winchester, VA 22604
(703) 665-4200**

Perks:
- DRIP
- 5 percent discount on reinvested dividends

▶ **Federal National Mortgage Association (NYSE:FNM)
3900 Wisconsin Ave., N.W.
Washington, DC 20016
(202) 752-7000 (202) 752-6605**

Perks:
- DRIP
- The company has made available free copies of *Remic Master* software (202-752-6604). The software provides assistance in understanding the complicated mortgage-backed securities market

▶ **Fifth Third Bancorp
(NASDAQ:FITB)
38 Fountain Square Plaza
Cincinnati, OH 45263
(513) 579-5300**

Perks:
- DRIP
- Electronic deposit of dividends

▶ **First Alabama Bancshares, Inc.
(NASDAQ:FABC)
417 N. 20th Street
Birmingham, AL 35203
(205) 832-8450 (205) 832-8011**

Perks:
- DRIP
- Electronic deposit of dividends
- First-time purchases of stock may be made directly from the company

**First American Corp.
(NASDAQ:FATN)
300 Union
Nashville, TN 37237-0721
(615) 748-2441**

Perks:
- DRIP
- 5 percent discount on reinvested dividends

▶ **First Bancorp. of Ohio**
  (NASDAQ:FBOH)
  106 South Main St.
  Akron, OH 44308-1444
  (216) 384-7347

Perks:
- ·DRIP
- Electronic deposit of dividends

First Bank System, Inc. (NYSE:FBS)
601 2nd Ave. South
Minneapolis, MN 55402-4302
(612) 973-1111 (612) 973-0334

Perks:
- DRIP
- 3 percent discount on reinvested dividends

First Chicago Corp. (NYSE:FNB)
30 W. Broadway
New York, NY 10007-2190
(212) 732-4000 (800) 446-2617

Perks:
- DRIP
- 3 percent discount on reinvested dividends
- Certificate safekeeping services

First Commerce Corp.
  (NASDAQ:FCOM)
210 Baronne St.
New Orleans, LA 70112
(504) 561-1371

Perks:
- DRIP
- 5 percent discount on reinvested dividends
- Electronic deposit of dividends

First Eastern Corp.
  (NASDAQ:FEBC)
11 West Market St.
Wilkes-Barre, PA 18768
(717) 821-4420

Perks:
- DRIP
- 5 percent discount on reinvested dividends

First Fidelity Bancorp. (NYSE:FFB)
550 Broad St., 10th Floor
Newark, NJ 07102
(609) 895-6800 (201) 565-3150
(201) 565-3200

Perks:
- DRIP
- 3 percent discount on reinvested dividends
- Electronic deposit of dividends

▶ **First Michigan Bank Corp.**
  (NASDAQ:FMBC)
  1 Financial Plaza
  Holland, MI 49423
  (616) 396-9000

Perks:
- DRIP
- 5 percent discount on reinvested dividends
- Electronic deposit of dividends

First Midwest Bancorp, Inc.
  (NASDAQ:FMB)
184 Shuman Blvd., Suite 310
Naperville, IL 60566
(708) 778-8700 (312) 427-2953

Perks:
- DRIP
- 3 percent discount on reinvested dividends

First of America Bank Corp.
  (NYSE:FOA)
211 S. Rose Street
Kalamazoo, MI 49007
(616) 376-9000

Perks:
- DRIP

- 5 percent discount on reinvested dividends
- Electronic deposit of dividends

First Security Corp. (NASDAQ:FSCO)
79 S. Main St.
Salt Lake City, UT 84111
(801) 350-5325

Perks:
- DRIP
- Electronic deposit of dividends

First Union Corp. (NYSE:FTU)
One First Union Center
301 S. College St., Suite 4000
Charlotte, NC 28288
(704) 374-6565

Perks:
- DRIP
- 2 percent discount on reinvested dividends
- 2 percent discount on optional cash payments
- Certificate safekeeping services
- Electronic deposit of dividends

▶ **First Virginia Banks, Inc. (NYSE:FVB)**
6400 Arlington Blvd.
Falls Church, VA 22042-2336
(703) 241-3669 (703) 241-4000

Perks:
- DRIP
- Electronic deposit of dividends

▶ **Firstar Corp. (NYSE:FSR)**
777 East Wisconsin Ave.
Milwaukee, WI 53202
(414) 765-4321

Perks:
- DRIP
- Electronic deposit of dividends

Fleet Financial Group, Inc. (NYSE:FLT)
50 Kennedy Plaza
Providence, RI 02903
(401) 278-5879 (401) 278-5149

Perks:
- DRIP
- 5 percent discount on reinvested dividends
- 3 percent discount on optional cash payments
- Electronic deposit of dividends

▶ **Fleming Companies, Inc. (NYSE:FLM)**
PO Box 26647
6301 Waterford Blvd.
Oklahoma City, OK 73126-0647
(405) 840-7200

Perks:
- DRIP
- 5 percent discount on reinvested dividends

Florida Progress Corp. (NYSE:FPC)
Barnett Tower
One Progress Plaza
St. Petersburg, FL 33701
(813) 824-6400

Perks:
- DRIP
- Certificate safekeeping services
- Residents of Florida may make initial purchases of stock directly

Fourth Financial Corp. (NASDAQ:FRTH)
100 N. Broadway
PO Box 4
Wichita, KS 67202
(316) 261-4256

Perks:
- DRIP
- Electronic deposit of dividends

FPL Group, Inc. (NYSE:FPL)
700 Universe Blvd.
Juno Beach, FL 33408
(407) 694-4000 (407) 694-4692

Perks:
- DRIP
- Certificate safekeeping services

Freeport-McMoRan, Inc. (NYSE:FTX)
1615 Poydras St.
New Orleans, LA 70112
(504) 582-4000

Perks:
- DRIP
- Certificate safekeeping services
- Electronic deposit of dividends

▶ **Fuller, H.B., Co. (NASDAQ:FULL)**
2400 Energy Park Drive
St. Paul, MN 55108-1591
(612) 645-3401

Perks:
- DRIP
- Certificate safekeeping services
- Electronic deposit of dividends

▶ **Gannett Co., Inc. (NYSE:GCI)**
1100 Wilson Blvd.
Arlington, VA 22234
(703) 284-6000

Perks:
- DRIP

▶ **General Electric Co. (NYSE:GE)**
3135 Easton Turnpike
Fairfield, CT 06431
(203) 373-2816 (203) 326-4040

Perks:
- DRIP

▶ **General Mills, Inc. (NYSE:GIS)**
Number One General Mills Blvd.
Minneapolis, MN 55426
(612) 540-2311

Perks:
- DRIP
- Certificate safekeeping services
- The company makes available a special holiday package of products and coupons—retail value of $50—for $18.95

General Motors Corp. (NYSE:GM)
3044 West Grand Blvd.
Detroit, MI 48202
(313) 556-5000 (212) 791-3909

Perks:
- DRIP
- 3 percent discount on reinvested dividends
- 3 percent discount on optional cash payments
- Certificate safekeeping services
- Electronic deposit of dividends
- Former shareholders of record may reestablish positions in the stock by buying shares directly from the company

▶ **General RE Corp. (NYSE:GRN)**
695 E. Main Street
Stamford, CT 06904
(203) 328-5000 (800) 524-4458

Perks:
- DRIP

▶ **Genuine Parts Co. (NYSE:GPC)**
2999 Circle 75 Parkway, N.W.
Atlanta, GA 30339
(404) 588-7822 (404) 953-1700

Perks:
- DRIP

Georgia-Pacific Corp. (NYSE:GP)
133 Peachtree St., N.E.
Atlanta, GA 30303
(404) 521-4000

Perks:
- DRIP
- Certificate safekeeping services

▶ Gerber Products Co. (NYSE:GEB)
445 State St.
Fremont, MI 49413
(616) 928-2000

Perks:
- DRIP
- Electronic deposit of dividends
- New shareholders receive discount coupons on products, as well as a catalog offering discounts on baby products

▶ Giant Food, Inc. (ASE:GFS.A)
6300 Sheriff Road
Landover, MD 20785
(301) 341-4100

Perks:
- DRIP

▶ Gillette Co. (NYSE:G)
Prudential Tower Building
Boston, MA 02199
(617) 421-7000

Perks:
- DRIP
- Certificate safekeeping services
- The company periodically includes discount coupons with quarterly and annual reports as well as with dividend checks

▶ Glaxo Holdings Plc (NYSE:GLX)
Lansdowne House
Berkeley Square
London W1XY 6BP8DH, England
(800) 524-4458

Perks:
- DRIP
- Certificate safekeeping services

Grace, W.R., & Co. (NYSE:GRA)
1 Town Center Road
Boca Raton, FL 33486
(407) 362-2000 (800) 647-4273

Perks:
- DRIP
- Certificate safekeeping services
- First-time purchases of stock may be made directly from the company

Graco, Inc. (NYSE:GGG)
4050 Olson Memorial Highway
Golden Valley, MN 55422
(612) 623-6000

Perks:
- DRIP
- Certificate safekeeping services
- Electronic deposit of dividends

Great Western Financial Corp.
(NYSE:GWF)
9200 Oakdale Ave., 7th Floor
Chatsworth, CA 91311
(818) 775-3411 (800) 522-6645

Perks:
- DRIP
- 3 percent discount on reinvested dividends

Green Mountain Power Corp.
(NYSE:GMP)
25 Green Mountain Dr.
South Burlington, VT 05402
(802) 864-5731

Perks:
- DRIP
- Certificate safekeeping services
- Electronic deposit of dividends

▶ GTE Corp.
(NYSE:GTE)
1776 Heritage Drive
North Quincy, MA 02171
(800) 225-5160

Perks:
- DRIP

Handy & Harman (NYSE:HNH)
250 Park Ave.
New York, NY 10177
(212) 661-2400

Perks:
- DRIP
- Certificate safekeeping services

▶ Hannaford Bros. Co.
  (NYSE:HRD)
  145 Pleasant Hill Rd.
  Scarborough, ME 04074
  (207) 883-2911

  Perks:
  - DRIP
  - Certificate safekeeping services
  - Electronic deposit of dividends

▶ Harcourt General, Inc.
  (NYSE:H)
  PO Box 1000
  27 Boylston St.
  Chestnut Hill, MA 02167
  (617) 232-8200

  Perks:
  - DRIP
  - Certificate safekeeping services

▶ Harley-Davidson, Inc.
  (NYSE:HDI)
  3700 West Juneau Ave.
  Milwaukee, WI 53201
  (414) 342-4680

  Perks:
  - Company tour/museum

Harris Corp. (NYSE:HRS)
1025 West NASA Blvd.
Melbourne, FL 32919
(407) 727-9100 (800) 542-7792

Perks:
- DRIP
- Certificate safekeeping services

Harsco Corp. (NYSE:HSC)
350 Poplar Church Road
Camp Hill, PA 17011
(717) 763-7064 (201) 296-4070
 (800) 526-0801

Perks:
- DRIP
- Certificate safekeeping services

Hartford Steam Boiler Inspection &
 Insurance Co. (NYSE:HSB)
One State Street
Hartford, CT 06102
(203) 722-1866 (800) 442-2001

Perks:
- DRIP
- Company museum with a collection of 19th- and 20th-century Connecticut antiques, paintings, and furniture

Hawaiian Electric Industries, Inc.
 (NYSE:HE)
900 Richard Street
PO Box 730
Honolulu, HI 96813
(808) 543-5662

Perks:
- DRIP
- Certificate safekeeping services
- Electronic deposit of dividends
- Residents of Hawaii may purchase initial shares directly from the firm

Health Care REIT, Inc.
 (NYSE:HCN)
One SeaGate, Suite 1950
Toledo, OH 43604
(419) 247-2800

Perks:
- DRIP
- 4 percent discount on reinvested dividends

► Heinz, H.J., Co. (NYSE:HNZ)
600 Grant St., 60th Floor
Pittsburgh, PA 15219
(412) 456-5700

Perks:
- DRIP
- The company periodically includes special deals on products and recipe books in shareholder mailings

► Helene Curtis Industries, Inc. (NYSE:HC)
325 North Wells St.
Chicago, IL 60610
(312) 661-0222

Perks:
- The company periodically includes discount coupons in shareholder mailings

► Hershey Foods Corp. (NYSE:HSY)
100 Crystal A Drive
Hershey, PA 17033
(717) 534-6799

Perks:
- DRIP
- Certificate safekeeping services
- Company tour
- Shareholders can order gifts for friends and relatives from a special holiday catalog, and Hershey will ship the package directly to the recipient
- Shareholders who attend the annual meeting usually receive product samples

► Home Depot, Inc. (NYSE:HD)
2727 Paces Ferry Rd.
Atlanta, GA 30339
(404) 433-8211

Perks:
- DRIP
- Certificate safekeeping services

► Honeywell, Inc. (NYSE:HON)
PO Box 524
Honeywell Plaza
Minneapolis, MN 55440
(612) 951-0095 (800) 647-4273

Perks:
- DRIP

► Hormel, Geo. A., & Co. (NYSE:HRL)
501 16th Ave. N.E.
PO Box 800
Austin, MN 55912
(507) 437-5737

Perks:
- DRIP
- Electronic deposit of dividends

Household International, Inc. (NYSE:HI)
2700 Sanders Rd.
Prospect Heights, IL 60070
(708) 564-5000

Perks:
- DRIP
- Electronic deposit of dividends

► Hubbell, Inc. (NYSE:HUB.B)
584 Derby Milford Rd.
Orange, CT 06477-4024
(203) 799-4100

Perks:
- DRIP
- Certificate safekeeping services

Huntington Bancshares, Inc. (NASDAQ:HBAN)
41 S. High St.
Columbus, OH 43287
(614) 476-8300

Perks:
- DRIP
- 5 percent discount on reinvested dividends

- Certificate safekeeping services
- Electronic deposit of dividends

Idaho Power Co. (NYSE:IDA)
PO Box 70
Boise, ID 83707
(800) 635-5406

Perks:
- DRIP
- Electronic deposit of dividends

IES Industries, Inc.
(NYSE:IES)
200 First St., S.E.
PO Box 351
Cedar Rapids, IA 52406
(800) 247-9785

Perks:
- DRIP
- Electronic deposit of dividends

Imperial Oil, Ltd. (ASE:IMO)
111 St. Clair Ave. West
Toronto, Ontario M5W 1K3 Canada
(416) 968-5076

Perks:
- DRIP

Inco, Ltd. (NYSE:N)
One New York Plaza
1 Water Street
New York, NY 10004
(212) 612-5500

Perks:
- DRIP
- 5 percent discount on reinvested dividends
- Electronic deposit of dividends

Independence Bancorp (PA)
(NASDAQ:INBC)
One Hillendale Rd.
Perkasie, PA 18944
(215) 257-2402

Perks:
- DRIP
- 5 percent discount on reinvested dividends

Independent Bank Corp. (MI)
(NASDAQ:IBCP)
230 W. Main St.
Ionia, MI 48846
(616) 527-9450

Perks:
- DRIP
- 5 percent discount on reinvested dividends

▶ **Indiana Energy, Inc.**
(NYSE:IEI)
1630 North Meridian St.
Indianapolis, IN 46202-1496
(317) 926-3351

Perks:
- DRIP
- Certificate safekeeping services
- Electronic deposit of dividends

Ingersoll-Rand Co. (NYSE:IR)
200 Chestnut Ridge Rd.
Woodcliff Lake, NJ 07675
(201) 573-0123

Perks:
- DRIP

▶ **Intel Corp. (NASDAQ:INTC)**
2200 Mission College Blvd.
Santa Clara, CA 95052-8119
(408) 765-8080

Perks:
- DRIP

Interchange Financial Services Corp.
(ASE:ISB)
Park 80 West/Plaza Two
Saddle Brook, NJ 07662
(201) 703-2265

Perks:
- DRIP
- First-time purchases of stock may be made directly from the company

International Business Machines Corp. (NYSE:IBM)
Old Orchard Rd.
Armonk, NY 10504
(914) 765-1900 (212) 791-4208
  (800) 426-3333

Perks:
- DRIP
- Certificate safekeeping services

▶ **International Dairy Queen, Inc.**
  (NASDAQ:INDQA)
  5701 Green Valley Drive
  Minneapolis, MN 55437
  (612) 830-0200

Perks:
- Shareholders who attend the annual meeting are treated to Dairy Queen products

International Multifoods Corp.
  (NYSE:IMC)
33 South Sixth St.
Minneapolis, MN 55402-0942
(612) 340-3300

Perks:
- DRIP
- Certificate safekeeping services

▶ **International Paper Co.**
  (NYSE:IP)
  2 Manhattanville Rd.
  Purchase, NY 10577
  (914) 397-1500 (212) 613-7147

Perks:
- DRIP
- Electronic deposit of dividends

Iowa-Illinois Gas & Electric Co.
  (NYSE:IWG)
206 E. 2nd St.
Davenport, IA 52801
(800) 373-4443

Perks:
- DRIP
- Electronic deposit of dividends

▶ **IPALCO Enterprises, Inc.**
  (NYSE:IPL)
  25 Monument Circle
  Indianapolis, IN 46204
  (317) 261-8394 (317) 261-8261

Perks:
- DRIP

IRT Property Co. (NYSE:IRT)
200 Galleria Pkwy., Suite 1400
Atlanta, GA 30339
(404) 955-4406

Perks:
- DRIP
- 5 percent discount on reinvested dividends

ITT Corp. (NYSE:ITT)
1330 Avenue of the Americas
New York, NY 10019
(201) 601-4202

Perks:
- DRIP
- Certificate safekeeping services
- Electronic deposit of dividends

Jefferson Bankshares, Inc.
  (NASDAQ:JBNK)
123 East Main St.
Charlottesville, VA 22902
(804) 972-1100

Perks:
- DRIP
- 5 percent discount on reinvested dividends

▶ **Jefferson-Pilot Corp. (NYSE:JP)**
100 North Greene St.
Greensboro, NC 27420
(919) 691-3000 (919) 691-3375
(704) 374-2697

Perks:
- DRIP
- Certificate safekeeping services

▶ **Johnson & Johnson (NYSE:JNJ)**
One Johnson & Johnson Plaza
New Brunswick, NJ 08933
(908) 524-0400

Perks:
- DRIP
- Certificate safekeeping services
- Electronic deposit of dividends

Johnson Controls, Inc. (NYSE:JCI)
5757 North Green Bay Ave.
PO Box 591
Milwaukee, WI 53201
(414) 228-1200 (800) 333-2222

Perks:
- DRIP
- Certificate safekeeping services
- Electronic deposit of dividends
- First-time purchases of stock may be made directly from the company

▶ **Jostens, Inc. (NYSE:JOS)**
5501 Norman Center Drive
Minneapolis, MN 55437
(612) 830-3366

Perks:
- DRIP
- Certificate safekeeping services
- Electronic deposit of dividends
- Shareholders usually receive a gift at the annual meeting

▶ **Kellogg Co. (NYSE:K)**
One Kellogg Square
PO Box 3599
Battle Creek, MI 49016-3599
(616) 961-2000 (800) 323-6138

Perks:
- DRIP
- Certificate safekeeping services
- New shareholders receive discount coupons on products
- Shareholders who attend the annual meeting usually receive a hospitality kit with product samples and discount coupons

Kemper Corp. (NYSE:KEM)
One Kemper Drive
Long Grove, IL 60049
(708) 540-2000

Perks:
- DRIP
- Certificate safekeeping services

Kennametal, Inc. (NYSE:KMT)
PO Box 231
Latrobe, PA 15650
(412) 539-5000

Perks:
- DRIP
- 5 percent discount on reinvested dividends

Kerr-McGee Corp. (NYSE:KMG)
123 Robert S. Kerr
PO Box 25861
Oklahoma City, OK 73102
(405) 231-6711 (405) 270-1313

Perks:
- DRIP
- Certificate safekeeping services

KeyCorp (NYSE:KEY)
One KeyCorp Plaza
PO Box 88
Albany, NY 12201-0088
(800) 888-7412

Perks:
- DRIP
- Electronic deposit of dividends

▶ **Keystone International, Inc.**
   (NYSE:KII)
   9600 W Gulf Bank Drive
   PO Box 40010
   Houston, TX 77240
   (713) 937-5301

Perks:
- DRIP

▶ **Kimberly-Clark Corp.**
   (NYSE:KMB)
   PO Box 619100
   D/FW Airport Station
   Dallas, TX 75261-9100
   (214) 830-1200

Perks:
- DRIP
- Certificate safekeeping services
- Electronic deposit of dividends
- The company gives shareholders the opportunity to buy a goody bag of products at a reduced price

▶ **Kmart Corp. (NYSE:KM)**
   3100 West Big Beaver Rd.
   Troy, MI 48084
   (313) 643-1000 (800) 336-6981

Perks:
- DRIP
- Certificate safekeeping services
- Electronic deposit of dividends

▶ **Knight-Ridder, Inc. (NYSE:KRI)**
   One Herald Plaza
   Miami, FL 33132
   (305) 376-3938 (212) 613-7147

Perks:
- DRIP
- Certificate safekeeping services

Lafarge Corp. (NYSE:LAF)
11130 Sunrise Valley Dr., Suite 300
Reston, VA 22091
(703) 264-3600

Perks:
- DRIP
- 5 percent discount on reinvested dividends

LG&E Energy Corp.
(NYSE:LGE)
220 W. Main
Louisville, KY 40202
(502) 627-3445 (800) 235-9705

Perks:
- DRIP
- Electronic deposit of dividends

▶ **Lilly, Eli, & Co.**
   (NYSE:LLY)
   Lilly Corporate Center
   Indianapolis, IN 46285
   (800) 833-8699 (317) 276-2000

Perks:
- DRIP

▶ **Limited, The, Inc.**
   (NYSE:LTD)
   Two Limited Parkway
   PO Box 16000
   Columbus, OH 43216
   (212) 791-6422 (614) 479-7000

Perks:
- DRIP

▶ **Lincoln National Corp.**
   (NYSE:LNC)
   1300 South Clinton St.
   Fort Wayne, IN 46802
   (219) 455-2000 (219) 455-2056

Perks:
- DRIP
- Certificate safekeeping services
- Electronic deposit of dividends
- Company museum consisting of the world's largest private collection of memorabilia devoted to Abraham Lincoln

▶ **Liz Claiborne, Inc. (NYSE:LIZ)**
1441 Broadway
New York, NY 10018
(212) 354-4900 (212) 791-6422

Perks:
▪ DRIP
▪ Certificate safekeeping services

▶ **Loctite Corp. (NYSE:LOC)**
Ten Columbus Blvd.
Hartford, CT 06106
(203) 520-5000

Perks:
▪ DRIP
▪ Shareholders who attend the
  annual meeting usually receive
  a gift

Louisiana Land and Exploration Co.
(NYSE:LLX)
909 Poydras St.
New Orleans, LA 70112
(504) 566-6500

Perks:
▪ DRIP
▪ Certificate safekeeping services

Louisiana-Pacific Corp. (NYSE:LPX)
111 SW Fifth Ave.
Portland, OR 97204-3699
(503) 221-0800

Perks:
▪ DRIP
▪ Certificate safekeeping services

▶ **Lowe's Companies, Inc.**
(NYSE:LOW)
PO Box 1111
N. Wilkesboro, NC 28656-0001
(919) 651-4000 (919) 651-4703

Perks:
▪ DRIP
▪ Certificate safekeeping services

▶ **Mark Twain Bancshares, Inc.**
(NASDAQ:MTWN)
8820 Ladue Rd.
St. Louis, MO 63124
(314) 727-1000 (216) 687-5745

Perks:
▪ DRIP

Marriott Corp. (NYSE:MHS)
1 Marriott Drive
Washington, DC 20058
(301) 380-9000 (301) 380-7770
(800) 442-2001

Perks:
▪ Shareholders receive $10 off weekend
  stays at certain *Marriott* hotels, 10 percent off on stays at the firm's *Fairfield
  Inn* chain (discount good every day of
  week), and 10 percent off on weekend
  stays at *Courtyard* hotels

▶ **Marsh & McLennan Companies,**
Inc. (NYSE:MMC)
1166 Avenue of the Americas
New York City, NY 10036
(212) 345-5000

Perks:
▪ DRIP
▪ Certificate safekeeping services

▶ **Marshall & Ilsley Corp.**
(NASDAQ:MRIS)
770 N. Water St.
PO Box 2035
Milwaukee, WI 53201
(414) 765-7801

Perks:
▪ DRIP
▪ Electronic deposit of dividends

Maxus Energy Corp. (NYSE:MXS)
717 North Harwood Street
Dallas, TX 75201-6594
(214) 953-2000

Perks:
- DRIP
- 3 percent discount on optional cash payments

▶ **May Department Stores Co. (NYSE:MA)**
611 Olive St.
St. Louis, MO 63101
(314) 342-6300 (800) 524-4458

Perks:
- DRIP
- Certificate safekeeping services

Maytag Corp. (NYSE:MYG)
403 West 4th St. North
Newton, IA 50208
(515) 792-8000

Perks:
- DRIP
- Certificate safekeeping services

▶ **McDonald's Corp. (NYSE:MCD)**
1 McDonald's Plaza
Oak Brook, IL 60521
(708) 575-7428

Perks:
- DRIP
- Certificate safekeeping services
- The company makes available "mock" certificates to give as gifts to new shareholders
- Company periodically makes available to shareholders newspaper/magazine articles and research reports done on the firm
- Company museum (Ray Kroc's first franchised outlet)

▶ **McGraw-Hill, Inc. (NYSE:MHP)**
1221 Avenue of the Americas
New York, NY 10020
(212) 512-4150 (212) 512-2000

Perks:
- DRIP

▶ **McKesson Corp. (NYSE:MCK)**
One Post St.
San Francisco, CA 94104
(415) 983-8367

Perks:
- DRIP

MCN Corp. (NYSE:MCN)
500 Griswold St.
Detroit, MI 48226
(313) 256-6324 (313) 256-5500

Perks:
- DRIP
- Certificate safekeeping services
- Electronic deposit of dividends

MDU Resources Group, Inc. (NYSE:MDU)
400 N. 4th St.
Bismarck, ND 58501
(701) 222-7621

Perks:
- DRIP
- Electronic deposit of dividends

Media General, Inc. (ASE:MEG.A)
333 E. Grace Street
Richmond, VA 23219
(804) 649-6000

Perks:
- DRIP
- Certificate safekeeping services

▶ **Medtronic, Inc. (NYSE:MDT)**
7000 Central Ave. N.E.
Minneapolis, MN 55432
(612) 574-4000 (800) 328-2518

Perks:
- DRIP

Mellon Bank Corp. (NYSE: MEL)
1 Mellon Bank Center
500 Grant St.
Pittsburgh, PA 15258
(412) 234-5000 (800) 756-3353

Perks:
- DRIP
- 3 percent discount on reinvested dividends
- 3 percent discount on optional cash payments
- Electronic deposit of dividends

Mercantile Bankshares Corp.
 (NASDAQ:MRBK)
2 Hopkins Plaza
Baltimore, MD 21201
(410) 237-5900

Perks:
- DRIP
- 5 percent discount on reinvested dividends

▶ **Merck & Co., Inc. (NYSE:MRK)**
 1 Merck Drive
 Whitehouse Station, NJ 08889
 (908) 423-6627

 Perks:
 - DRIP
 - Certificate safekeeping services
 - Electronic deposit of dividends

Meridian Bancorp, Inc.
 (NASDAQ:MRDN)
35 N Sixth St.
PO Box 1102
Reading, PA 19603
(215) 655-2000

Perks:
- DRIP
- 5 percent discount on reinvested dividends
- Electronic deposit of dividends
- Local residents may make initial purchases directly from the firm

Merry Land & Investment Co., Inc.
 (NYSE:MRY)
624 Ellis St.
PO Box 1417
Augusta, GA 30903
(404) 722-6756

Perks:
- DRIP
- 5 percent discount on reinvested dividends

Middlesex Water Co.
 (NASDAQ:MSEX)
1500 Ronson Road
Iselin, NJ 08830-0452
(908) 634-1500

Perks:
- DRIP
- Electronic deposit of dividends

Millipore Corp. (NYSE:MIL)
80 Ashby Rd.
Bedford, MA 01730
(617) 275-9200 (617) 575-2900

Perks:
- DRIP
- Certificate safekeeping services

▶ **Minnesota Mining &**
 Manufacturing Co. (NYSE:MMM)
3M Center
St. Paul, MN 55144
(612) 733-1110 (612) 450-4064

Perks:
- DRIP
- Certificate safekeeping services
- Electronic deposit of dividends
- New shareholders receive a welcome package consisting of company products such as *Post-it* notes, tape, and household products

▶ **Minnesota Power & Light Co.**
 (NYSE:MPL)
30 W. Superior St.
Duluth, MN 55802-2093
(218) 723-3974 (218) 722-2641

Perks:
- DRIP

- Electronic deposit of dividends
- Customers of the utility may make initial purchases directly from the firm

▶ **Mobil Corp. (NYSE:MOB)**
3225 Gallows Road
Fairfax, VA 22037-0001
(800) 648-9291 (703) 849-3000

Perks:
- DRIP
- Certificate safekeeping services

Mobile Gas Service Corp.
(NASDAQ:MBLE)
2828 Dauphin Street
Mobile, AL 36606
(205) 476-2720

Perks:
- DRIP
- Electronic deposit of dividends

▶ **Monsanto Co. (NYSE:MTC)**
800 N. Lindbergh Blvd.
St. Louis, MO 63167
(314) 694-5353 (314) 694-1000

Perks:
- DRIP

Montana Power Co. (NYSE:MTP)
40 East Broadway
Butte, MT 59701-9989
(800) 245-6767 (406) 723-5421

Perks:
- DRIP
- Certificate safekeeping services
- Electronic deposit of dividends
- Customers of the utility may purchase initial shares directly from the firm

▶ **Morgan, J.P., & Co. Inc. (NYSE:JPM)**
60 Wall St.
New York, NY 10260-0060
(212) 483-2323 (212) 791-6422

Perks:
- DRIP
- 3 percent discount on reinvested dividends
- Certificate safekeeping services

Moto Photo, Inc. (NASDAQ:MOTO)
4444 Lake Center Drive
Dayton, OH 45426
(513) 854-6686

Perks:
- Shareholders receive a complimentary membership to the Moto Photo club. Members receive discounts on film, film processing, picture frames, and special gifts as well as special deals on cruises and car rentals

▶ **Motorola, Inc. (NYSE:MOT)**
1303 E. Algonquin Road
Schaumburg, IL 60196
(708) 576-5000

Perks:
- DRIP
- Certificate safekeeping services
- Company museum

▶ **Nalco Chemical Co. (NYSE:NLC)**
One Nalco Center
Naperville, IL 60563-1198
(708) 305-1000 (800) 446-2617

Perks:
- DRIP
- Electronic deposit of dividends

National Bancorp of Alaska, Inc.
(NASDAQ:NBAK)
301 W. Northern Lights Blvd.
PO Box 100600
Anchorage, AK 99510
(907) 276-1132

Perks:
- Company museum with over 8000 artifacts, sculptures, and paintings emphasizing history of the area and native Alaskan arts

National City Corp. (NYSE:NCC)
1900 East 9th Street
Cleveland, OH 44114-0900
(216) 575-2640

Perks:
- DRIP
- Certificate safekeeping services
- Electronic deposit of dividends

National Fuel Gas Co. (NYSE:NFG)
30 Rockefeller Plaza
New York, NY 10112
(212) 541-7533

Perks:
- DRIP
- Electronic deposit of dividends
- Customers of the utility may purchase initial shares directly from the firm

National Medical Enterprises, Inc. (NYSE:NME)
2700 Colorado Ave.
PO Box 4070
Santa Monica, CA 90404
(310) 998-8000

Perks:
- DRIP
- Certificate safekeeping services

National Penn Bancshares, Inc. (NASDAQ:NPBC)
Philadelphia & Reading Aves.
Boyertown, PA 19512
(215) 367-6001

Perks:
- DRIP
- The company serves a family-style meal to shareholders at the annual meeting

▶ **National Service Industries, Inc. (NYSE:NSI)**
1420 Peachtree St., N.E.
Atlanta, GA 30309
(404) 853-1000

Perks:
- DRIP
- Certificate safekeeping services

NationsBank Corp. (NYSE:NB)
100 N. Tryon St.
Charlotte, NC 28255
(704) 386-5000

Perks:
- DRIP
- 5 percent discount on reinvested dividends
- Certificate safekeeping services

▶ **NBD Bancorp, Inc. (NYSE:NBD)**
611 Woodward Ave.
Detroit, MI 48226
(313) 225-1000 (800) 257-1770

Perks:
- DRIP
- Electronic deposit of dividends

Nevada Power Co. (NYSE:NVP)
6226 West Sahara Ave.
Las Vegas, NV 89102
(702) 367-5000

Perks:
- DRIP
- Electronic deposit of dividends
- Customers of the utility may purchase initial shares directly from the firm

New England Electric System (NYSE:NES)
25 Research Drive
Westborough, MA 01582
(508) 366-9011

Perks:
- DRIP
- Certificate safekeeping services
- Electronic deposit of dividends

New Jersey Resources Corp.
  (NYSE:NJR)
1350 Campus Parkway
Wall, NJ 07719
(908) 938-1480

Perks:
- DRIP
- Customers of the utility may purchase initial shares directly from
  the firm

New Plan Realty Trust (NYSE:NPR)
1120 Avenue of the Americas
New York, NY 10036
(212) 869-3000

Perks:
- DRIP
- 5 percent discount on reinvested
  dividends

New York State Electric & Gas Corp.
  (NYSE:NGE)
4500 Vestal Parkway East
Binghamton, NY 13902-3607
(607) 729-2551

Perks:
- DRIP
- Certificate safekeeping services
- Electronic deposit of dividends
- Residents of the state of New York
  may make initial purchases of
  stock directly from the company

▶ New York Times Co. (ASE:NYT.A)
229 W. 43rd St.
New York, NY 10036
(212) 556-1234 (212) 791-6422

Perks:
- DRIP
- Certificate safekeeping services

Newell Co. (NYSE:NWL)
29 E. Stephenson St.
Freeport, IL 61032
(815) 235-4171

Perks:
- DRIP
- Certificate safekeeping services
- Shareholders usually receive a new
  product sample at the annual meet-
  ing (firm markets *Anchor Hocking*
  cookware and *Stuart Hall* and
  Sanford office supplies)

NICOR, Inc. (NYSE:GAS)
1844 Ferry Road
Naperville, IL 60563
(708) 305-9500

Perks:
- DRIP
- Electronic deposit of dividends

Nordson Corp. (NASDAQ:NDSN)
28601 Clemens Rd.
Westlake, OH 44145-1148
(216) 892-1580

Perks:
- DRIP
- Electronic deposit of dividends

▶ Norfolk Southern Corp.
  (NYSE:NSC)
Three Commercial Place
Norfolk, VA 23510-2191
(804) 629-2600

Perks:
- DRIP
- Electronic deposit of dividends

North Carolina Natural Gas Corp.
  (NYSE:NCG)
PO Box 909
Fayetteville, NC 28302-0909
(919) 483-0315

Perks:
- DRIP
- 5 percent discount on reinvested
  dividends
- Electronic deposit of dividends

North Fork Bancorp., Inc. (NYSE:NFB)
9025 Route 25
Mattituck, NY 11952-9339
(516) 298-5000

Perks:
- DRIP
- 5 percent discount on optional cash payments

▶ Northern States Power Co.
  (NYSE:NSP)
414 Nicollet Mall
Minneapolis, MN 55401
(800) 527-4677

Perks:
- DRIP
- Certificate safekeeping services
- Electronic deposit of dividends
- Residents in Minnesota, North Dakota, South Dakota, Wisconsin, and Michigan may purchase initial shares directly from the company

▶ Northern Telecom Ltd. (NYSE:NT)
3 Robert Speck Parkway
Mississauga, Ontario L4Z 3C8
  Canada
(416) 897-9000

Perks:
- DRIP

▶ Novo-Nordisk A/S (NYSE:NVO)
Novo Alle
DK-2880
Bagsvaerd, Denmark
(212) 867-0131

Perks:
- DRIP

▶ Nucor Corp. (NYSE:NUE)
2100 Rexford Rd.
Charlotte, NC 28211
(704) 366-7000 (704) 374-6531

Perks:
- DRIP

NUI Corp. (NYSE:NUI)
PO Box 760
550 Route 202-206
Bedminster, NJ 07921-0706
(908) 781-0500

Perks:
- DRIP
- 5 percent discount on reinvested dividends

▶ NYNEX Corp. (NYSE:NYN)
335 Madison Avenue
New York, NY 10017
(212) 370-7400 (800) 358-1133

Perks:
- DRIP
- Certificate safekeeping services
- Electronic deposit of dividends

Ohio Casualty Corp.
  (NASDAQ:OCAS)
136 N. Third St.
Hamilton, OH 45025-0001
(513) 867-3903

Perks:
- DRIP

Oklahoma Gas & Electric Co.
  (NYSE:OGE)
101 North Robinson
Oklahoma City, OK 73101
(405) 272-3216

Perks:
- DRIP
- Certificate safekeeping services
- Electronic deposit of dividends
- Customers of the utility may buy initial shares directly from the firm

Old National Bancorp (IN)
  (NASDAQ:OLDB)
420 Main Street
Evansville, IN 47708
(812) 464-1200

Perks:
- DRIP
- 3 percent discount on reinvested dividends
- 2½ percent discount on optional cash payments
- Certificate safekeeping services

Oneida Ltd. (NYSE:OCQ)
Kenwood Ave.
Oneida, NY 13421
(315) 361-3636

Perks:
- DRIP
- Electronic deposit of dividends

▶ **Orange & Rockland Utilities, Inc. (NYSE:ORU)**
One Blue Hill Plaza
Pearl River, NY 10965
(914) 352-6000 (914) 577-2512
(914) 577-2457

Perks:
- DRIP
- Electronic deposit of dividends

Otter Tail Power Co. (NASDAQ:OTTR)
215 S. Cascade St.
Fergus Falls, MN 56537
(218) 739-8479

Perks:
- DRIP
- Company gives away several door prizes at the annual shareholders meeting

▶ **Pacific Telesis Group (NYSE:PAC)**
130 Kearny St.
San Francisco, CA 94018
(415) 394-3000 (800) 637-6373

Perks:
- DRIP

- 3½ percent discount on reinvested dividends
- 3½ percent discount on optional cash payments
- Certificate safekeeping services
- Electronic deposit of dividends

PacifiCorp (NYSE:PPW)
700 N.E. Multnomah St.
Portland, OR 97232-4107
(800) 233-5453

Perks:
- DRIP
- Electronic deposit of dividends

▶ **Pall Corp. (NYSE:PLL)**
2200 Northern Blvd.
East Hills, NY 11548
(516) 484-5400 (800) 633-4236

Perks:
- DRIP
- Certificate safekeeping services
- Electronic deposit of dividends

Panhandle Eastern Corp. (NYSE:PEL)
5400 Westheimer Ct.
Houston, TX 77056-5310
(713) 627-5400

Perks:
- DRIP
- Electronic deposit of dividends

▶ **Paramount Communications, Inc. (NYSE:PCI)**
15 Columbus Circle
New York, NY 10023-7780
(212) 373-8100

Perks:
- DRIP
- Certificate safekeeping services

▶ Penney, J.C., Co., Inc. (NYSE:JCP)
6501 Legacy Drive
Plano, TX 75024
(800) 842-9470

Perks:
- DRIP
- Certificate safekeeping services

Pennsylvania Power & Light Co.
(NYSE:PPL)
Two North Ninth St.
Allentown, PA 18101-1179
(800) 345-3085

Perks:
- DRIP
- Certificate safekeeping services
- Electronic deposit of dividends

Pentair, Inc. (NASDAQ:PNTA)
1500 County Road B2
St. Paul, MN 55113-3105
(612) 636-7920

Perks:
- DRIP
- Certificate safekeeping services
- Electronic deposit of dividends

Peoples Energy Corp. (NYSE:PGL)
122 S. Michigan Ave.
Chicago, IL 60603
(312) 431-4292 (800) 228-6888

Perks:
- DRIP
- Certificate safekeeping services
- Electronic deposit of dividends

▶ PepsiCo, Inc. (NYSE:PEP)
700 Anderson Hill Rd.
Purchase, NY 10577
(914) 253-3055

Perks:
- DRIP
- Certificate safekeeping services

Perkin-Elmer Corp. (NYSE:PKN)
761 Main Ave.
Norwalk, CT 06859-0001
(203) 762-1000 (617) 575-2900

Perks:
- DRIP

▶ Pfizer, Inc. (NYSE:PFE)
Shareholders Services
235 E. 42nd St.
New York, NY 10017-5755
(212) 573-3704

Perks:
- DRIP
- Certificate safekeeping services
- Electronic deposit of dividends
- Shareholders who attend the annual meeting usually receive a gift bag with a new consumer product (the company markets *Ben-Gay, Visine, Plax,* and *Burbasol*)

▶ Phelps Dodge Corp.
(NYSE:PD)
2600 N. Central Ave.
Phoenix, AZ 85004-3014
(602) 234-8199 (602) 234-8100

Perks:
- DRIP
- Certificate safekeeping services
- Electronic deposit of dividends

Philadelphia Electric Co.
(NYSE:PE)
2301 Market St.
Philadelphia, PA 19101
(215) 841-4000 (800) 626-8729

Perks:
- DRIP
- Certificate safekeeping services
- Electronic deposit of dividends

Philadelphia Suburban Corp.
 (NYSE:PSC)
762 Lancaster Ave.
Bryn Mawr, PA 19010
(215) 527-8000

Perks:
- DRIP
- 5 percent discount on reinvested dividends
- Customers of the utility periodically have the opportunity to purchase initial shares directly from the firm

▶ Philip Morris Companies, Inc.
 (NYSE:MO)
120 Park Ave.
New York, NY 10017
(212) 880-5000 (800) 442-0077

Perks:
- DRIP
- Certificate safekeeping services
- Electronic deposit of dividends
- Company periodically includes discount coupons in shareholder mailings
- Shareholders who attend the annual meeting usually receive a gift package containing company products (brand names include *Kraft, Jell-O, Birds Eye, Oscar Mayer,* and *Maxwell House*)

Piccadilly Cafeterias, Inc.
 (NASDAQ:PICC)
PO Box 2467
Baton Rouge, LA 70821-2467
(504) 293-9440

Perks:
- DRIP
- 5 percent discount on reinvested dividends
- Electronic deposit of dividends

Piedmont Natural Gas Co., Inc.
 (NYSE:PNY)
1915 Rexford Road
Charlotte, NC 28211
(704) 364-3120

Perks:
- DRIP
- 5 percent discount on reinvested dividends
- Certificate safekeeping services
- Electronic deposit of dividends

Pitney Bowes, Inc. (NYSE:PBI)
World Headquarters
Stamford, CT 06926-0700
(203) 356-5000

Perks:
- DRIP
- Certificate safekeeping services

PMC Capital, Inc. (ASE:PMC)
18301 Biscayne Blvd., 2nd Floor South
North Miami Beach, FL 33160
(305) 933-5858 (800) 937-5499

Perks:
- DRIP
- 2 percent discount on reinvested dividends
- 2 percent discount on optional cash payments

PNC Bank Corp. (NYSE:PNC)
Fifth Avenue & Wood Street
Pittsburgh, PA 15222
(800) 843-2206

Perks:
- DRIP
- Electronic deposit of dividends

Portland General Corp. (NYSE:PGN)
One World Trade Center
121 S.W. Salmon St.
Portland, OR 97204
(503) 464-8820

Perks:
- DRIP
- Certificate safekeeping services

▶ **Potomac Electric Power Co.**
(NYSE:POM)
1900 Pennsylvania Ave., N.W.
Washington, DC 20068
(800) 527-3726

Perks:
- DRIP
- Certificate safekeeping services
- Electronic deposit of dividends

▶ **PPG Industries, Inc. (NYSE:PPG)**
One PPG Place
Pittsburgh, PA 15272
(412) 434-2120 (412) 434-3131

Perks:
- DRIP
- Electronic deposit of dividends

▶ **Premier Industrial Corp. (NYSE:PRE)**
4500 Euclid Ave.
Cleveland, OH 44103-3780
(216) 391-8300

Perks:
- DRIP
- Certificate safekeeping services

Presidential Realty Corp. (ASE:PDL.B)
180 S. Broadway
White Plains, NY 10605
(914) 948-1300

Perks:
- DRIP
- 5 percent discount on reinvested dividends

▶ **Procter & Gamble Co. (NYSE:PG)**
1 Procter & Gamble Plaza
Cincinnati, OH 45202
(513) 983-1100 (800) 742-6253

Perks:
- DRIP
- Electronic deposit of dividends
- The company periodically includes discount coupons in shareholder mailings
- Shareholders who attend the annual meeting usually receive product samples as well as snacks and refreshments

PSI Resources, Inc.
(NYSE:PIN)
1000 East Main St.
Plainfield, IN 46168
(317) 839-9611 (800) 446-2617

Perks:
- DRIP
- Certificate safekeeping services

Public Service Co. of Colorado
(NYSE:PSR)
1225 17th St., Suite 300
Denver, CO 80202
(303) 571-7511

Perks:
- DRIP
- 3 percent discount on reinvested dividends
- Certificate safekeeping services
- Electronic deposit of dividends

Public Service Co. of North
Carolina, Inc. (NASDAQ:PSNC)
Dividend Reinvestment Service
PO Box 1398
Gastonia, NC 28053-1398
(704) 864-6731

Perks:
- DRIP
- 5 percent discount on reinvested dividends

Public Service Enterprise Group, Inc. (NYSE:PEG)
80 Park Plaza
Newark, NJ 07101
(800) 526-8050

Perks:
- DRIP
- Electronic deposit of dividends

Puget Sound Power & Light Co. (NYSE:PSD)
PO Box 97034
Bellevue, WA 98009-9734
(206) 454-6363

Perks:
- DRIP
- Electronic deposit of dividends
- Customers of the utility may purchase initial shares directly from the firm

▶ **Quaker Oats Co. (NYSE:OAT)**
Quaker Tower
321 North Clark St.
Chicago, IL 60610
(312) 222-7111 (312) 222-7818

Perks:
- DRIP
- Certificate safekeeping services
- Electronic deposit of dividends
- New shareholders receive a packet of discount coupons. Company also periodically includes discount coupons in shareholder mailings

▶ **Ralston Purina Co. (NYSE:RAL)**
Checkerboard Square
St. Louis, MO 63164
(314) 982-1000

Perks:
- DRIP

- Certificate safekeeping services
- Shareholders are eligible for discounts on accommodations, lift tickets, and ski lessons at the company's Keystone Resort in Keystone, CO

▶ **Raytheon Co. (NYSE:RTN)**
141 Spring St.
Lexington, MA 02173
(617) 862-6600 (617) 575-2900

Perks:
- DRIP
- Certificate safekeeping services

Right Start, Inc. (NASDAQ:RTST)
Right Start Plaza
5334 Sterling Center Drive
Westlake Village, CA 91361
(818) 707-7100

Perks:
- Company periodically includes special deals or product discounts in shareholder mailings, especially the annual report

▶ **Rite Aid Corp. (NYSE:RAD)**
30 Hunter Lane
Camp Hill, PA 17011
(717) 761-2633 (212) 701-7608

Perks:
- DRIP

▶ **Roadway Services, Inc. (NASDAQ:ROAD)**
1077 Gorge Blvd.
PO Box 88
Akron, OH 44309-0088
(216) 384-8184

Perks:
- DRIP

▶ **Rochester Telephone Corp.**
  (NYSE:RTC)
  180 South Clinton Ave.
  Rochester, NY 14646-0700
  (716) 777-1000

  Perks:
  ▪ DRIP
  ▪ Certificate safekeeping services

Rockwell International Corp.
  (NYSE:ROK)
  625 Liberty Ave.
  Pittsburgh, PA 15222-3123
  (412) 565-7120 (412) 236-8000

  Perks:
  ▪ DRIP

▶ **Rollins, Inc. (NYSE:ROL)**
  2170 Piedmont Rd., N.E.
  Atlanta, GA 30324
  (404) 888-2000

  Perks:
  ▪ DRIP

▶ **RPM, Inc. (NASDAQ:RPOW)**
  PO Box 777
  Medina, OH 44258
  (216) 225-3192 (216) 737-5745

  Perks:
  ▪ DRIP

▶ **Rubbermaid, Inc.**
  (NYSE:RBD)
  1147 Akron Rd.
  Wooster, OH 44691
  (216) 264-6464

  Perks:
  ▪ DRIP
  ▪ Certificate safekeeping services
  ▪ Shareholders receive three free passes to shop at the employee store located at the company's headquarters

▶ **Russell Corp. (NYSE:RML)**
  1 Lee Street
  Alexander City, AL 35010
  (205) 329-4832

  Perks:
  ▪ DRIP

Ryder System, Inc. (NYSE:R)
  3600 NW 82nd Ave.
  Miami, FL 33166
  (305) 593-3726 (212) 791-6422

  Perks:
  ▪ DRIP
  ▪ Certificate safekeeping services

▶ **Safety-Kleen Corp. (NYSE:SK)**
  777 Big Timber Rd.
  Elgin, IL 60123
  (708) 697-8460

  Perks:
  ▪ DRIP

St. Paul Companies, Inc.
  (NYSE:SPC)
  385 Washington St.
  St. Paul, MN 55102
  (612) 221-7911

  Perks:
  ▪ DRIP
  ▪ Certificate safekeeping services

Salomon, Inc. (NYSE:SB)
  7 World Trade Center
  New York, NY 10048
  (800) 772-7865 (212) 791-6422

  Perks:
  ▪ DRIP

▶ **San Diego Gas & Electric Co.**
  (NYSE:SDO)
  101 Ash St.
  San Diego, CA 92101
  (800) 522-6645 (619) 696-2020

Perks:
- DRIP
- Certificate safekeeping services
- Customers of the utility may purchase initial shares directly from the firm

Santa Anita Companies (NYSE:SAR)
333 City Blvd. West, Suite 2100
Orange, CA 92613-1560
(714) 634-7575

Perks:
- Shareholders of 100 or more shares receive 30 complimentary Club House admission tickets each year; shareholders with fewer than 100 shares receive six free tickets

▶ **Sara Lee Corp. (NYSE:SLE)**
3 First National Plaza
Chicago, IL 60602-4602
(312) 726-2600

Perks:
- DRIP
- Certificate safekeeping services
- Shareholders who attend the annual meeting usually receive a bag of the company's products (brand names include *Ball Park, Sara Lee, Hanes, L'eggs, Sheer Energy, Playtex,* and *Kiwi*)

SCANA Corp. (NYSE:SCG)
1426 Main Street
Columbia, SC 29201
(803) 748-3669 (800) 763-5891

Perks:
- DRIP
- Certificate safekeeping services
- Permits first-time purchases of stock directly for residents in 44 states

▶ **SCEcorp (NYSE:SCE)**
2244 Walnut Grove Avenue
Rosemead, CA 91770
(800) 347-8625

Perks:
- DRIP
- Certificate safekeeping services

▶ **Schering-Plough Corp.**
(NYSE:SGP)
One Giralda Farms
Madison, NJ 07940-1000
(201) 822-7000 (800) 524-4458

Perks:
- DRIP
- Certificate safekeeping services

▶ **Scott Paper Co. (NYSE:SPP)**
Scott Plaza
Philadelphia, PA 19113
(215) 522-5942 (212) 791-6422

Perks:
- DRIP
- The company makes available to shareholders, for a reduced price, a special holiday gift box of products

Sears, Roebuck & Co.
(NYSE:S)
3333 Beverly Road
Hoffman Estates, IL 60179
(312) 875-2500 (212) 791-3357

Perks:
- DRIP
- Certificate safekeeping services

Shawmut National Corp.
(NYSE:SNC)
777 Main Street
Hartford, CT 06115
(203) 728-2000

Perks:
- DRIP
- 3 percent discount on optional cash payments
- Certificate safekeeping services

▶ **Sherwin-Williams Co.**
   (NYSE:SHW)
   101 Prospect Ave., N.W.
   Cleveland, OH 44115-1075
   (216) 566-2000 (216) 566-2140

   Perks:
   - DRIP
   - Certificate safekeeping services

Signet Banking Corp. (NYSE:SBK)
7 North Eighth St.
Richmond, VA 23219
(800) 451-7392 (804) 747-2000

Perks:
- DRIP
- 5 percent discount on reinvested dividends

SmithKline Beecham Plc (NYSE:SBE)
New Horizons Court
Brentford
Middlesex TW8 9EP, England
(800) 428-4237

Perks:
- DRIP
- Certificate safekeeping services

▶ **Smucker, J.M., Co. (NYSE:SJMA)**
   Strawberry Lane
   Orrville, OH 44667-0280
   (216) 682-3000 (800) 622-6757

   Perks:
   - DRIP
   - Certificate safekeeping services
   - Shareholders who attend the annual meeting usually receive a gift package consisting of three or four new products and spreads

▶ **South Jersey Industries, Inc.**
   (NYSE:SJI)
   One S. Jersey Plaza, Route 54
   Folsom, NJ 08037
   (609) 561-9000

Perks:
- DRIP
- 3 percent discount on reinvested dividends
- 3 percent discount on optional cash payments

Southeastern Michigan Gas
Enterprises, Inc. (NASDAQ:SMGS)
405 Water St.
Port Huron, MI 48060
(313) 987-2200

Perks:
- DRIP
- Certificate safekeeping services

Southern California Water Co.
(NASDAQ:SWTR)
630 E. Foothill Blvd.
San Dimas, CA 91773
(714) 394-3600

Perks:
- DRIP

▶ **Southern Indiana Gas & Electric**
   Co. (NYSE:SIG)
   20 N.W. 4th St.
   Evansville, IN 47741-0001
   (812) 464-4553 (812) 424-6411

   Perks:
   - DRIP

▶ **Southern New England**
   Telecommunications Corp.
   (NYSE:SNG)
   227 Church Street
   New Haven, CT 06510
   (800) 243-1110

   Perks:
   - DRIP

SouthTrust Corp. (NASDAQ:SOTR)
420 N. 20th St., 34th Floor
Birmingham, AL 35203
(205) 254-5509

Perks:
- DRIP

Southwest Gas Corp.
 (NYSE:SWX)
5241 Spring Mountain Rd.
Las Vegas, NV 89193
(702) 876-7252

Perks:
- DRIP
- Certificate safekeeping services
- Customers of the utility may purchase initial shares directly from the firm

Southwest Water Co.
 (NASDAQ:SWWC)
16340 E. Maplegrove St.
La Puente, CA 91744-1399
(818) 918-1231

Perks:
- DRIP
- 5 percent discount on reinvested dividends
- Certificate safekeeping services

▶ **Southwestern Bell Corp.**
 (NYSE:SBC)
One Bell Center
St. Louis, MO 63101-3099
(314) 235-9800

Perks:
- DRIP
- Certificate safekeeping services

Southwestern Electric Service Co.
 (NASDAQ:SWEL)
1717 Main St., Suite 3300
Dallas, TX 75201
(214) 741-3125

Perks:
- DRIP
- 5 percent discount on reinvested dividends

Southwestern Public Service Co.
 (NYSE:SPS)
Tyler at 6th
PO Box 1261
Amarillo, TX 79101
(806) 378-2841

Perks:
- DRIP

▶ **Sprint Corp. (NYSE:FON)**
2330 Shawnee Mission Pkwy.
Westwood, KS 66205
(913) 624-3000

Perks:
- DRIP

Standex International Corp.
 (NYSE:SXI)
6 Manor Parkway
Salem, NH 03079
(603) 893-9701

Perks:
- DRIP

Stanhome, Inc. (NYSE:STH)
333 Western Ave.
Westfield, MA 01085
(800) 628-1918 (413) 562-3631

Perks:
- DRIP
- Certificate safekeeping services
- Shareholders who attend the annual meeting usually receive a gift bag of the company's products (the firm markets giftware, including *Precious Moments* collectibles)

Stride Rite Corp. (NYSE:SRR)
5 Cambridge Center
Cambridge, MA 02142
(617) 491-8800 (617) 575-2900

Perks:
- DRIP
- Certificate safekeeping services

Suffolk Bancorp (NASDAQ:SUBK)
6 West 2nd St.
Riverhead, NY 11901
(516) 727-5667

Perks:
- DRIP
- 3 percent discount on reinvested dividends
- 3 percent discount on optional cash payments

Summit Bancorporation (NJ)
  (NASDAQ:SUBN)
1 Main Street
Chatham, NJ 07928
(201) 701-2666

Perks:
- DRIP
- 3½ percent discount on reinvested dividends
- 3½ percent discount on optional cash payments

Supervalu, Inc. (NYSE:SVU)
11840 Valley View Road
Eden Prairie, MN 55344
(612) 828-4000

Perks:
- DRIP
- Electronic deposit of dividends
- Shareholders who attend the annual meeting usually receive a gift bag of products "unique to Supervalu"

Synovus Financial Corp.
  (NYSE:SNV)
Corporate Trust Dept.
PO Box 120
Columbus, GA 31902
(706) 649-2387

Perks:
- DRIP
- Electronic deposit of dividends

▶ **Tambrands, Inc. (NYSE:TMB)**
777 Westchester Ave.
White Plains, NY 10604
(914) 696-6000 (800) 446-2617

Perks:
- DRIP
- Certificate safekeeping services

Tandy Corp. (NYSE:TAN)
1800 One Tandy Center
Fort Worth, TX 76102
(817) 390-3700

Perks:
- Around the Christmas holiday, shareholders receive a 10 percent discount on purchases up to $10,000 at *Radio Shack* stores

▶ **TECO Energy, Inc. (NYSE:TE)**
702 N. Franklin St.
Tampa, FL 33602
(813) 228-4111

Perks:
- DRIP
- Certificate safekeeping services

Telephone & Data Systems, Inc.
  (ASE:TDS)
30 North LaSalle St.
Chicago, IL 60602
(312) 461-2339

Perks:
- DRIP
- 5 percent discount on reinvested dividends

▶ **Texaco, Inc. (NYSE:TX)**
2000 Westchester Ave.
White Plains, NY 10650
(914) 253-4000 (800) 283-9785

Perks:
- DRIP
- Certificate safekeeping services

- First-time purchases of stock may be made directly from the company
- Shareholders may buy stock for friends or family under the company's convenient "gift membership" plan

Texas Utilities Co. (NYSE:TXU)
1506 Commerce St., 12 West
Dallas, TX 75201
(800) 828-0812

Perks:
- DRIP
- 5 percent discount on reinvested dividends
- Certificate safekeeping services

► **Thomas & Betts Corp. (NYSE:TNB)**
1001 Frontier Rd.
Bridgewater, NJ 08807-0993
(908) 685-1600

Perks:
- DRIP
- Certificate safekeeping services

► **Time Warner, Inc. (NYSE:TWX)**
75 Rockefeller Plaza
New York, NY 10019
(212) 484-8000

Perks:
- DRIP
- 5 percent discount on reinvested dividends
- Certificate safekeeping services

Timken Co. (NYSE:TKR)
1835 Dueber Ave. S.W.
Canton, OH 44706-2798
(216) 471-3376

Perks:
- DRIP
- 5 percent discount on reinvested dividends

Toro Co. (NYSE:TTC)
8111 Lyndale Ave. South
Bloomington, MN 55420
(612) 888-8801

Perks:
- DRIP
- Certificate safekeeping services

Transamerica Corp. (NYSE:TA)
600 Montgomery St.
San Francisco, CA 94111
(415) 983-4000 (800) 446-2617

Perks:
- DRIP
- Certificate safekeeping services

TransCanada PipeLines Ltd.
 (NYSE:TRP)
PO Box 1000
Station M
TransCanada Tower
Calgary, Alberta T2P 4K5 Canada
(403) 267-6100 (403) 267-6555

Perks:
- DRIP
- 5 percent discount on reinvested dividends

► **Tribune Co. (NYSE:TRB)**
 435 North Michigan Ave.
 Chicago, IL 60611
 (312) 222-9100

Perks:
- DRIP
- Certificate safekeeping services
- Company tour

TRW, Inc. (NYSE:TRW)
1900 Richmond Rd.
Cleveland, OH 44124
(800) 442-2001 (216) 291-7000

Perks:
- DRIP
- Certificate safekeeping services

UGI Corp. (NYSE:UGI)
PO Box 858
Valley Forge, PA 19482
(215) 337-1000

Perks:
- DRIP
- 5 percent discount on reinvested dividends
- Certificate safekeeping services

Union Bank (NASDAQ:UBNK)
350 California St.
San Francisco, CA 94104
(415) 445-0200 (213) 239-0672

Perks:
- DRIP
- 5 percent discount on reinvested dividends

Union Electric Co. (NYSE:UEP)
1901 Chouteau Ave.
St. Louis, MO 63103
(314) 621-3222

Perks:
- DRIP
- Certificate safekeeping services
- Customers of the utility may purchase initial shares directly from the firm

► Union Pacific Corp.
(NYSE:UNP)
Martin Tower
Eighth and Eaton Aves.
Bethlehem, PA 18018
(212) 791-6422 (215) 861-3200

Perks:
- DRIP
- Certificate safekeeping services

Union Planters Corp. (NYSE:UPC)
7130 Goodlett Farms Parkway
Cordova, TN 38018
(901) 383-6000 (800) 238-5028

Perks:
- DRIP
- 5 percent discount on reinvested dividends

United Cities Gas Co.
(NASDAQ:UCIT)
5300 Maryland Way
Brentwood, TN 37027
(615) 373-0104

Perks:
- DRIP
- 5 percent discount on reinvested dividends

U.S. Bancorp (NASDAQ:USBC)
111 Southwest 5th Ave.
U.S. Bancorp Tower
Portland, OR 97204
(503) 275-6472

Perks:
- DRIP
- Electronic deposit of dividends

► United Water Resources, Inc.
(NYSE:UWR)
200 Old Hook Rd.
Harrington Park, NJ 07640
(201) 784-9434

Perks:
- DRIP
- 5 percent discount on reinvested dividends
- 5 percent discount on optional cash payments
- Certificate safekeeping services
- The company's customers may make first-time purchases of stock directly

► Universal Corp. (NYSE:UVV)
1501 N. Hamilton Street
Richmond, VA 23230
(804) 359-9311 (804) 254-1303

Perks:
- DRIP

Universal Foods Corp. (NYSE:UFC)
433 E. Michigan St.
Milwaukee, WI 53202
(414) 271-6755

Perks:
- DRIP
- Shareholders who attend the annual meeting usually receive a new product sample

UNUM Corp. (NYSE:UNM)
2211 Congress St.
Portland, ME 04122
(207) 770-2211

Perks:
- DRIP
- Certificate safekeeping services

Upjohn Co. (NYSE:UPJ)
7000 Portage Rd.
Kalamazoo, MI 49001
(800) 253-8600 (800) 323-1849

Perks:
- DRIP
- Certificate safekeeping services

USF&G Corp. (NYSE:FG)
100 Light St.
Baltimore, MD 21202
(410) 547-3000

Perks:
- DRIP
- Certificate safekeeping services

▶ **UST, Inc. (NYSE:UST)**
  100 W. Putnam Ave.
  Greenwich, CT 06830
  (203) 622-3656

  Perks:
  - DRIP
  - Certificate safekeeping services

- Shareholders who attend the annual meeting usually receive a grab bag of the company's products (*Skoal* smokeless tobacco and key chains with the company emblem)

▶ **U S West, Inc. (NYSE:USW)**
  7800 East Orchard Road
  Englewood, CO 80111
  (303) 793-6500 (800) 537-0222

  Perks:
  - DRIP
  - Certificate safekeeping services
  - The company offers a continuous odd-lot buyback program for owners of fewer than 100 shares. The firm charges a fee of $6 plus $0.06 per share sold

UtiliCorp United, Inc. (NYSE:UCU)
Dividend Reinvestment
PO Box 13287
Kansas City, MO 64199-3287
(816) 421-6600

Perks:
- DRIP
- 5 percent discount on reinvested dividends

▶ **V.F. Corp. (NYSE:VFC)**
  1047 North Park Road
  Wyomissing, PA 19610
  (212) 791-6422 (215) 378-1151

  Perks:
  - DRIP
  - Certificate safekeeping services
  - The company periodically gives fashion shows, featuring its clothing lines (*Lee, Girbaud,* and *Wrangler* jeans, *Bassett-Walker* and *Jantzen* activewear, *Red Kap* and *Big Ben* occupational apparel, and *Vanity Fair* intimate apparel) at the annual meeting

▶ **Wachovia Corp. (NYSE:WB)**
301 North Main St.
Winston-Salem, NC 27150
(919) 770-5787

Perks:
- DRIP
- Certificate safekeeping services

▶ **Wal-Mart Stores, Inc.
(NYSE:WMT)**
702 Southwest 8th St.
Bentonville, AR 72716
(501) 273-4000

Perks:
- Company museum (the first store that shared Sam Walton's name)

▶ **Walgreen Co. (NYSE:WAG)**
200 Wilmot Rd.
Deerfield, IL 60015
(312) 461-5535

Perks:
- DRIP
- Certificate safekeeping services
- Attendees to the company's 1993 annual meeting received free admission to the Art Institute of Chicago

▶ **Warner-Lambert Co.
(NYSE:WLA)**
201 Tabor Rd.
Morris Plains, NJ 07950
(201) 540-2000 (212) 791-6422

Perks:
- DRIP
- Certificate safekeeping services

**Washington National Corp.
(NYSE:WNT)**
1630 Chicago Ave.
Evanston, IL 60201
(708) 570-5500

Perks:
- DRIP
- 5 percent discount on reinvested dividends

▶ **Washington Real Estate
Investment Trust (ASE:WRE)**
4936 Fairmont Ave.
Bethesda, MD 20814
(301) 652-4300

Perks:
- DRIP

▶ **Weis Markets, Inc.
(NYSE:WMK)**
1000 S. Second St.
Sunbury, PA 17801
(717) 286-4571

Perks:
- DRIP

Wells Fargo & Co. (NYSE:WFC)
420 Montgomery St.
San Francisco, CA 94163
(415) 477-1000 (415) 399-7535

Perks:
- DRIP
- Certificate safekeeping services
- Company museum featuring western memorabilia, including some of the firm's famous Wells Fargo stage wagons

**Wendy's International, Inc.
(NYSE:WEN)**
4288 West Dublin-Granville Rd.
Dublin, OH 43017
(614) 764-3100

Perks:
- DRIP
- Certificate safekeeping services
- Company periodically includes discount coupons in shareholder mailings

Westcoast Energy, Inc.
 (NYSE: WE)
1333 West Georgia St.
Vancouver, BC V6E 3K9 Canada
(604) 691-5500

Perks:
- DRIP
- 5 percent discount on reinvested dividends

▶ **Weyerhaeuser Co. (NYSE:WY)**
 33663 Weyerhaeuser Way South
 Federal Way, WA 98003
 (206) 924-2345

   Perks:
   - DRIP
   - Certificate safekeeping services

▶ **Whirlpool Corp. (NYSE:WHR)**
 Administrative Center
 2000 M-63
 Benton Harbor, MI 49022
 (616) 926-5000 (312) 461-2544

   Perks:
   - DRIP

Whitman Corp. (NYSE:WH)
3501 Algonquin Road
Rolling Meadows, IL 60008
(708) 818-5000

Perks:
- DRIP
- Certificate safekeeping services

WICOR, Inc. (NYSE:WIC)
626 E. Wisconsin Ave.
Milwaukee, WI 53202
(414) 291-7026

Perks:
- DRIP
- Residents of Wisconsin may make first-time purchases directly from the company

▶ **Winn-Dixie Stores, Inc. (NYSE:WIN)**
 PO Box B
 5050 Edgewood Ct.
 Jacksonville, FL 32203-0297
 (904) 783-5000

Perks:
- DRIP
- The company pays dividends monthly rather than quarterly

▶ **Wisconsin Energy Corp. (NYSE:WEC)**
 231 West Michigan St.
 Milwaukee, WI 53201
 (414) 221-2345

Perks:
- DRIP
- Certificate safekeeping services
- Residents of Wisconsin may purchase initial shares directly from the firm

▶ **WMX Technologies (NYSE:WMX)**
 3003 Butterfield Rd.
 Oak Brook, IL 60521
 (708) 572-8800

Perks:
- DRIP
- Certificate safekeeping services

▶ **Worthington Industries, Inc.**
 (NASDAQ:WTHG)
 1205 Dearborn Drive
 Columbus, OH 43085
 (614) 438-3210 (800) 442-2001

Perks:
- DRIP
- Certificate safekeeping services

▶ **WPL Holdings, Inc. (NYSE:WPH)**
 222 W. Washington Ave.
 Madison, WI 53703
 (800) 356-5343 (800) 622-2258

Perks:
- DRIP
- Certificate safekeeping services

▶ **Wrigley, William, Jr. Co.**
   (NYSE:WWY)
   410 North Michigan Ave.
   Chicago, IL 60611
   (312) 644-2121

   Perks:
   - DRIP
   - Certificate safekeeping services
   - Shareholders are sent a box of 20 packs (100 sticks) of the company's chewing gum each year

York Financial Corp.
(NASDAQ:YFED)
PO Box 15068
101 S. George St.
York, PA 17405-7068
(717) 846-8777

Perks:
- DRIP
- 10 percent discount on reinvested dividends

▶ **Zurn Industries, Inc.**
   (NYSE:ZRN)
   One Zurn Place
   Erie, PA 16514-2000
   (814) 452-2111

   Perks:
   - DRIP
   - Certificate safekeeping services

References

Chapter One

Better Investing, September 1992.

Exxon Corporation Dividend Reinvestment Prospectus, February 3, 1992.

Investor's Business Daily, June 3, 1992.

Investor's Business Daily, September 30, 1992.

Philadelphia Business Journal, February 22–28, 1993.

The Wall Street Journal, March 11, 1992.

The Wall Street Journal, March 3, 1993.

Chapter Two

Bill Staton's Money Advisory, December 9, 1992.

Forbes, June 22, 1992.

Fortune, March 8, 1993.

Kiplinger's Personal Finance Magazine, February 1993.

Kiplinger's Personal Finance Magazine, December 1992.

Kiplinger's Personal Finance Magazine, May 1992.

Money, May 1992.

Shareholder Freebies by Eamonn Fingleton and Roland Turner.

The Wall Street Journal, June 23, 1992.

Chapter Three

100% No-Load Mutual Fund Investment Guide and Member Fund Directory, 1993.

5-Star Investor, October 1992.

Barron's, July 13, 1992.

Business Week, August 17, 1992.

Business Week, August 24, 1992.

Buying Treasury Securities at Federal Reserve Banks, 15th ed., December 1990.

Donoghue's MONEYLETTER, July 1992.

Dow Jones and Co. 1991 Annual Report.

Exxon Corporation Dividend Reinvestment Prospectus, February 3, 1992.

Forbes, June 8, 1992.

Individual Investor, December 1992.

Individual Investor, August 1992.

Investor's Business Daily, April 24, 1992.

Investor's Business Daily, August 1, 1990.

Investor's Business Daily, May 26, 1992.

Investor's Business Daily, July 15, 1992.

Kiplinger's Personal Finance Magazine, September 1992.

Kiplinger's Personal Finance Magazine, August 1992.

Kiplinger's Personal Finance Magazine, October 1992.

McDonald's Third-Quarter Report (1991).

Money, October 1991.

Money, July 1992.

NACHA/S&P Electronic Deposit of Dividends Report.

New York Times, August 4, 1992.

Philadelphia Inquirer, May 15, 1992.

The New York Times, August 4, 1992.

The Wall Street Journal, September 29, 1992.

The Wall Street Journal, September 24, 1992.

The Wall Street Journal, July 15, 1992.

The Wall Street Journal, March 5, 1992.

The Wall Street Journal, May 18, 1992.

The Wall Street Journal, May 1, 1991.

U S West, 1991 Annual Report.

Worth, August/September 1992.

Chapter Four   •

Barron's, July 27, 1992.

Barron's, December 28, 1992.

Barron's, March 23, 1992.

Boardroom Reports, August 1, 1992.

Business Week, July 27, 1992.

Business Week, January 25, 1993.

Business Week, October 19, 1992.

Business Week, September 28, 1992.

Business Week, November 2, 1992.

Consumers Digest, November/December 1992.

Consumers Digest, September/October 1991.

Donoghue's MONEYLETTER, September 1992.

Donoghue's MONEYLETTER, October 1992.

Forbes, February 15, 1993.

Forbes, January 4, 1993.

Forbes, June 22, 1992.

Fortune 1993 Investor's Guide.

FW, May 12, 1992.

FW, November 10, 1992.

Information from the American Arbitration Association.

Investor's Business Daily, December 3, 1992.

Investor's Business Daily, September 28, 1992.

Investor's Business Daily, October 29, 1992.

Kiplinger's Personal Finance Magazine, April 1993.

Kiplinger's Personal Finance Magazine, January 1988.

Money, September 1992.

Money, June 1992.

Money, December 1992.

Newsweek, February 1, 1988.

Personal Finance, June 10, 1992.

Smart Money, February 1993.

St. Petersburg Times, November 16, 1992.

Sylvia Porter's Personal Finance, September 1987.

The New York Times, February 20, 1993.

The New York Times, May 12, 1992.

The New York Times, May 1, 1992.

The Wall Street Journal, April 30, 1992.

The Wall Street Journal, April 6, 1992.

The Wall Street Journal, December 24, 1992.

The Wall Street Journal, June 19, 1992.

The Wall Street Journal, March 16, 1992.

The Wall Street Journal, February 20, 1992.

The Wall Street Journal, July 15, 1991.

The Wall Street Journal, February 14, 1992.

The Wall Street Journal, April 21, 1992.

The Wall Street Journal, April 27, 1992.

The Wall Street Journal, March 5, 1992.

The Wall Street Journal, January 7, 1993.

The Wall Street Journal, May 19, 1992.

The Wall Street Journal, January 11, 1993.

The Wall Street Journal, August 7, 1992.

The Wall Street Journal, September 18, 1992.

Worth, August/September 1992.

Worth, April/May 1992.

Chapter Five

1992 Hay/Huggins Benefits Report.

Business Week, July 27, 1992.

Business Week, December 14, 1992.

Chicago Tribune, December 7, 1992.

Forbes, July 20, 1992.

FW, September 15, 1992.

Individual Investor, August 1992.

Investor's Business Daily, December 3, 1992.

Journal of Financial Economics 23, 1989.

Journal of Financial Economics 6, 1978.

The Wall Street Journal, December 4, 1992.

The Wall Street Journal, December 2, 1992.

The Wall Street Journal, August 4, 1992.

The Wall Street Journal, December 16, 1992.

The Wall Street Journal, December 3, 1992.

The Wall Street Journal, December 2, 1992.

Chapter Six

AAII Journal, October 1992.

Barron's, December 28, 1992.

Better Investing, August 1992.

Boardroom Reports, December 15, 1992.

Business Week, February 8, 1993.

Business Week, Reinventing America 1992.

Business Week, May 11, 1992.

Business Week, November 2, 1992.

Business Week, March 15, 1993.

Chicago Sun-Times, April 12, 1992.

Chicago Tribune, November 26, 1992.

Chicago Tribune, November 30, 1992.

Chicago Tribune, January 1, 1993.

Forbes, February 15, 1993.

Forbes, June 22, 1992.

Fortune, November 16, 1992.

Fortune, January 11, 1993.

H.J. Heinz Company, Fiscal First Quarter 1993.

Investor's Business Daily, September 21, 1992.

Investor's Business Daily, September 2, 1992.

Investor's Business Daily, June 23, 1992.

Investor's Business Daily, July 8, 1992.

Investor's Business Daily, September 6, 1992.

Investor's Business Daily, October 16, 1992.

Investor's Business Daily, January 22, 1993.

Investor's Business Daily, June 10, 1992.

Investor's Business Daily, December 24, 1992.

Investor's Business Daily, November 3, 1992.

Investor's Business Daily, November 9, 1992.

Investor's Business Daily, December 28, 1992.

Investor's Business Daily, November 30, 1992.

Kiplinger's Personal Finance Magazine, December 1992.

Kiplinger's Personal Finance Magazine, May 1992.

McDonald's 1992 First Quarter Report.

Money, July 1992.

The New York Times, September 18, 1992.

The Economist, July 4, 1992.

The Georgeson Report, Second Quarter 1992.

The 100 Best Stocks to Own in America (Dearborn), by Gene Walden.

The Quaker Oats Company, First Quarter Fiscal 1993.

The Right Start, Inc., 1992 Annual Report.

The Right Start, Inc., Prospectus, October 11, 1991.

The Wall Street Journal, February 2, 1993.

The Wall Street Journal, December 3, 1992.

The Wall Street Journal, October 9, 1992.

The Wall Street Journal, October 5, 1992.

The Wall Street Journal, September 1, 1992.

The Wall Street Journal, September 21, 1992.

The Wall Street Journal, August 27, 1992.

The Wall Street Journal, June 18, 1992.

The Wall Street Journal, April 27, 1992.

The Wall Street Journal, January 22, 1993.

The Wall Street Journal, July 24, 1992.

The Wall Street Journal, September 22, 1992.

The Wall Street Journal, November 3, 1992.

The Wall Street Journal, May 21, 1992.

The Wall Street Journal, June 5, 1992.

The Wall Street Journal, June 8, 1992.

The Wall Street Journal, May 15, 1992.

The Wall Street Journal, November 23, 1992.

The Wall Street Journal, October 30, 1992.

The Wall Street Journal, October 28, 1992.

The Wall Street Journal, May 11, 1992.

The Wall Street Journal, December 9, 1992.

The Wall Street Journal, September 3, 1992.

The Wall Street Journal, January 21, 1993.

The Wall Street Journal, October 1, 1992.

The Wall Street Journal, October 16, 1992.

The Wall Street Journal, December 4, 1992.

The Wall Street Journal, January 29, 1993.

Worth, October/November 1992.

Chapter Seven

Business Week, August 10, 1992.

Forbes, October 26, 1992.

Fortune, January 11, 1993.

Fortune, January 27, 1992.

Kiplinger's Personal Finance Magazine, May 1992.

The New York Times, April 27, 1992.

The New York Times, September 11, 1992.

Norwest Modernism Pamphlet.

The Wall Street Journal, April 10, 1992.

The Wall Street Journal, July 15, 1992.

The Wall Street Journal, July 28, 1992.

Touring America, June 1992.

Chapter Eight

Abbott Laboratories, First Quarter Report 1992.

American Federal Community Reinvestment Act Statement, 1992.

AT&T Annual Report 1991.

Barron's, July 27, 1992.

Business Week, November 2, 1992.

Business Week, October 19, 1992.

Chicago Sun Times, December 20, 1992.

Chicago Tribune, January 14, 1993.

Companies With a Conscience (Birch Lane Press), by Mary Scott and Howard Rothman.

Environmental Business Journal, August 1992.

Exxon Education Foundation Report, 1991.

Forbes, November 9, 1992.

Forbes, March 29, 1993.

Fortune, November 16, 1992.

Fortune, February 8, 1993.

FW, September 1, 1992.

Inc., April 1992.

Individual Investor, October 1992.

Investing from the Heart (Crown), by Jack A. Brill and Alan Reder.

Investing with Your Conscience (Wiley), by John C. Harrington.

Investor's Business Daily, October 21, 1992.

Investor's Business Daily, July 22, 1992.

Investor's Business Daily, June 25, 1992.

Investor's Business Daily, December 28, 1992.

Kiplinger's Personal Finance Magazine, September 1992.

Kiplinger's Personal Finance Magazine, January 1993.

McDonald's Fourth Quarter Report.

PepsiCo Support Education Programs.

Personal Investing News, March/April 1992.

Sears 1991 Annual Report.

The Clean Yield Newsletter, February 1993.

The Clean Yield Newsletter, March 1993.

The New York Times, September 9, 1992.

The Wall Street Journal, December 24, 1992.

The Wall Street Journal, October 5, 1992.

The Wall Street Journal, April 20, 1992.

The Wall Street Journal, February 11, 1993.

The Wall Street Journal, July 7, 1992.

The Wall Street Journal, November 20, 1992.

The Wall Street Journal, April 6, 1992.

The Wall Street Journal, July 16, 1992.

The Wall Street Journal, July 8, 1992.

The Wall Street Journal, November 19, 1992.

The Wall Street Journal, July 15, 1992.

The Wall Street Journal, September 30, 1992.

USA Today, January 19, 1993.

Worth, October/November 1992.

Worth, April/May 1992.

Chapter Nine

Bill Staton's Money Advisory, February 17, 1993.

Bottom Line Personal, October 15, 1992.

Business Week, July 20, 1992.

Business Week, August 3, 1992.

Consumers Digest, November/December 1992.

Forbes, March 29, 1993.

Forbes, January 18, 1993.

Forbes, August 17, 1992.

Forbes, June 22, 1992.

Kiplinger's Personal Finance Magazine, March 1993.

Kiplinger's Personal Finance Magazine, January 1993.

Kiplinger's Personal Finance Magazine, February 1993.

Mercantile Pathfinders Travelogue, 1993.

Money, August 1992.

Money, November 1992.

Money, Forecast 1993.

Money, January 1993.

Naisbitt Trend Letter, June 25, 1992.

National Association of Unclaimed Property Administrators Information Pamphlet.

St. Petersburg Times, November 16, 1992.

The Bull & Bear, October 1991.

The Dolans' *Straight Talk on Your Money*, December 1992.

The Moneypaper, July 1991.

The Wall Street Journal, February 18, 1992.

The Wall Street Journal, November 24, 1992.

The Wall Street Journal, January 19, 1993.

The Wall Street Journal, December 10, 1992.

The Wall Street Journal, November 11, 1992.

The Wall Street Journal, January 7, 1993.

The Wall Street Journal, November 23, 1992.

The Wall Street Journal, April 6, 1992.

USA Today, December 14, 1992.

Chapter Ten

AAII Journal, November 1992.

Business Week, December 7, 1992.

Kiplinger's Personal Finance Magazine, October 1992.

Money, November 1992.

Paul Merriman's Fund Exchange, October 1992.

The Moneypaper, November 1992.

The Wall Street Journal, November 20, 1992.

Worth, August/September 1992.

Index

Note: The *f.* after a page number refers to a figure.

About the Author

Charles B. Carlson is editor of *Dow Theory Forecasts*, the widely followed investment newsletter, and author of the best-selling book, *Buying Stocks Without a Broker*. A Chartered Financial Analyst, he is often quoted in the media and appears frequently on radio and television.

Special Deals
and Freebies

No book on investor perks, freebies, and giveaways would be complete without offering readers a little something extra. Consider this section the "surprise inside."

The following pages contain 28 "reader-only" coupons providing freebies and special deals on leading financial publications, software, and services. The list of coupon sponsors falls into three major groups.

Financial Newspapers/Magazines
- *The Wall Street Journal*
- *Barron's*
- *Business Week*
- *Forbes*
- *Money*
- *Worth*
- *FW (Financial World)*
- *Investor's Business Daily*

Financial Newsletters
- *Dow Theory Forecasts*
- *The Low-Priced Stock Survey*
- *DRIP Investor*
- Morningstar's *5-Star Investor*
- *Bottom Line Personal*
- *Boardroom Reports*

Financial Software, Databases, and Research Services
- Microsoft Excel
- Quicken
- Andrew Tobias' Managing Your Money
- Metastock
- Dow Jones News/Retrieval
- CompuServe
- Signal
- QuoTrek

- America On-Line
- Reality's Smart Investor
- Retire ASAP
- LiveWire
- Alexander Steele's Mutual Fund Expert
- Daily Graphs

I think it's important that you know that none of these companies paid a cent to put a coupon in this book. I had complete control over what products are listed, which means no product is listed merely because the company was willing to pay an appearance fee.

Naturally, I do use many of the products and find them very helpful. I've also included products that fit nice niches within the investment world. I think you'll find many of the deals attractive, especially the free trial subscriptions on newsletters and magazines, as well as major reductions on software and database services.

With information being everything in the investment game, you owe it to yourself to become as knowledgeable as possible. A good—and inexpensive—way to increase your knowledge is by taking advantage of these discount offers to sample some of the finest investment resources on Wall Street.

THE WALL STREET JOURNAL.

☐ YES. Send me four weeks of The Wall Street Journal to enjoy free. AT the same time, reserve an additional 26 weeks (30 weeks in all) at the trial rate of $78. That's the regular price of a 26 week subscription, so my first four weeks cost me nothing. Note: Offer good for new subscribers in the Continental U.S. only. Limit: Only four free weeks of The Wall Street Journal per household.

Name_____

Address_____Suite/Apt._____

City_____State_____Zip_____

Mail To: Dow Jones & Co., Inc., ATTN: H. Magill, P.O. Box 300
         Princeton, NJ 08543-0300

28CA

BARRON'S

☐ YES. Send me four weeks of Barron's to enjoy free. At the same time, reserve an additional 13 weeks (17 weeks in all) at the trial rate of $32. That's the regular price of a 13 week subscription, so my first four weeks cost me nothing. Note: Offer good for new subscribers in the Continental U.S. only. Limit: Only four free weeks of Barron's per household.

Name_____

Address_____Suite/Apt._____

City_____State_____Zip_____

Mail To: Dow Jones & Co. Inc., ATTN: H. Magill, P.O. Box 300
         Princeton, NJ 08543-0300

27DE

... Yes, if you could make only one request of your stockbroker, it might well be ..

"Just give me one good stock under $10."

Why low priced stocks anyway? Simple, because that's where the action is. These stocks provide tremendous leverage! In plain words, they have further to go. They have more potential than big, bloated blue chips that have reached their maturity.

There's no point in getting low priced stock information if it's going to cost you a bundle, so *The Low Priced Stock Survey* is only $35 for six months, a $13 savings from the regular rate.

You must be fully satisfied ... you may cancel within 30 days at no obligation. After that you may cancel at any time for a refund of the paid, unused portion.

To begin your *Low Priced Stock Survey* introductory subscription, just complete the back of this coupon today. You will receive as your bonus a complimentary copy of Charles Carlson's book, *The 60 Second Investor* ... yours to keep no matter what.

SAVE OVER $100 IN TEN SECONDS
AND USE YOUR SAVINGS
TO BUY LUNCH ON US!

Even at full cover price **Business Week** is a bargain.
But at savings of *over $100,* it is an absolute *must* buy.

If the world of business waited a month to happen, Business Week would
be less vital than it is. But in a changing environment, at home and abroad,
Business Week is necessary to anyone who intends to succeed. That's why
more top management read it than any other business publication.

Business Week's mix of articles that focus on companies, analysis and
trends makes it uniquely able to affect your daily business decisions—
whether it's news from Washington, around the nation, or the globe.
Business Week's weekly frequency makes the reporting more timely than
the biweeklies, more analytical than the dailies.

**Return the coupon today. You'll save over $100 and make
even better informed business decisions—with Business Week.**

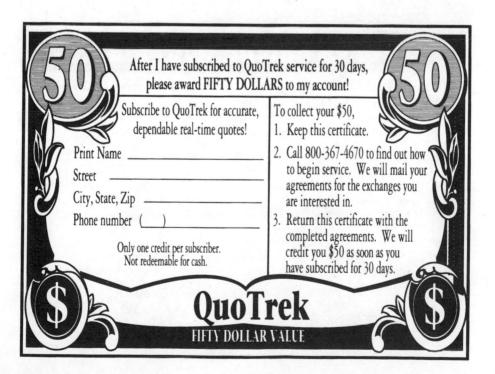

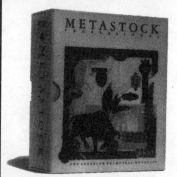

Please send my copy of Microsoft Excel 4.0 for Windows.

Choose the order option that's easiest for you:
- See your local reseller.
- Complete below and send in an envelope with payment and proof of purchase (see requirements below) to Microsoft Excel 4.0 Upgrade Offer, P.O. Box 3011, Bothell, WA 98041-3011.

Name _____

Shipping address _____

City _____ State _____ ZIP _____

Daytime phone (in case we have a question about your order)

Please check one disk option:
5.25" high-density (Kit No. 065-150-400)
3.5" high-density (Kit No. 065-151-400)

Please send me _____ copy(ies) of Microsoft Excel 4.0 for Windows at $129 each $ _____

Sales tax* (see list below) $ _____

Freight ($7.50 per unit) $ _____

Total cost $ _____

Method of payment:
   Check or money order enclosed
   MasterCard   VISA   American Express

Check or credit card number:

☐☐☐☐ ☐☐☐☐ ☐☐☐☐ ☐☐☐☐

Expiration date:

☐☐☐☐

Cardholder's signature _____

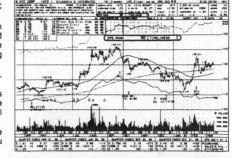

Profit from CompuServe today.

All you need to join CompuServe is a personal computer, a modem, and a telephone line. Through this special offer, you'll receive:

- FREE CompuServe basic services— including our basic stock quotes—for one month.
- A $15 usage credit good toward exploring our many extended and premium services.
- Plus a complimentary subscription to *CompuServe Magazine*, our monthly journal that will help you get the most out of CompuServe.

Call **800 848-8199** and ask for Representative **425.**

Offer expires August 31, 1994 and is limited to first-time members only. One per customer.

NO COST. NO OBLIGATION.

☐ **YES!** Please send me the next three issues of FINANCIAL WORLD — absolutely free. If I like them, I'll pay just $19.95 and receive 21 additional issues (for a total of 24). That's a savings of 44% off the regular subscription rate.

Name

Company

Address

City/State   Zip

HLUN

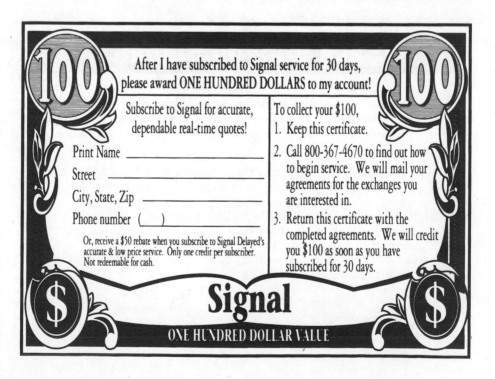

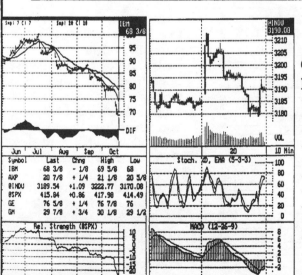

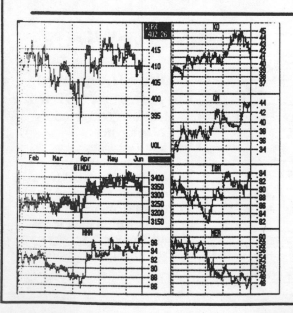

Your Monthly Guide To
Buying Stocks Without A Broker

DRIP Investor, edited by Charles Carlson, CFA, author of the best-selling *Buying Stocks Without A Broker* and editor of the highly respected *Dow Theory Forecasts*, covers all aspects of dividend reinvestment programs (DRIPs) — how to buy stocks without a broker, how to buy stocks at a discount, and how to buy blue-chips on the "installment plan" for as little as $10 a month. For a limited time receive the Charter Rate of only $59 for a full year — a 25% savings. <u>Money-back guarantee.</u> You may cancel any time for a full refund.

With your subscription you will receive a *DRIP Investor* customized 3-ring binder, our Special 12-page Report, *Why You Don't Need Wall Street* plus a complimentary copy of the best seller, *Buying Stocks Without A Broker.*

To take advantage of this generous "FREE LUNCH" offer, fill out the back of this card and mail today.

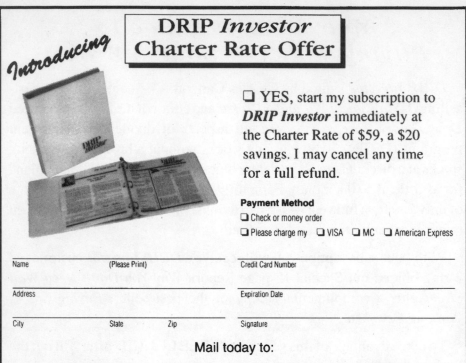